North Carolina

Sheila Turnage
Photography by Jim Hargan

COMPASS AMERICAN GUIDES
An imprint of Fodor's Travel

Compass American Guides: North Carolina

Compass Senior Editor: Jennifer Paull
Editor: Shannon Kelly
Design: Nora Rosansky, Tigist Getachew
Creative Director: Fabrizio La Rocca
Photo Editor and Archival Researcher: Melanie Marin
Editorial Production: Astrid deRidder
Manufacturing Production: Amanda Bullock
Map Design: Mark Stroud, Moon Street Cartography

Cover photo, Jim Hargan, Bodie Island Lighthouse

Fifth Edition
Copyright © 2010 Fodor's Travel, a division of Random House, Inc.
Maps copyright © 2010 Fodor's Travel, a division of Random House, Inc.

Fifth Edition

ISBN 978–1–4000–0904–6
ISSN 1549–4543

Compass American Guides, 1745 Broadway, New York, NY 10019
PRINTED IN CHINA
10 9 8 7 6 5 4 3 2 1

Whitewater Falls thunder through
Nantahala National Forest.

*To Rodney, whose
joy and respect
lighten my step.*

C O N T E N T S

TOPICAL ESSAYS AND SIDEBARS

LITERARY EXTRACTS

A pastoral scene in Lickskillit Community, Yancey County.

MAPS

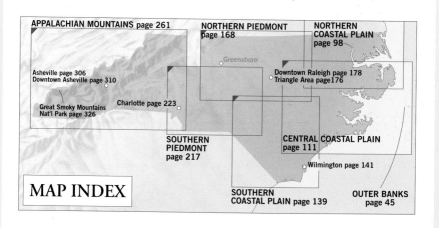

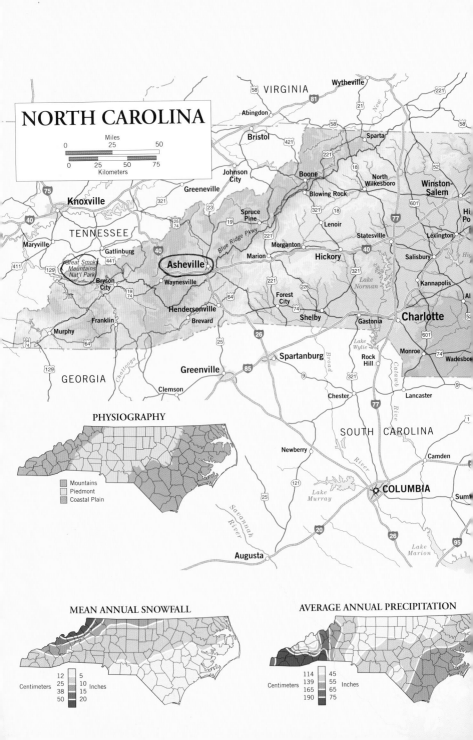

NORTH CAROLINA

Miles
0   25   50

0   25   50   75
Kilometers

PHYSIOGRAPHY

Mountains
Piedmont
Coastal Plain

MEAN ANNUAL SNOWFALL

Centimeters
12   5
25   10   Inches
38   15
50   20

AVERAGE ANNUAL PRECIPITATION

Centimeters
114   45
139   55   Inches
165   65
190   75

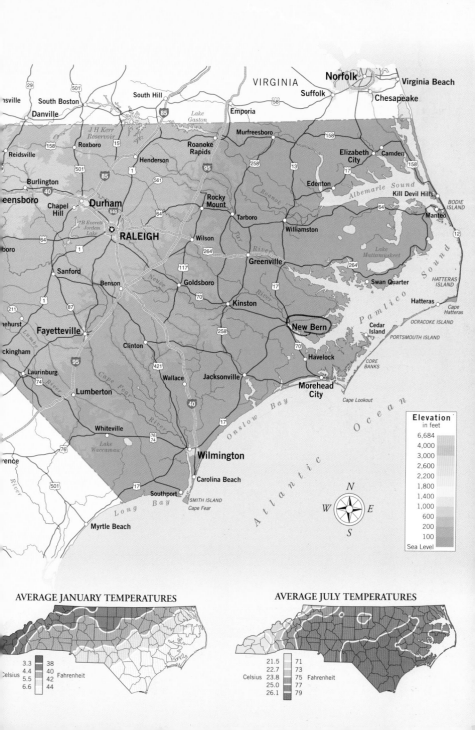

Elevation
in feet

6,684	
4,000	
3,000	
2,600	
2,200	
1,800	
1,400	
1,000	
600	
200	
100	
Sea Level	

N
W E
S

AVERAGE JANUARY TEMPERATURES

Celsius		Fahrenheit
3.3	38	
4.4	40	
5.5	42	
6.6	44	

AVERAGE JULY TEMPERATURES

Celsius		Fahrenheit
21.5	71	
22.7	73	
23.8	75	
25.0	77	
26.1	79	

Azaleas scatter color along Greenfield Lake, near Wilmington.

OVERVIEW

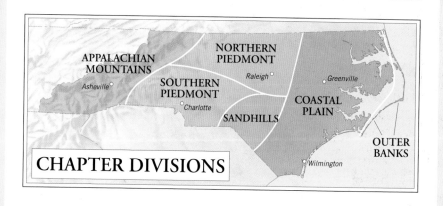

APPALACHIAN
MOUNTAINS

Asheville

NORTHERN
PIEDMONT

Raleigh

Greenville

SOUTHERN
PIEDMONT

Charlotte

SANDHILLS

COASTAL
PLAIN

OUTER
BANKS

CHAPTER DIVISIONS

Wilmington

OUTER BANKS

A long strip of barrier islands running from the Virginia border to Cape Fear, the Outer Banks are known for their miles of pristine beaches, fishing villages, lighthouses, and vacation homes. It was here that English colonists settled under the sponsorship of Sir Walter Raleigh in 1585. Reminders of their "Lost Colony" can be visited on Roanoke Island today.

A golden moment on the Outer Banks.

Cypress stand sentinel at Lake Waccamaw, on the Coastal Plain.

NORTHERN PIEDMONT

This region includes Winston-Salem, once the marketplace for North Carolina tobacco farms. The prosperous cities of Durham, Chapel Hill, and Greensboro are located here, as is the state's capital, Raleigh. Famous universities, including Duke, UNC–Chapel Hill, and NC State University, can also be found here.

COASTAL PLAIN

The Coastal Plain is home to the state's colonial era towns, including Edenton, New Bern, Bath, and Beaufort; and to hundreds of tobacco farms. The port of Wilmington, the region's largest city, is surrounded by beaches, resorts, and sights of interest. Inland, farms and small towns dot the flat, often swampy landscape.

Charlotte—a skyline shaped by business.

SOUTHERN PIEDMONT

Charlotte, the state's largest city, is the center of one of America's fastest-growing metropolitan areas. The region is also famous for NASCAR racing, Seagrove pottery, Asheboro's zoo, the reservoirs of the Pee Dee River, and the large Uwharrie National Forest.

This kitchen scene, from the Duke Homestead and Tobacco Museum near Durham, reflects the early days of the tobacco industry.

Pines whisper along a Sandhills path.

THE SANDHILLS

Geographically part of the Coastal Plain, the Sandhills are defined by their sandy soils and sharp-smelling long-leaf pine forests. The towns of Pinehurst and Southern Pines are home to some of the world's finest golf courses and country clubs. The region has long been a vacation destination and second home to some of America's rich and famous.

THE APPALACHIANS

The highest mountains east of the Mississippi, the heavily forested Appalachians stretch across the western eighth of North Carolina and are preserved in America's most visited national park, the Great Smoky Mountains National Park. The best skiing resorts cluster around Boone and Banner Elk. Asheville, the region's largest city, has long been a favorite with vacationers escaping the summer heat of the lowlands. One of those vacationers from "up north," George Vanderbilt, built America's grandest mansion, Biltmore, just outside of Asheville.

Rhododendrons overlook the gentle Appalachians.

Mist fills the valleys
in the heart of the
Smoky Mountains.

CULTURE AND HISTORY

By nature's design, four distinct North Carolinas coexist within the Tar Heel State, running in wide bands parallel to the Atlantic coast. Geologic tides of stone, ice, water, and time sculpted these four North Carolinas: the rugged Appalachians to the west, a red-clay Piedmont plateau, a sandy coastal plain, and to the east, the Outer Banks, with their shallow sounds and treacherous shoals.

By history's more fleeting decree, North Carolina shares borders with Virginia, to the north, and South Carolina and Georgia to the south. East to west, the state stretches 503 miles, from the Atlantic Ocean to Tennessee, which lies just beyond the crooked backbone of the Great Smoky Mountains.

European settlers began pushing into the state in the 1600s, staking out land farmed and hunted by Algonquin, Sioux, and Iroquois people. When the wagon dust settled a century later, North Carolina's four geographic zones had become home to four new, distinct cultures, each rising from a unique history, each facing a unique future.

THE LAY OF THE LAND

North Carolina's geologic beginnings lie to the west, in North America's oldest mountains.

The mineral-rich Appalachians, which rose up like granite giants about 450 million years ago, cover only an eighth of North Carolina's 52,712 square miles. But their rushing waters have helped shape all that lies to the east: the Piedmont, plains, sounds, Outer Banks, and even the Atlantic shelf, which extends 60 miles into the ocean.

The Appalachians are a braid of ancient mountain chains—the Great Smoky Mountains to the west and Blue Ridge to the east—crisscrossed by smaller chains. They include the highest peak east of the Mississippi (Mt. Mitchell, at 6,684 feet), thundering waterfalls, mountaintop meadows, and rugged gorges. As you'd expect, they've mellowed over the past half-billion years, trading stark granite planes for weathered faces and gentler curves.

Many rivers tumble to life in the Appalachian region and arc southeast to the ocean, but they haven't always traveled great distances to do so. The Atlantic has wandered inland at least seven times over millions of years, sculpting a series of gentle terraces that underlie today's coastal plain. As recently as 25,000 years ago, melting polar ice caps sent the Atlantic far inland. The ocean eventually receded, leaving behind its thick seabed—today's coastal plain. As rivers flowed down from the mountains, dropping their sediments, they created a massive system of sounds, barrier islands, and the Atlantic shelf.

North Carolina's seven broad, shallow sounds make up the largest system of inland sounds in the United States. Beyond lie the Outer Banks, a narrow chain of sandy barrier islands that reach from Virginia toward the South Carolina line.

NATIVE AMERICAN SETTLEMENT

Geology's tides moved from west to east, but most of the early Native American migrations flowed from north to south.

Archaeologists believe the Algonquins swept into the area around 10,000 years ago, settling small villages on the coastal plain. Centuries later the first wave of Iroquois immigrants, the Cherokee, moved south. Many settled along the streams of the Piedmont plateau and in the Appalachian foothills. Others spread as far south as Alabama.

Later the Sioux—notably the Catawba and Cheraw—pushed into those same hills and rich valleys, elbowing the Cherokee deep into the Appalachians. Finally, in a second Iroquois migration around AD 1100, the Tuscarora wedged into the coastal plain, shoving the Algonquins east into tidewater marshlands and onto the barrier islands.

By the 16th century North Carolina's four major native nations lived roughly within the four geographic zones. Contrary to myth, they were not peaceful. The Sioux warred endlessly with their hereditary enemies the Iroquois—the Cherokee in the mountains, and the Tuscarora on the plain. The Algonquin tribes, including the Secotan, warred against the fierce Tuscarora. Yet within their own communities they led settled lives, built houses, grew crops, and made clothing and jewelry. Early European explorers recorded meeting hospitable people who lived orderly and materially comfortable lives.

This engraving by Theodore de Bry was based on a watercolor made by John White in 1585, during Ralph Lane's expedition. The drawing depicts the Indian village of Secoton, believed to have stood on the central coastal plain near the modern-day town of Aurora.

EUROPEANS ARRIVE

In the early 1500s a new tide lapped against North Carolina's barrier islands, and then against a mainland charted by French, Spanish, and English adventurers hungry for land, souls, glory, and gold.

Giovanni da Verrazano, a Florentine sailing under a French flag, explored the Cape Fear area in 1524 and eagerly promoted the land's "faire fields and plains," trees, plentiful game, and easily charmed natives. The land, he wrote, was "as pleasant and delectable to behold, as is possible to imagine." Although the Cape Fear Coast Convention and Visitor's Bureau wouldn't think so, Verrazano may have exaggerated slightly. Royal interest translated into funding—the 16th-century equivalent of grant money.

Spain visited next in the person of Lucas Vásquez de Allyón, who tried in 1526 to plant a colony on the Cape Fear River. Natives, furious at having their children enslaved, contributed to the colony's painful demise.

Hernando de Soto looped through western North Carolina around 1540 searching for "gold-bearing mountains." But the Spanish, in their quest for wealth and slaves, soon focused colonization efforts on gold-rich Central America. Enter England.

Sir Walter Raleigh, soldier, explorer, poet, investor, and alleged lover of Queen Elizabeth I, sent two English ships to the New World in 1584. On July 2 captains Philip Amadas and Arthur Barlowe anchored in Pamlico Sound, rowed ashore, and claimed all before them for Queen Elizabeth I of England—known to everyone (except perhaps the amorous Sir Walter Raleigh) as the Virgin Queen. Hence North Carolina's first name, Virginia.

Days later, a Secotan warrior paddled his dugout over to greet the English, who came bearing gifts: a hat, a shirt, wine, and meat. He reciprocated with a boatload of fish. The next day he returned with 40 or 50 friends, including Granganimeo, brother of the Secotan chief Wingina.

The English found the natives "very handsome, goodly people, and in their behavior as mannerly and civil as any in Europe." Granganimeo "made all signs of joy and welcome," they wrote, "striking on his head and his breast, and afterwards on ours, to show we were all one, smiling and making show the best he could of all love, and familiarity."

They set up a lively trade, the Secotan swapping furs for tin plates (used as breastplates), copper kettles, hatchets, axes, and knives. Granganimeo's generosity fed the English, literally: "He sent us every day a brace or two of fat bucks, conies, hares, fish, the best in the world," they wrote. He also sent root crops, fruit, and corn.

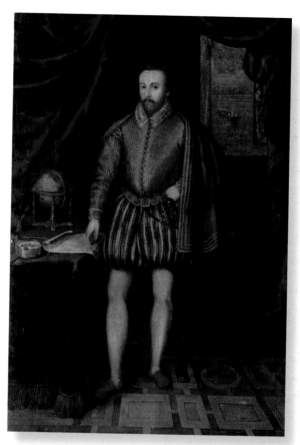

Sir Walter Raleigh provided funds and ships for the first English settlement in America, on Roanoke Island, in 1585. Raleigh himself never crossed the Atlantic. (NC Museum of Art, Raleigh)

Encouraged, the English pressed on, discovering on Roanoke Island a palisaded Secotan village fortified for war against enemy Indian nations. The Englishmen, however, received only kind treatment. After a two-month stay they headed for London. "We brought home also two of the savages, lusty men, whose names were Wanchese and Manteo," they wrote.

History doesn't say what Wanchese and Manteo thought of London's cobble-stone streets and lace-collared poets, or of Queen Elizabeth I and her court. But we do know this: Manteo came home a year later as the colonists' friend and ally. Wanchese came home the same day, a deadly enemy.

THE LOST COLONY

Sir Walter Raleigh's first colony, led by a military officer named Ralph Lane, landed at Roanoke Island in July 1585. They quickly built an earth fort, dubbed Fort Raleigh.

Lane's colony included artist John White, whose drawings open a rare window into the world of the Secotan and their neighbors, but most of Lane's 108 colonists were soldiers of fortune, more interested in wealth than in culture.

Lane explored northeast Carolina, trading brutality for hospitality as he moved from village to village. He torched one village and its corn crop in reprisal for the alleged theft of a silver cup. At a Chowan village he kidnapped the chief's son.

His deteriorating reputation preceded him up the Roanoke River. He found villages he counted on for food deserted, their corncribs empty. His army straggled back to Fort Raleigh half starved from their exploration of a river teeming with fish.

Wanchese and the Secotan chief Wingina united the mainland tribes, planning to ambush Lane's men. But Lane struck first, ambushing and beheading several men, including Wingina.

A few weeks later Lane and company hitched a ride home with Sir Francis Drake, leaving 15 luckless souls to guard Fort Raleigh.

Raleigh intended his next settlement to be England's first permanent New World colony. Led this time by Governor John White, a diplomat, the colony's hundred-odd members included women, children, tradesmen, and farmers. Sailing from England in 1587, they planned to settle in Chesapeake Bay to the north, but stopped first at Roanoke Island to pick up Lane's men, who had been left behind at Fort Raleigh.

The stunned colonists found Fort Raleigh razed, its houses occupied by a lone skeleton, the only sign of Lane's men. When they attempted to reboard their ship and continue northward, they learned that their captain had no intention of taking them any further. Only Governor White was able to gain passage back to England with the captain. There White began to gather supplies for the stranded colony that included his daughter, son-in-law, and new granddaughter, Virginia Dare, the first English child born in America.

When White returned three years later, he found the colonists' houses destroyed. The word "Croatoan" carved into a doorpost. Finding no Maltese cross, the colonists' distress signal, White hoped his colony had joined Manteo and the friendly Croatan people, on Ocracoke Island.

Searches turned up rumors, but no colonists. They simply walked into history, never to be heard from again.

ENGLAND'S INROADS

With the Lost Colony's demise, England shifted colonization efforts north, to modern-day Virginia and the Chesapeake. Coastal Virginia and South Carolina (as we know them today) were settled in the 1600s by wealthy Europeans with massive land grants—the basis of their plantation system. Not so North Carolina. Because of the navigational hazards of the Outer Banks, transatlantic ships usually avoided North Carolina's harbors, landing instead to the south in Charleston. It wasn't until English naturalist John Lawson chronicled his 1701 journey from Charleston to the North Carolina Piedmont, and to Bath on Pamlico Sound, that Europeans eyed North Carolina's promising—and relatively unsettled—lands.

North Carolina's earliest settlers went first to Virginia. Some worked their way over as indentured servants, others booked passage as free men and women. Most were yeomen farmers who came for the modest land grant given to anyone willing to claim the New World for England. Eventually, they drifted south.

The natives could not stem this seeping tide. Settlers trickled steadily into the Albemarle region beginning in the mid-1600s, buying or taking land and driving the natives inland toward hostile tribes. Smallpox and other Old World diseases wiped out native villages, opening even more land.

In 1663, when England's Charles II deeded the Carolina coast to the eight Lords Proprietor to pay off political debts, settlement quickened. One pamphlet invited craftsmen and laborers to Carolina—named for Charles II (Carolus is the Latin for Charles)—offering indentured servants land, tools, clothes, and a rare chance to "raise their fortunes." They recruited women, too: "If any Maid or single Woman have a desire to go over, they will think themselves in the Golden Age, when Men paid a Dowry for their Wives; for if they be but Civil, and under 50 years of Age, some honest Man or other, will purchase them for their wives."

In 1710 Baron Christoph von Graffenried bought 17,500 acres on the Neuse River, and established a colony of 400 Swiss settlers at New Bern. In response, the

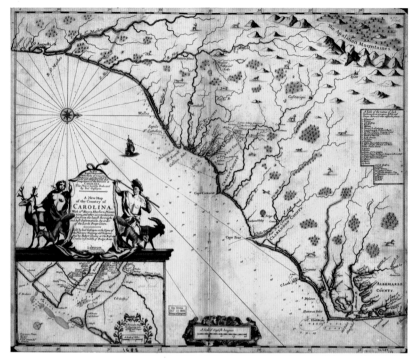

Map of the "country of Carolina" ca. 1682

Tuscarora formed an alliance with their neighbors, and in September 1711 they attacked white settlers across the plain, butchering families and burning homes.

The Tuscarora War raged for two years until, in March 1713, the last of the Tuscarora retreated to a palisade fort at Nooherooka, near Grifton. An army of colonials and Indians bombed and burned the fort, taking 392 prisoners into slavery, scalping 192, killing 200 in the fort, and 166 more as they fled.

With the destruction of the region's strongest tribe, settlers surged south to the Cape Fear River, establishing Brunswick Town—colonial North Carolina's most important port—and grabbing rich plantation lands along the river. Wealthy South Carolinians, too, established massive rice plantations along Cape Fear.

North Carolina's settlement began in earnest. When North Carolina's royal governor, Gabriel Johnston—a Scot—invited his countrymen over, they came in kilted droves. Settling along the Upper Cape Fear, they established Cross Creek, known today as Fayetteville.

The New Garden Moravian Mission in the late 18th century.
(Courtesy, Friends Historical Collection, Guilford College)

The greatest migration began in the 1730s, when German, Quaker, and Ulster Scot immigrants headed south from Pennsylvania. Traveling first singly and then in fleets of Conestoga wagons, they followed the Great Wagon Road through the Shenandoah Valley into North Carolina. In 1752 the Moravians bought a 100,000-acre tract of land and established several mission towns including Old Salem—an oasis of civilization on the American frontier, and the seed of present-day Winston-Salem. Two years later Gov. Arthur Dobbs, an Ulster Scot, encouraged a second wave of "Scotch-Irish" immigrants.

As for the native people, those who had not been killed by war and new diseases either fled before the approaching tides or bowed their heads. Only the Cherokee survived intact, clinging to the peaks of the Appalachians. And even their lands were threatened as settlers surged against the foothills.

REVOLUTIONARY ERA

As Britain's 13 American colonies grew more restless with British taxes and restrictions in the mid-18th century, arguments for rebellion, democracy, and independence circulated by pamphlet and by word of mouth through city taverns and New England village meeting halls, Virginia manor houses, and backwoods hollows. Many aristocrats and American yeomen were growing increasingly confident of their own abilities to fight and to govern.

North Carolina at this time was a colony divided culturally, politically, and financially, east against west. In the east the farmers, plantation owners, timbermen, and merchants of the coastal plain led relatively comfortable lives. They had access to their royal governor, William Tryon, and controlled the parliament, which met at Tryon's Palace in New Bern. Many were English by heritage, and maintained vital financial ties with English markets.

The "backcountrymen" led different lives and told a different story—often in German, or with a thick Scottish brogue.

Many of the Piedmont's German, Quaker, and Scotch-Irish citizens had no love for an English king. More importantly, they found themselves overtaxed by their eastern neighbors and poorly represented in a provincial parliament, which

Storming a Redoubt at Yorktown by Eugene Lami shows the Revolutionary soldiers overrunning British breastworks, leading to the surrender of Cornwallis. (Virginia State Library and Archives)

met in New Bern—a town they'd never seen, thanks to the southeastern swoop of the rivers, which sent much of their trade to Charleston.

Unfair taxes, repression, and a thieving tax collector named Edmund Fanning finally pushed the Piedmont's backcountry "Regulators" to arms. They stormed a Hillsborough courthouse in 1770, horse-whipped Fanning, beat up the attorneys, and ran the judge out of town.

The rebellion escalated until Tryon marched his militia west, routing a ragtag throng of 2,000 rebels at Alamance County Courthouse. Tryon, an astute politician, returned to his palace, packed his bags, and hightailed it to New York.

As revolutionary ideas continued to brew, eastern Carolinians grew increasingly hostile to the English Parliament's taxes. When war finally erupted in Lexington, Massachusetts, in April 1776, North Carolina's loyalties were divided. By July, when representatives of the 13 colonies met in Philadelphia to sign the Declaration of Independence, North Carolina sent three delegates—Joseph Hewes, John Penn, and William Hooper.

Ironically, it was the comfortable easterners, with commercial and family ties to England, who swayed the colony toward independence as taxes rose. The backcountry men more often opposed war—the Quakers on moral grounds—although they felt the sting of British taxes as keenly as tidewater settlers.

The Ulster Scots along the Cape Fear remained loyal to the Crown and marched to the aid of Lord Cornwallis. After Patriots sent the Scots packing, the English steered clear of North Carolina for another four years, but Cornwallis marched back in 1780, to the Battle of Guilford Courthouse near Greensboro. After losing a fourth of his army there, he staggered to Wilmington and then to Yorktown, where he surrendered.

The Revolution gave the redcoats the boot, but did little to unify North Carolina. Wrangling North Carolina politicians took so long to ratify the U.S. Constitution that the state briefly earned the status of a foreign country, and the tariffs to prove it. North Carolina finally joined the Union in 1789, claiming the flag's 12th star.

ANTEBELLUM ERA

Who were we in the period between the establishment of the Republic and the Civil War? With nearly 400,000 people in 1790, North Carolina ranked third among the 13 states in population, behind Virginia and Pennsylvania.

Across the state most whites worked on small family farms where self-reliance was the rule. They grew their own food, wove their own cloth, and minded their own business.

In the east a few planters produced labor-intensive cash crops like tobacco, rice, indigo, and cotton, using slave labor. Slavery was less common in North Carolina than in neighboring states, but by 1790, 100,000 slaves made up nearly a quarter of the population.

In the far west, meanwhile, pioneers—including North Carolinian Daniel Boone—began pressing into the Appalachians. Land grants to Revolutionary War veterans increased settlement, and America's first gold rush—to western North Carolina—added to the push. Until 1829 all the native gold minted in the U.S. came from North Carolina; the Cherokee's shrinking homelands became increasingly valuable.

Culturally and educationally, North Carolina lagged behind her neighbors, earning the nickname "Rip Van Winkle State."

The state's small, independent-minded farmers couldn't have funded a public school system if they'd wanted one—which they didn't. They needed children with strong backs. To them, book learning was a luxury.

In 1811 in Edgecombe County only half the white men and a third of the white women could write their names. Legislators controlled their unlettered population with a penal code designed to chill even 19th-century blood: 28 crimes were hanging offenses.

This pitcher made in Liverpool in 1790 outlines the population of the United States at that time. Note that North Carolina's population was 393,751. South Carolina's population was actually 249,000 or so, not 24,973 as cited. (National Museum of American History, Smithsonian Institution)

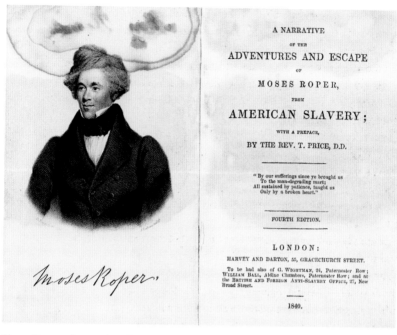

A NARRATIVE
OF THE
ADVENTURES AND ESCAPE
OF
MOSES ROPER,
FROM
AMERICAN SLAVERY;
WITH A PREFACE,
BY THE REV. T. PRICE, D.D.

" By our sufferings since ye brought us
To the man-degrading mart;
All sustained by patience, taught us
Only by a broken heart."

FOURTH EDITION.

LONDON:
HARVEY AND DARTON, 55, GRACECHURCH STREET.
To be had also of G. WIGHTMAN, 24, Paternoster Row;
WILLIAM BALL, Aldine Chambers, Paternoster Row; and at
the BRITISH AND FOREIGN ANTI-SLAVERY OFFICE, 27, New
Broad Street.

1840.

Moses Roper, a former slave from Caswell County, sold the story of his escape to a London publisher in 1838. (North Carolina Collection)

In the decades preceding the Civil War the Rip Van Winkle State awakened, establishing, for white citizens at least, public schools, institutions for the mentally and physically handicapped, roads, and a railroad.

For slaves life became more brutal. In 1831, after Nat Turner led a slave uprising in Virginia, legislators outlawed slave education, social gatherings, and black-led churches.

Native Americans also suffered. In 1835 the federal government ordered the 15,000-member Cherokee nation to abandon their homes in the Appalachian Mountains and walk to a reservation in Oklahoma. The forefathers of today's Eastern Cherokee refused to go, hiding high in the mountains. A fourth of those who walked what became known as the "Trail of Tears" died on the way, and the Cherokee homeland opened to white settlers.

Whites in the east began to fear slave uprisings, as a larger and larger percentage of the population lived in slavery. In 1860, when North Carolina's population reached 992,622, a third of that population was owned by 34,658 slaveholders.

Abolitionists in Congress argued that slavery was immoral and must be outlawed, but most free North Carolinians maintained that slavery was a political rather than a moral issue. Although most didn't own slaves, they believed the federal government had no right to interfere in a state's political affairs.

THE CIVIL WAR: FIGHTING FOR HOME, HONOR, AND SOMEONE ELSE'S WAY OF LIFE

North Carolina's leaders, slow to join the Union in 1783, were just as hesitant to leave in 1861. The state, known for its Union sympathies, adopted a "watch and wait" attitude as seven southern states seceded. In an early 1861 election only a third of North Carolina's counties sent secessionist candidates to the General Assembly. But when Confederate "fire-eaters" fired on Fort Sumter and Abraham Lincoln ordered North Carolina troops to march against their neighbors, Governor Ellis replied, "You can get no troops from North Carolina." North Carolina was, reluctantly, at war.

The state paid dearly for its role in the "War for Southern Independence."

North Carolina, which was home to one-ninth of the South's population, supplied a sixth of all Southern troops, and a quarter of all Southern dead—a particularly shocking casualty rate since only one major battle was fought in North Carolina.

By the war's end North Carolina was in shambles. The eastern part of the state, occupied throughout the war, lay in ruins.

In 1861, less than two weeks after the adoption of the Ordinance of Secession, 18-year-old Charles Powell volunteered to fight for the Confederacy. He was enlisted as first sergeant of Company E of the Fourteenth Regiment of Volunteers. (Courtesy William S. Powell)

When North Carolinians joined the Confederate Army they earned the nickname "Tar Heels," probably for their willingness to stand their ground. (Southern Historical Collection, Julius Leinbach Papers)

Washington, New Bern, and Wilmington were torched by exiting Union soldiers. As William T. Sherman's massive army rambled north to Appomattox Courthouse in Virginia, his cavalry slashed through the mountains, destroying millions of dollars' worth of factories, railroads, homes, churches, and schools and stealing food and supplies. Smoke hung over Raleigh, Asheville, Salem, Greensboro, Waynesville, Salisbury, Shelby, and other western towns.

Still, some northerners thought North Carolina got off too easy. One newspaper opined, "More fire would have made more healthy spirit in the State."

In all, some 125,000 North Carolina men—more than could vote—marched to war, earning the nickname "Tar Heels," probably for their willingness to stand their ground. Forty thousand died—half in battle, half from disease.

Those who came home found their houses burned, their fields fallow, their businesses smoldering, and their taxes impossible to pay. Thousands of acres of land changed hands, and thousands of families plunged into poverty.

The slaves—a third of the population—had been freed. But with no money, property, or education, they had nowhere to go. Many stayed put, working for ex-masters as sharecroppers.

The bitter years that followed saw the rise of the Ku Klux Klan and of a Reconstructionist government whose primary legacy would be a century of anti-Republican, anti-Yankee sentiment.

ECONOMIC AWAKENING

Textiles and tobacco—small industries in prewar North Carolina—paved the way for North Carolina's emergence from economic and social chaos.

By 1880 North Carolina farmers tripled their prewar cotton production. More importantly, 49 new mills—new elements of North Carolina economy—cranked

A CIVIL WAR LETTER

Dear Burwell

Yours of the 26th reached me a few days since, and I expect you begin to want to hear from home by this time, so I will write you a few lines.

I wonder if your uncle Tom has told you about his sheep getting drowned, he may not know of it himself. Every one he had was drowned in the big fresh, and all your uncle John's with them except the house lamb. They were all found in a raft together frozen, some ten days after the water fell. There was between 30 and 40 of them, and it was the very last of the month that they thawed enough to get them out and save the wool. That is a considerable misfortune [in] these hard times. Ours happened not to be in the low ground.

. . . All this talk of armistice and peace etc is very cheering to despondents, I don't know how we shall all feel when it blows over. . . .

Mat has been ordered into service twice and only got as far as the depo [sic] each time. I shall not commence gardening this month I guess. A great many soldiers pass here now, they generally stop at your uncle Sam's. Pat Sherrin is knitting fancy gloves for some of them, who happen to fall in love with her, or she with them, or both we tell her. . . . Your Pa gets on slowly with his plowing and other work I expect. Your Grand Ma is going to see Mrs. Cheek. She went to John Newells [sic] the other day, she says it is a sad looking place. Write soon and a little more.

As ever your
Ma
Feb 5th, 1865

—**Author unknown**, excerpted from *Awakenings: Writings and Recollections of Eastern North Carolina Women,* published 1978

out $2.5 million worth of textiles. Mill towns, with all their faults, sprang to life across the Piedmont, employing entire families. By 1900 women constituted 34 percent and children 24 percent of the mills' labor force.

Across the east, more and more farmers were planting bright-leaf, flue-cured tobacco for the factories of the Piedmont. The invention of the cigarette rolling machine in 1881 shifted the economy into high gear as tobacco barons, including James B. Duke of the American Tobacco Company and R. J. Reynolds, grabbed

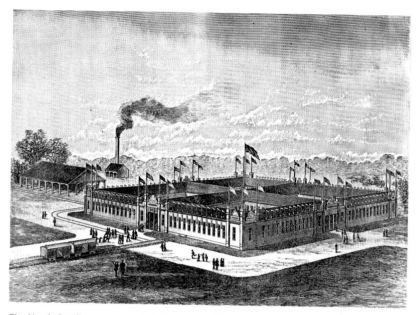

The North Carolina Agricultural Society erected this building near the present site of Raleigh's Little Theater for the North Carolina State Exposition of 1884. The four inner courts held a variety of displays of industrial products, livestock, handicrafts, and minerals. Tens of thousands of North Carolinians attended the fair. (North Carolina Collection)

control of the world tobacco market. Their factories in Greensboro, Winston-Salem, and Reidsville employed thousands.

Riding a rising economic tide, furniture factories rumbled to life around Hickory and Lenoir, while in the Pine Belt timbermen harvested turpentine, tar, and pitch.

Asheville, in the southern Appalachians, boomed. Building on its history as a health resort, the city attracted a monied clientele. The most prominent resident was George Vanderbilt, who built his 255-room mountain hideaway there. The creation of the Biltmore Estate single-handedly jump-started the local economy.

Generally affluent (and privately educated) legislators did little for public schools, but created three colleges for white students and four for blacks—all of them in the Piedmont or eastern North Carolina. In the Appalachians educational opportunities remained "few and far between" until private schools began accepting labor and crafts as tuition. Still, as the 20th century dawned some 19.5 percent of all white North Carolinians and 47.6 percent of all black North Carolinians were unable to read.

TOBACCO: A 1930s PERSPECTIVE

Durham (405 alt., 52,307 pop.) is a modern industrial city in the eastern piedmont. The universal demand for tobacco, coupled with the genius of the Duke family and other business leaders, is exemplified in long rows of factories where thousands work daily, filling whole trains with their products. Here was created the fortune that endowed Duke University.

Often the air is permeated by the pungent scent of tobacco from the stemmeries and the sweetish odor of tonka bean used in cigarette manufacture. From 9 to 5 o'clock Durham's streets reflect the activity of its business houses and professional offices. When the American Tobacco and the Liggett and Myers whistles blow, an army of workers pours forth—men and women, white and colored. Buses and trucks, heavily laden, rumble along the thoroughfares. For an hour or two the streets are alive with the hurry and noise of a big city. Then the bustle subsides and relative calm is resumed.

—*WPA Guide to North Carolina, 1930s*

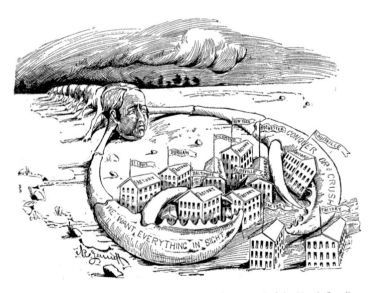

A satirical cartoon of James B. Duke grasping for control of the North Carolina tobacco industry. (Southern Historical Collection, University of North Carolina)

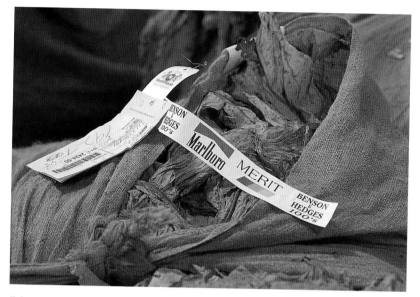

Tobacco manufacturing became a major industry in North Carolina in the 1880s, and by the turn of the 19th century the Tar Heel State had gained world dominance in the trade.

THE 20TH CENTURY AND BEYOND

The first half of the 20th century saw a 350-percent increase in the production of tobacco, whose value jumped from $8 million in 1900 to $356 million in 1945. Tobacco's impact didn't stop with paychecks for factory workers and farmers. Tobacco money helped fund universities, museums, symphonies, and medical facilities.

The Great Depression staggered the economies of the east and Piedmont, but on the isolated Outer Banks and in most of the Appalachians the Depression years looked pretty much like other years—except that the WPA came calling. WPA workers sculpted the Blue Ridge Parkway through the mountains, knocking on cabin doors that opened in on the 18th century, and laying the groundwork for preserving some of the state's most scenic wilderness areas.

World War II changed North Carolina more than any single event except, perhaps, the Civil War. Military bases, including Camp Lejeune (Jacksonville), Cherry Point (Havelock), and Fort Bragg (Fayetteville) sprang up almost over-night and entered the national consciousness. Some, like Operation Bumblebee on Topsail Island, would become closely guarded secrets.

Wartime industries pitched their tents alongside. In all, 83 North Carolina plants sold over $1 billion worth of war goods to defense agencies. Ultimately, though, war's greatest impact didn't come through the 362,000 North Carolina men and women who marched off to war, or from the $2 billion pumped into local economies by Uncle Sam. The war rode in on a tidal wave of new ideas. For the first time Tar Heels were forced to deal as comrades-in-arms with people of different faiths, accents, skin tones, and opinions. White soldiers worked alongside African-American and Native American soldiers, and together they won.

At home Carolina women let the kitchen door slap shut behind them and found jobs that paid "cash money." They raised families alone, made decisions alone, and succeeded alone.

When North Carolina came marching home, it was to another season of change.

Ezell Blair, Franklin McCain, David Richmond, and Joseph McNeil refused service at a lunch counter at a Woolworth's in Greensboro in 1960, staging the first "sit-in" of the Civil Rights movement. (Courtesy Jack Moebes, Greensboro News & Record Photo Archives)

Military men flocked to North Carolina's colleges and universities to take advantage of the G.I. Bill and a revised workplace. For the first time an across-the-board mix of white Tar Heels had access to education.

For African-Americans, however, frustrations grew. North Carolina's "separate but equal" school system ran heavy on separate, short on equal, and education wasn't the only inequity. Jim Crow laws segregated hospitals, restaurants, businesses, even water fountains. The laws were hard to change: until 1965 African-Americans had to pass a literacy test before they could vote, and few were willing to risk stepping forward to try.

Integration came slowly, but for the most part peacefully, to North Carolina. Although The University of North Carolina at Chapel Hill began admitting African-Americans to its law, medicine, and graduate schools in 1951, the public school system as a whole wouldn't be fully integrated for another 20 years.

It was in Greensboro, where Quakers had opposed slavery and spirited slaves north in false-bottomed wagons, that North Carolina's most noted Civil Rights leaders took their first public stand—or seat, actually—for equality.

On February 1, 1960, four black students from the Agricultural and Technical College of North Carolina walked into Woolworth's, on Elm Street, and quietly sat at the lunch counter, asking to be served. Their months-long sit-in worked, and the technique spread across the South.

One by one, the Jim Crow laws toppled.

The latter part of the 20th century and the dawn of the 21st brought still more change to North Carolina. The textile industry, a Piedmont bread and butter enterprise for generations, faltered as manufacturers set their sights on cheaper labor markets. Public opinion, public policy, and public funding led to a diminished call for tobacco from North Carolina's Tobacco Road.

Commerce abhors a vacuum, however. Medicine, research, and finance have stepped forward in the Piedmont. In the east, movie production and retirement- and vacation-oriented development are making giant strides as farmers continue to grow and harvest tobacco for newly structured markets.

SO, HERE WE ARE

Today around 9 million people live in North Carolina, evenly divided between rural and urban areas. As of 2006, 67.9 percent of us were White but not Hispanic, 21.7 percent African-American, 1.3 percent Native American, 1.9 percent Asian, and 6.7 percent Hispanic or of Latino origin.

Overall, our median age is 35.8 years; nearly half of us are between 18 and 44. When you come to visit, you'll find that 63 percent of us have a North Carolina accent, and some of us will sport license plates letting you know we're native Tar Heels.

One in three North Carolinians, then, are simply "not from around here," as we tactfully say. A little over 5 percent of us were born outside the United States. Nearly 31 percent of us came here from other states, often to take advantage of job opportunities in the Piedmont's fast-growing urban centers or to retire. Those retirees often chat on Appalachian porches, swing golf clubs in Southern Pines, or kick back along a lazy waterway in the east.

North Carolina began as a state of farmers, and farming remains important. As of 2007 the state's farms ranked number one nationally in the production of tobacco, Christmas trees, pigs, and sweet potatoes; and second in the production of trout and turkeys.

Still, the number of farms continues to shrink. From 2003 until 2007, for instance, the number of farms in the Tar Heel state dropped from 53,500 to 48,000. Their average size rose slightly, from 170 acres to 183, but North Carolina farms still remain small compared to the national average of 449 acres. The vast majority of our farms generate less than $10,000 in sales annually.

Meanwhile, our cities continue to grow. From 2000 to 2006, the population in and around Charlotte grew by 11.2 percent; that in and around Raleigh grew by 25 percent. Greenville, in the eastern part of the state, expanded by 16.2 percent. North Carolina cities including Charlotte, Raleigh, Wilmington, Asheville, and Winston-Salem are often listed in "top places to relocate" surveys.

Historically, education has been a glaring weakness in the Tar Heel state. Only 78.1 percent of us are high school graduates; 22.5 percent of us are college graduates. Still, North Carolina is known for its excellent universities, including Duke University, Wake Forest University, the University of North Carolina at Chapel Hill, and NC State University in Raleigh, among others.

North Carolina remains a state of modest means. Our median personal income in 2006 was just over $31,000—a little under the national average. Around 13.8 percent of us live in poverty—about 1 percent higher than the national average. Of the businesses in North Carolina, about 8 percent are owned by African-Americans and 27 percent by women.

Though we've changed in some respects, we remain the same in others. Native North Carolinians still eat barbecue, collards, and grits (not in the same meal),

Participants in the Easter Bonnet Festival of Dillsboro watch the annual parade from the town hall.

and you'll find those items on the menus of the many small, "down-home" restaurants and cafés scattered across the state.

We say "hey" instead of "hi," and most of us say "y'all," meaning two or more of you all.

Some of us golf at Pinehurst, but more of us prefer NASCAR, a sport founded by North Carolina moonshiners who once sped bootleg liquor up and down the Eastern Seaboard.

But if you really want to understand who we are, consider the highest of Tar Heel compliments: "Good people." We often, but not always, apply the label singularly, and we draw the word out flat: "He's gooood people," we say, nodding once for emphasis. Or even, "She's just plain good people."

We won't say it very often, but when you hear it, take note. It tells you who we are, what we value, and that we trust you to value those things, too.

It's not an assessment of wealth or social standing; it's an evaluation of the heart.

BARBECUE: THE STATE FOOD
OF NORTH CAROLINA

Barbecue may or may not have originated in North Carolina, but try to tell that to a native North Carolinian. From the coast to the mountains, a plate of pig is the food of choice for casual dining. Some say that North Carolinians have had a long-standing love affair with barbecue since the Colonial period, when local Indians showed the colonists how they cooked meat over hot coals.

Since then, two distinctive types of North Carolina barbecue have evolved, one on either side of the state, and proponents of each continue to bicker over which is better. In both schools pork is the required meat, and hush puppies, or fried corn bread, are served alongside. But from there the camps are split, more or less along the Fall Line (the border between the coastal plain and the Piedmont).

On the eastern side, the barbecuer uses a vinegar-and-pepper-based sauce to season the whole hog as it cooks slowly over hot coals—traditionally hickory and oak, though today propane gas is more commonly used. (The absence of tomatoes from the eastern sauce may be related to the fact that early colonists along the eastern seaboard believed the tomato to be poisonous.)

Eastern barbecue, because it consists of the entire hog, tends to be lean and slightly dry, so it is served finely chopped and brought to the table with a bottle of sauce and a side of Brunswick stew—a slightly sweet mixture of corn, tomatoes, okra, and meat and/or fish—an ideal complement to the drier, somewhat salty barbecue. Another common side dish is white potatoes, chunks of which are boiled in water seasoned with onions, tomato sauce, sugar, and bacon drippings.

In the East, coleslaw—made with shredded cabbage, mayonnaise, and sometimes mustard or sweet pickle—is

Barbecue—NC's down-home dish of choice—served hot and spicy at the Annual Memorial Day Riverfest in Bryson City.

commonly used as a garnish rather than as a major side dish.

Western, or **Piedmont, barbecue** is made from pork shoulders, a dark, marbled cut of pork that results in moister meat. While being cooked slowly over a wood fire, the meat is rarely basted. In the West barbecue is normally cut into chunks or slices, although it is occasionally chopped as finely as the eastern variety.

Western barbecue comes with a "dip," a sweet-and-sour sauce that is the same as the eastern variety save for the addition of small amounts of ketchup or Worcestershire sauce: just enough to add a reddish tint. In most western barbecue houses the only side dish is coleslaw—coarsely chopped cabbage with just the barbecue sauce itself and a little sugar.

Despite the tussle between advocates of eastern and western styles, barbecue is the ethnic food of most native North Carolinians: it is and has always been closely tied to the state's heritage. As Bob Garner writes, "within North Carolina . . . barbecuing was, with a few exceptions, the occupation of farmers and journeymen, white and black, and its arts, methods, and mysteries were endlessly discussed and debated."

EASTERN NORTH CAROLINA BARBECUE SAUCE

1 quart apple-cider vinegar
½ to 1 oz. crushed red pepper *(to taste)*
1 tablespoon salt
1 teaspoon ground black pepper

Mix all ingredients and baste pork as it cooks. After meat has cooked, use this sauce to season to taste.

HUSH PUPPIES

3 cups yellow cornmeal
1 cup all-purpose flour
2 tablespoons sugar
2 teaspoons baking powder
1 teaspoon onion flakes or powder *(optional)*
1 or 2 eggs
2 cups low-fat buttermilk
¼ cup shortening

Mix all dry ingredients, add milk, egg, and shortening. Stir mixture until smooth, about one minute. If mixture is too thick, add more milk. Pour 3 or 4 inches of cooking oil into deep fryer and heat to 375°. Spoon batter into hot oil. As hush puppies float, turn them for even browning. Remove from oil, drain (on paper towels), and eat while hot.

—Thomas Ross

HISTORY TIMELINE

1500s Algonquin people flourish in eastern North Carolina, living in organized villages, hunting, and planting pumpkins, tobacco, and sunflowers.

1585-1590 English settlers build a fort on Roanoke Island. Two years later a second group of settlers find no trace of the first. The second group also disappears, becoming known as the Lost Colony.

1600s Small groups of English settlers establish farms in North Carolina. Some try to enslave Native American children, earning tribal enmity.

1709 John Lawson, English naturalist, publishes a book describing his travels among Native Americans, whom he admires. Two years later the Tuscarora capture him along with two companions, and execute Lawson with fire.

1711 Tuscaroras attack settlements along the Neuse and Pamlico Rivers, killing settlers and burning farms and villages. Two years later they are crushed.

Blackbeard

1718 Blackbeard, the most infamous of NC pirates, is killed.

1774 Women of Edenton refuse to drink English tea as a patriotic gesture, and are satirized in the English press.

1776 Three North Carolinians, Joseph Hewes, John Penn, and William Hooper, sign the Declaration of Independence.

1789 North Carolina becomes the 12th state to join the Union. During the Revolution, Patriot soldiers rout Lord Cornwallis near Greensboro, NC.

1838 Failing to reverse the 1835 federal government mandate, the Cherokee in western NC are force-marched to Oklahoma on "The Trail of Tears."

Naturalist John Lawson and Baron Christoph von Graffenried are taken captive by Indians in 1709.

1861 North Carolina joins the Confederacy after some hesitation. Volunteers line up to defend states' rights.

1862 New Bern is captured and occupied by Union troops.

1865 The Battle of Bentonville, fought between C.S.A. General Johnston and U. S. General Sherman, results in 4,000 casualties. Johnston surrenders to Sherman 17 days after Lee surrenders at Appomattox.

1884 North Carolina, a primary tobacco state, leads the world in cigarette production.

1903 The Wright brothers fly the first plane near Kitty Hawk on the Outer Banks. Flight lasts 12 seconds and goes 120 feet.

Greensboro sit-in

1930s Construction begins on the Blue Ridge Parkway, a WPA project designed to help lift the country out of the Depression. Working on the Parkway brings economic relief to laborers in nearby counties and unwanted commotion to highland farmers.

1960 The state's Civil Rights movement begins with a sit-in at the lunch counter in Greensboro by four students from North Carolina Agricultural and Technical College.

1950–2000 The Research Triangle Park, created in the 1950s to help plug North Carolina's "brain drain," becomes the largest planned research park in the United States, giving rise to a host of business parks specializing in pharmaceuticals, biotechnology, and other related fields. Late-20th-century changes in the textile and tobacco industries lead to further adjustments in North Carolina's economy.

Wright brothers

1926 John Coltrane is born in Hamlet and later moves to High Point. He goes on to become one of the country's most famous tenor saxophonists.

1929 Novelist Thomas Wolfe publishes *Look Homeward, Angel,* based on life in his hometown of Asheville.

OUTER BANKS

A photograph snapped in space shows North Carolina's Outer Banks as a thin arm of sand nudging its way into the Atlantic. Time-lapse photography would create a more fluid image.

For centuries, these barrier islands have shielded North Carolina's low, mainland coast from pounding surf, ravenous currents, and the storm surge of hurricanes. How do the islands stand against such force? They don't.

The banks' survivability is founded not on resistance, but on their ability to change. Geologically, the islands are an endlessly elegant tumble of sand, wind, and sea.

THE ISLANDS' DANCE

When Tar Heels say they're going to the Outer Banks, they're usually heading for the sandy spits of land that stretch from Virginia to Ocracoke's southern inlet. But barrier islands protect the length of the North Carolina coast.

Two strong underwater rivers continually shape the barrier islands. The Labrador Stream's chill fingers slide south to Cape Hatteras, while the warmer, inky-blue Gulf Stream flows north. The collision of these two currents creates some of the world's most consistently turbulent waters and winds, and the shiftiest real estate on the East Coast.

Inlets and land change place like magic among the islands. The "inlets," named by sailors looking for a way "in" to the mainland, are actually "outlets" carved by sound waters pushing to the sea. Inlets typically wander slowly, spewing ever-changing fans of sand into the ocean, but hurricanes, which can swallow towns and pitch ships into mainland peanut fields, can send the ocean crashing over the islands, bulldozing new inlets in a very short time. The hurricanes of 1848 and 1899 created the Oregon and Hatteras inlets overnight.

Despite fierce storms and strolling inlets, some islands are so heavily developed that the honk of cars drowns out the honk of wild geese. Fortunately, Cape Hatteras and Cape Lookout National Seashores alone include much of the barrier islands' 300-mile oceanfront. The U.S. Fish and Wildlife Service maintains several wildlife refuges. The state owns several natural areas, historic sites, and estuarine reserves. In these protected areas sea turtles trudge ashore to nest on moonlit beaches, wild ponies gallop along the sound, and migrating snow geese fuss and flap beneath wintry skies. Like us, they come in response to the undiminished call of the sea.

HISTORY

English explorers Philip Amadas and Arthur Barlowe visited North Carolina's Outer Banks in 1584, landing on a low, sandy island about 20 miles long—probably Hatteras. Along the sound, they wrote, flocks of white cranes rose with a cry like a rising army. The sound-side forest contained the "highest and reddest Cedars of the world," pines, cypress, sassafras, deer, rabbits, hare, fowl, and a "profusion of grapes."

ALGONQUIN HOSPITALITY

Algonquins, who lived in small villages, soon came to trade with the explorers, paddling fire-hollowed canoes shaped with metal from "Christian ships." They brought coral, leather, and "divers[e] kinds of dies very excellent." Among the traders was a Secotan leader, Granganimeo, who brought his family along.

OUTER BANKS

Moyock, Knotts Island, Sligo, Barco, Corolla, Currituck Lighthouse, Whalehead Club, Bertha, Old Trap, Sanderling, Sanderling Inn, Duck, Mamie, Southern Shores, Point Harbor, Kitty Hawk, Albemarle Sound, COLINGTON ISLAND, Wright Brothers National Monument, Elizabeth Gardens, Lost Colony, Kill Devil Hills, Nags Head Woods, Jockey's Ridge State Park, Nags Head, Ft. Raleigh Nat'l Hist Site, N.C. Aquarium, Manteo, Roanoke Island Festival Park, Whalebone, East Lake, White Doe Inn, ROANOKE ISLAND, BODIE ISLAND, Manns Harbor, Wanchese, Bodie Island Lighthouse, Bodie Island Visitors Center, Oregon Inlet, Coquina Beach, PEA ISLAND, Stumpy Point, Pea Island National Wildlife Refuge, Stumpy Pt Bay, Sandy Point, Rodanthe, Chicami Comino Life-Saving Station, Salvo, Long Shoal Point, Lake Mattamuskeet, Engelhard, New Holland, Long Point, Swan Quarter, Wysocking Bay, CAPE HATTERAS NATIONAL SEASHORE, HATTERAS ISLAND, Avon, JUDITH ISLAND, Bluff Point, Pamlico Point, GREAT ISLAND, Buxton, Buxton Woods, Cape Hatteras Lighthouse, Frisco, Graveyard of the Atlantic Museum, Cape Hatteras, Mesic, Bay Point, Free Ferry, Hatteras, Maribel, Maw Point, Hatteras Inlet, Diamond Shoals, Point of Marsh, Backdoor, Ocracoke, OCRACOKE ISLAND, Island Inn, Teach's Hole, Ferry (toll), Free Ferry, Portsmouth, Ocracoke Island Lighthouse, Ocracoke Inlet, Cedar Island, PORTSMOUTH ISLAND, Minnesott Beach, West Bay, Lola, Swash Inlet, South River, Neuse River, Atlantic, North Harlowe, To New Bern, Davis, Otway, Maritime Museum, Morehead City, Beaufort, CAPE LOOKOUT NATIONAL SEASHORE, Harkers Island, Rachel Carson Estuary, N.C. Aquarium, Salter Path, Atlantic Beach, Fort Macon State Park, SHACKLEFORD BANKS, Cape Lookout Lighthouse, Cape Lookout, CORE BANKS, Core Sound, Drum Inlet, Pamlico Sound, Atlantic Ocean

Miles 0 15 30
Kilometers 0 15 30 45

THE BARRIER ISLANDS' FERRY SYSTEM

North Carolina's barrier islands have given rise to the most extensive ferry system in the United States. Since World War II the state has snaked bridges from the mainland to once-remote islands like Hatteras. Until World War II the islands were connected only by ferries, and many, including Ocracoke, still are.

North Carolina's pug-nosed ferries are the best deal on the coast. You can drive on, bike on, or walk on. You need reservations for ferries connecting Ocracoke and the mainland.

The most serene way to visit the Outer Banks may be to begin on the mainland at Swan Quarter or Cedar Island and take the ferry to Ocracoke village. This route not only bypasses the jarring development around Whalebone, it puts you in touch with the rhythm of the sea before you set foot on the islands.

If you like the water, it's great: whitecaps roll across the sound, teasing the ferry from side to side, while on the upper deck sunburned vacationers doze as the laughing gulls wheel around the ship's broad stern, hoping for bits of bread. If you have a tendency to get seasick, on the other hand, bring something to soothe your stomach.

Once you're on the islands, a half-hour ferry run links Ocracoke and Hatteras islands. You can't make reservations for this ferry, so come early, be patient, and

The Ocracoke ferry: in touch with rhythm of the sea.

bring a book. And always bring a gift for the laughing gulls. The gulls that follow these ferries appreciate a piece of bread or a cracker; a few will eat from your hand.

In addition to the big ferries, there's an unofficial fleet of smaller, private ferries and water taxis taking vacationers over to the smaller islands for day trips. Look for them along the waterfront of any village on the island, or any town along the shore. They aren't shy about offering their services, and they allow you to boat across to deserted beaches, peaceful marshlands, a lighthouse, and lost towns.

For ferry information, contact the North Carolina Department of Transportation (800-BY FERRY; www.ncferry.org).

Reconstruction of *Elizabeth II,* the British ship that brought around 116 colonists to Roanoke Island in 1587. Three years later, the colony had disappeared.

The Englishmen did not record Granganimeo's wife's name (we can only wonder what Queen Elizabeth thought of that), but noted she was a pretty, bashful woman. Like her husband, she wore a leather cloak and shift, and a headband decorated with white coral. Her pearl earrings hung to her waist and, the metal-hungry English noted, Granganimeo wore a gold or copper headpiece.

Soon the Englishmen became bold enough to visit Granganimeo's village, whose nine cedar houses sat in a palisade on Roanoke Island. Being English, they arrived unannounced.

Southern hospitality began here.

Granganimeo's wife "came running out to meet us very cheerfully and friendly," they wrote. Her husband was absent, but she ordered her people to pull their boat ashore, and carry the men to land. Then she invited them home for lunch.

In the outer room of her five-room house, by a great fire, she washed and dried their clothes. In an inner room, she laid out a feast: wheat porridge, venison, fish, melons, vegetables, fruits, wine, and teas. During the visit, armed hunters entered, setting the Englishmen's nerves on edge. Noting her guests' discomfort, their hostess broke the hunters' arrows, and had the hunters run from the village.

A DITTY ON A PIRATE'S DUTY

Blackbeard the Pirate.

The "Ned Teach" in this 1718 ditty is Blackbeard the pirate. The songwriter may have been a young printer's apprentice named Ben Franklin.

Then each man to his gun
For the work must be done
With cutlass, sword, and pistol.
And when we no longer can strike a blow
Then fire the magazine, boys, up we go.
It is better to swim in the sea below
Than to hang in the air and feel the crow,
Sang jolly Ned Teach of Bristol.

Artist John White visited the following year with Sir Walter Raleigh's disastrous first colony. His watercolors capture the details of life among a people rapidly approaching extinction.

Today place names of the northern islands echo Algonquin voices: Hatteras, Roanoke, Manteo, Wanchese. In rare cases Algonquin words have crept into everyday language. If you camp in Cape Hatteras National Seashore and your trash is raided by a masked bandit, when you mutter "raccoon" you are using an Algonquin word.

LOST COLONY ON ROANOKE ISLAND

In 1585 Sir Walter Raleigh's first colony plundered this land and its people, changing a climate of peace to one of rage. In 1587 he sent a second colony of around 116 men, women, and children. The colonists planned to settle on Virginia's Chesapeake Bay, but their ill-tempered pilot, Simon Fernandes, refused to take them farther than Roanoke Island. He allowed their leader, Governor John White, to return to England with him for supplies, but left the colonists in a fragile skeleton-occupied fort, surrounded by murderous natives. When Governor White returned with supplies three long years later, the colony had disappeared.

Some say the colonists merged with friendly tribes. Some say they were lost at sea or massacred. The Lost Colony's demise and the treacheries of the North Carolina shoals stymied colonization attempts for generations. And that suited the pirates just fine.

PIRATES

Blackbeard, Gentleman Stede Bonnet, Calico Jack Rackham, Ann Bonney, Mary Reed, Charles Vane, and Israel Hands all plied their trades along the North Carolina coast in the early 1700s. In fact, more than one island village claims among its founders pirates who washed ashore, retired ashore, or fled ashore. (For more on Blackbeard, see the Coastal Plains chapter.)

Many pirates—including Blackbeard, who lost his head at Ocracoke—began as privateers. At first, colonial politicians welcomed pirates for the same reasons today's politicians might welcome outlet malls: in the short-run they were good for the economy. Pirates sold pilfered, cut-rate cargoes to grateful merchants in Charleston, New York, Norfolk, Philadelphia, and Boston.

But by 1718, 2,000 pirates were working the Eastern Seaboard. Piracy begat more pirates as legitimate sailors chose to become buccaneers rather than walk the plank themselves. Carolina shipping lanes made easy pickings, and the North Carolina coast became a haven for pirates, whose light sloops waltzed across the shallow sounds.

As the pirates became bolder, ports closed, business suffered, and the colonial navies stepped in. Some pirates went down fighting. Some sailed away. Others were executed. Maritime history's most colorful chapter died with a blast of gunpowder, a glint of steel, and the snap of a hangman's noose.

VALIANTLY SAVING THE SHIPWRECKED

The steamer *Metropolis* was wrecked off Currituck Beach in January 1878 with the loss of 85 lives. The account of the incident was later reported in *Harper's Monthly*.

Peculiar cries, like that of many human voices mingled with the shrieks of the sea, led to the discovery of the stranded vessel by persons on the shore, who could see nothing through the fog. A boy was sent running to the nearest house, a half a mile inland, the occupant of which mounted his horse and galloped to the nearest station, some four and a half miles away. . . .

...... ● · ● · ● ......

Three or four precious hours had already been consumed; the water was filled with floating fragments of the wreck. Efforts to throw the shot-line failed, and the despairing people, giving up all hope of rescue before the ship should break entirely in pieces, accepted their last alternative, plunging into the treacherous waves. The surf was running high, and the struggling drowning mass of human beings drifted toward the shore. The lifesavers and citizens ran into the water to meet them and save them, and strove nobly in the inner breakers and undertow, dragging them ashore in great numbers. The incidents of that awful hour defy any attempts at description. The air was filled with encouraging shouts and agonizing screams. Upward of a hundred were rescued, and many were restored from apparent death.

A handsome Newfoundland dog participated in the work, incited by the example of his master, and came dripping through the surf, bringing safely ashore a half-drowned man.

The steamship *Metropolis,* wrecked in a gale off Currituck Beach, 1878.

The Baywatch of Nags Head, circa 1890s, is this Life Saving Patrol. (Southern Historical Collection, University of North Carolina Library)

GRAVEYARD OF THE ATLANTIC

Off the barrier islands the Atlantic has swallowed over 2,300 ships since colonial days, but the loss of life would have been much greater without lighthouses, lifesaving stations, and islanders willing to risk their lives to snatch strangers from the sea.

Every inch of island beachfront can recall some kind of shipwreck. But some shipwrecks are anchored so firmly in history that people talk about them as if they happened last Tuesday. Stop by a country store some February night, when the wind's so cold the marsh grass wears ice shackles, and someone's likely to say, "It's as cold as the night the *Crissie Wright* came ashore."

The *Crissie Wright* ran aground on Shackleford Banks one screaming, icy day over 100 years ago. As horrified islanders watched, the three-masted schooner rolled onto her side and the storm's waves poured over her. The islanders tried twice to launch a rescue boat, but the storm slammed them back to shore.

In desperation, they sang hymns to comfort the trapped sailors. As night fell, the temperature dropped into the single digits, and the freezing crewmen slipped into the sea. When a whaling crew finally fought their way to the *Crissie Wright*,

The controversy over the serene Carolina seashore is best illustrated in these two photographs, one a subdivision on Pine Island in Currituck County . . .

. . . the other the MacKay Island National Wildlife Refuge, also in Currituck County.

ABOUT THAT ACCENT

Until the 1950s the Outer Banks really were islands unto themselves.

Change bypassed the islands for centuries, preserving 17th-century traditions, like the celebration of Old Christmas on January 6th. The language didn't change much either. Islanders speak a dialect close to the Elizabethan English spoken by the Lost Colonists.

You'll know the dialect when you hear it, though you may not immediately understand it. Islanders speak with their lips close together, and their tongues near the roofs of their mouths. "Ou" sounds like "oo," as in "aboot the hoose." (About the house.) They pronounce "i" as "oi," and short "a" and "ar" sounds as "ah," as in, "The toid's so hoigh, the shahks ahr eatin'the cahbbahge."(The tide's so high, the sharks are eating the cabbage.)

People who use this musical dialect "have high tide in their voices." Today, that high tide is being washed away by outsiders' influences. But spend time around the docks, hardware stores, or churches, and you'll still hear high tide in the island voices.

---

they found every man on board frozen stiff except the overweight cook, Cookie Johnson, who was saved by the warmth of his own fat.

Lighthouses began guiding ships around treacherous waters in the late 1700s. Today six lighthouses help mariners get their bearings at sea. Each flashes a distinct light pattern and each sports a different painted design, clearly visible by day.

The Graveyard of the Atlantic is dangerous to swimmers, too. The Outer Banks are noted for deadly riptides, which can snatch swimmers out to sea.

NATIONAL SEASHORES ESTABLISHED

Islanders have always fished, raked clams, set crab pots, and netted shrimp, but until refrigeration came ashore, most islanders took little more from the sea than their sustenance. After World War II some villages became commercial fishing centers.

The Park Service came ashore around the same time, and the government's creation of the islands' natural areas remains a sore topic at the bait shop. Beginning in the 1950s, the government condemned thousands of island acres for the two national seashores, forcing islanders to sell land for as little as under $2 an acre.

Today beachfront property easily fetches several million dollars per acre. You see the problem.

This unhappy history explains the islands' development pattern: small villages nestled between pristine beaches and maritime forests; and beyond the preserves, tracts of privately owned land developed with a vengeance. Ironically, it's the undeveloped, endless golden beaches and vibrant estuaries that call visitors and tourism dollars to the islands.

Times have changed since folks vacationing on the Outer Banks ferried over from the mainland, bringing along children, aunts, uncles, servants, even chickens who'd live under the cottage until their time came to grace the dinner table. People drive onto Hatteras Island today, and "fast food" no longer means the chickens under the cottage outran you.

The once-isolated Outer Banks are extremely popular—offering cottages rented by the week, golf courses, historic B&Bs, shopping complexes, and seascape campgrounds—so make your reservations well in advance. (*See* Local Favorite Places to Stay, at the end of this chapter.) A year ahead is not too early for cottage reservations.

EXPLORING ROANOKE ISLAND   *map page 45, upper-middle*

Roanoke Island is surrounded by sounds which, depending on Nature's mood, may glitter like sapphires, or glower like a gray-faced god as you drive over them. The island itself is a place of quiet neighborhoods, pine forests, and the village of Manteo, on Shallowbag Bay. Historically, the Lost Colony put Roanoke Island on the map; the modern island returns the favor. Four sites focus on Sir Walter Raleigh's Lost Colonists.

★ FORT RALEIGH NATIONAL HISTORIC SITE

Soon after you cross the Croatan Sound on US 64, signs will point the way to Fort Raleigh National Historic Site. From its visitors center and museum, you have access to the Elizabethan Gardens, Fort Raleigh, and the Lost Colony outdoor drama. This is also a good place to pick up information on activities within Cape Hatteras National Seashore.

Standing by **Fort Raleigh,** a tiny, star-shaped earthwork in a forest of whispering pines, one can easily imagine the Lost Colony's men, women, and children facing an angry New World, protected only by this fragile outpost of empire.

Today families stroll these gentle walkways, passing between the museum and this re-created fort, or rambling along a nature trail that leads to the sound.

Another trail leads a few yards north to the amphitheater for *The Lost Colony,* premiered by Pulitzer Prize–winning playwright Paul Green in 1937. The production incorporates drama, dance, and music to tell the story of the Lost Colonists, including Virginia Dare, the first English child born in America. You need reservations for this popular play, which runs during summer only. Bring industrial-strength mosquito repellent. *1409 National Park Dr.; 252/473–3414 or 800/488–5012.*

The adjacent 10-acre **Elizabethan Gardens,** created by landscape artists Umberto Innocenti and Richard Webel, include a rose garden, wildflower garden, formal sunken garden, herb garden, 16th-century statues, and a great lawn laced with live oaks, hollies, dogwood, and magnolias. Colonists who built Fort Raleigh in 1585 may have rested beneath the live oak in this garden. Queen Elizabeth and Sir Walter Raleigh never set a velvet slipper on American soil, but they may have strolled through a pleasure garden like this one while planning their New World. *1411 National Park Dr.; 252/473–3234.*

NORTH CAROLINA AQUARIUM

The North Carolina Aquarium on Roanoke Island focuses on the "Waters of the Outer Banks"—freshwater, brackish, and ocean waters. You'll meet everything from otters to alligators to sea turtles in this facility. The 285,000-gallon centerpiece

The Elizabethan Gardens at Fort Raleigh National Historic Site in Manteo.

exhibit features a re-creation of the USS *Monitor*, which sank off the NC coast during the Civil War. Sharks, cobia, drum, groupers, sea turtles, and other reef species make themselves at home among the re-created wreckage.

Ask about the aquarium's special programs, including collecting cruises, beach walks, and canoe trips. *374 Airport Rd.; 252/473–3494.*

★ ROANOKE ISLAND FESTIVAL PARK

If Fort Raleigh didn't give you a sense of the vulnerability of England's early colonists, the *Elizabeth II*, a replica of one of the ships Sir Walter Raleigh's colonists sailed to America in 1584, will. And you'll find her in this park. Her billowing white sails may make her *feel* large, but this ship is a mere 69 feet long—and she was trusted to cross the Atlantic.

Colonists traveled as cargo, crammed into a 4½-foot-tall space between decks for the 42-day voyage to the West Indies, where ships took on fresh water and supplies, and then sailed up the coast to Carolina. Ask the costumed interpreters for details.

What did the colonists wear? Drop by the park's Roanoke Adventure Museum, check the costume trunk, and slip into some 16th-century garb to find out. The museum includes a hands-on trip through 400 years of area history; visit an Algonquin house while you're there. (There's an "American Indian Town" on the boards for 2009.) At the park's Settlement Site you can get a sense of life in the colony. Chat with a carpenter, try out a straw bed, or watch a blacksmith at work.

Other attractions in this 25-acre park include an art gallery, theater events, and boardwalks along the marshes. *1 Festival Park, across from the Manteo waterfront; 252/475–1500.*

OUTER BANKS NORTH OF WHALEBONE   *map page 45*

North from Whalebone, NC 12 pushes through an area of dense, uninspired development where cottages, condos, restaurants, and shops seem to stand on each other's shoulders, vying for attention. There's an ocean in there somewhere: You'll pass a beach access on your way to Nags Head, one of the islands' first resort communities.

NAGS HEAD   *map page 45, upper-middle*

Nags Head has long been known for its 30 or so relaxed, 19th-century cottages, whose wraparound porches usually shelter rocking chairs. These old cottages stare

STEDE BONNET: GENTLEMAN PIRATE

Major Bonnet, a wealthy planter from Barbados, came to piracy in midlife as modern men of a certain age come to red sports cars. One day in 1718 he looked at his wife and their high-society friends, strolled down to the waterfront, bought a fast sloop, hired a seedy crew, and sailed away.

Bonnet hijacked several ships off the North Carolina and Virginia coasts, and then set his sights on a large warship, the *Queen Anne's Revenge*. He realized his error the moment Blackbeard peered over the warship's gunwale, his jet-black beard billowing in the wind. When Blackbeard invited him on board the *Queen Anne's Revenge* as his partner, Bonnet quickly agreed.

Blackbeard now captured several other ships, imprisoning passengers and crews, and blockaded Charleston Harbor. For four days he held Charleston hostage, demanding medicine for his prisoners' lives. Why? Some say he was addicted to laudanum (an opium extract). Others say wife number twelve's dowry included syphilis.

Charleston came through with the drugs, but the blockade left the city in a murderous mood. Once Blackbeard set him free, Bonnet made up for lost time, sacking ten ships and then heading for the Lower Cape Fear for repairs. It was a rookie's choice: one way in and one way out. South Carolina's navy attacked on September 27, 1718, taking Bonnet and his crew. Charleston's judges, still smarting from the blockade, welcomed Bonnet's crew to the gallows.

Bonnet spent his last days begging for a reprieve. In a letter displayed at the Southport Maritime Museum, he offered to forfeit his arms and legs if he could keep his life. Once again, he had no luck.

---

serenely out to sea, ignoring the newer cottages, amusements, and eateries that have elbowed in alongside.

In the early days shipwrecks helped keep Nags Head's economy afloat. The law was "finders keepers," and islanders were enthusiastic finders. Story is, they'd drop a corpse en route to the graveyard if someone shouted "Ship Ashore!"

In fact, Nags Head may have taken its name from the practice of local land pirates, who hung a lantern around a nag's neck and walked her along a starlit

Summer visitors stroll the boardwalk at Nags Head, a popular beach resort in the 19th century. (Southern Historical Collection, University of North Carolina)

beach. Sea captains, mistaking the bobbing light for a ship rocked by safe waters, headed inland and their ships foundered on the shoals. Islanders then waited for salvageable cargoes to wash ashore.

★ JOCKEY'S RIDGE STATE PARK   *map page 45, upper-middle*

From Nags Head, US 158 heads north to the East Coast's tallest sand dune, protected by Jockey's Ridge State Park. In 1975 developers planned to flatten and pave Jockey's Ridge. Fortunately, the Nature Conservancy stepped in. Today the 10-story dune is still great to climb up, and even greater to roll down. This park includes a picnic area, an exhibit hall, and self-guided nature trails that let you wind through the dunes to the sound. *158 Bypass at milepost 12; 252/441–7132.*

NAGS HEAD WOODS   *map page 45, upper-middle*

Continuing north, US 158 crosses West Ocean Acres Drive. Take a left to Nags Head Woods, one of the islands' last maritime forests. Parts of the islands were once thick with forests, but early shipbuilding and lumbering industries have taken their toll.

Along these quiet, dune-sheltered trails you may see a pileated woodpecker flipping among red oaks 500 years old, and an osprey nesting on a piling in the sound. Unless you're a Nature Conservancy member, you can visit only from 10 AM to 3 PM on weekdays.

KILL DEVIL HILLS   *map page 45, upper*

Kill Devil Hills is a resort community possibly named by colonist William Byrd, who said its people drank rum "so bad and unwholesome, that it is not improperly called 'Kill-Devil.'" If you grow lonely for the ocean, head a few blocks east and drive along NC 12, known locally as Beach Road.

★**Wright Brothers National Memorial,** about 3 miles north on US 158 at milepost 7.75, offers respite from the midday sun. Its museum houses a replica of Orville and Wilbur's 1903 airplane, a glider, and other exhibits. Word is that Orville and Wilbur built theirs in six months for under $1,000—a sum that included round-trip tickets from Dayton—and that it took 50 craftsmen three years to build the half-million-dollar replica.

On the East Coast's highest sand dune at Jockey's Ridge State Park, hang gliders take advantage of the same conditions that attracted the Wright brothers to the area: strong winds and soft sand.

THE WRIGHT STUFF

The dawn of the 20th century found mankind racing for the heavens, with scientists in Europe and the Americas rushing to perfect flying contraptions. But the world paid scant attention to Orville and Wilbur Wright, amateurs who designed gliders in their Dayton, Ohio, bike shop. In 1900 the Wright Brothers wrote to the National Weather Bureau, seeking a test site for their gliders. The Kitty Hawk–Kill Devil Hills area, with its soft dunes and strong winds, looked promising. They contacted the lifesaving station.

Captain Bill Tate wrote back: "If you decide to try your machine here and come I will take pleasure in doing all I can for your convenience and success and pleasure, and I assure you you will find a hospitable people when you come among us." Wilbur arrived on September 13, after a hideous two-day schooner voyage from Elizabeth City, and pitched his tent near Tate's home.

The brothers' first visit caused a stir, not because of their cockamamy notions, but because they brought gasoline to the island. Islanders, who found the brothers amusing and their cash endearing, worried about having the explosive near their homes.

That first year the brothers flew their glider like a giant kite, studying its wing motion. When they returned in 1901 their improved plane had a 22-foot wingspan, almost twice that of their first glider, and flew without lines. On their 1902 glider, whose tail featured a moveable rudder, the brothers made over 1,000 test flights, gliding up to 600 feet per flight.

Finally, in 1903, the brothers unveiled their masterpiece. The airplane sported a 40-foot wingspan, a rudder control, and an aileron control to adjust direction and altitude. No glider, this. A four-cylinder gasoline engine powered the propellered craft, and a launching system made flat land take-offs possible.

On December 14 they raised their signal flag, calling neighbors to witness the flight, and pull them from the wreckage if necessary. They launched the plane, but Wilbur raised the nose too high, stalled, and fell to earth.

On December 17 the brothers raised the flag again. This time Orville launched the plane into freezing 27 mph winds. As stunned islanders watched, the plane rose above the sand. Orville flew 120 feet in 12 seconds, Wilbur running alongside, flapping his arms and screeching encouragement.

The brothers made three more flights that day, the last one made it a distance of 852 feet. Ironically, the witnesses to this landmark feat were men so isolated from the 20th century that they told the story in a dialect similar to the Elizabethan English their forebears spoke.

John Daniels, a member of the Kill Devil Hills Lifesaving Station, took this famous photograph of the first mechanized flight on December 17, 1903. Daniels had never operated a camera before the Wright brothers asked him to witness and record their first successful flight. Years later he recalled the historic moment, "The machine looked like some big, graceful golden bird sailing off into the wind. I think it made us feel kind o' meek and prayerful like." (Library of Congress)

Outside, trails lead across the dunes to the brothers' camp, rebuilt from old photos, and to a granite memorial marking the site of their historic first flight. This memorial hosts kite-flying contests and other events occasionally throughout the year. (Wear real shoes. This sand sprouts prickly pear cacti.) *1000 Croatan Highway; 252/441–7430.*

The villages to the north of Kill Devil Hills are now more in tune with summering tourists than migrating geese. The condos and quick-stop groceries disappear as you drive through **Pine Island Sanctuary**, but as you approach Corolla you'll enter another thicket of shops and cottages.

The Currituck Lighthouse and the lightkeeper's noble house in Corolla.

COROLLA   *map page 45, upper*

Pronounced cor-*ah*-lah, this village is literally the end of the road. The unpainted **Currituck Lighthouse** stood on this sandy shore in isolation until a few years ago, when the state paved NC 12 about a mile beyond its door. Now development crowds its way up the coast. Still, for a few dollars you can climb the 1875 lighthouse for a view of the ocean and sound. *1101 Corolla Village Rd.; 252/453–4939.*

Currituck County takes its name from the Algonquin word "coratank," which means wild geese. In the early 1900s wealthy northerners established hunting clubs here, protecting thousands of acres of land. You can visit one of those clubs today. After years of fundraising and restorations, the **Whalehead Club** has opened its doors again. Built in 1925 as a getaway for Edward and Marie Louise Knight, the 36-room house underwent several reincarnations under six owners, even serving a stint as a Coast Guard facility. Guided tours cover the history and architecture of the structure as well as the folklore associated with it. *1100 Club Dr.; 252/453–9040.*

The grounds include a free boat ramp, a shoreline where families perch on the rocks and go crabbing, a picnic area, and a boardwalk to the Currituck Lighthouse.

BIRDS FLY. MEN DRINK.

Every December, on the anniversary of the Wright brothers' first flight, a motley fraternity of pilots, aerospace engineers and writers about aviation gathers at Kitty Hawk, North Carolina. After an all-night party, these celebrants assemble bleary-eyed on the sand dunes where Wilbur and Orville's craft of hickory sticks stuck together with Arnstein's Bicycle Cement first started forward into the wind. At the precise moment of the Wrights' liftoff in 1903, two Navy jets representing the two brothers come roaring in low from the sea, rise to clear the sand dunes, kick in their afterburners over the Wright monument, and then, in a thundering instant that rattles the earth, turn straight up into the sky and climb until they are out of sight. The day is often raw and windy, but the faithful club members are always out there for this small, moving ceremony. They style themselves the "Man Will Never Fly Society." Their motto is, "Birds fly. Men drink."

I am not a member, but when I am bouncing around up there among thunderstorms, I always recall the society's name and credo with profound appreciation.

—**Charles Kuralt**,
A Life on the Road, 1990

The sand banks to the north contain some of the highest, most restless dunes on the East Coast, extensive maritime forests, and rich estuaries. For better or worse (my money's on better), the small protected areas on Currituck Banks are accessible only by four-wheel-drive, or boat.

FROM WHALEBONE SOUTH TO OCRACOKE
map page 45, middle

From Whalebone on Bodie Island, NC 12 heads south into Cape Hatteras National Seashore, where you can look for a public beach access every few miles. There are four popular camping areas within the seashore: at Oregon Inlet, Cape Point near Buxton, Frisco, and Ocracoke. **Coquina Beach,** on the southern tip of Bodie Island, is named for the millions of tiny coquina clamshells along the shore.

BODIE ISLAND LIGHTHOUSE *map page 45, middle*

Bodie Island's black-and-white striped lighthouse is the third built to watch over the Oregon Inlet. The first, built in 1848, tipped over. Retreating Confederate soldiers blew up the second. This one first flashed its light seaward in 1872.

The lighthouse keeper's home, where children once schemed to tame wild island ponies, is now inhabited by nature exhibits and ecology films. A nature walk winds through the marshes to an observation platform overlooking yaupon, cattails, wax myrtle, bayberries, and "profusions" of wild grapes like those Amadas and Barlowe reported in 1584. *Hwy. 12, milepost 22; 252/441–5711.*

HATTERAS ISLAND *map page 45, middle*

At the south end of Bodie Island, the Herbert C. Bonner Bridge spans **Oregon Inlet** to Hatteras Island. The Oregon Inlet Campground and Oregon Inlet Fishing Center (charters, public launch) are popular with fishermen.

This inlet is historically one of the most important deep-water inlets along the Outer Banks, and one of the most dangerous. Waters near inlets are deadly. Out-flowing currents will sweep you out to sea.

Hatteras Island is named for the Native Americans who once lived here. In the villages along the sound are cottages, motels, shops, restaurants, fishing charters, and piers.

PEA ISLAND NATIONAL WILDLIFE REFUGE *map page 45, middle*

Along the northern section of the island, NC 12 meanders beside the grass-edged sound in the ★**Pea Island National Wildlife Refuge**, which offers excellent birding year-round. Listen for the mellow bugling of whistling swans and the high-pitched hownk-hownk of snow geese, as they end their several-thousand-mile journeys and settle into the refuge.

An architectural rendering of the interior of Bodie Island's lighthouse.

Houses damaged by the encroaching sea at Rodanthe.

The refuge's water habitats (ocean, brackish, and sound) attract more than 260 bird species each year. Another 50 species are accidental tourists, driven in on the wings of storms. Spring brings egrets, ibises, herons, yellow legs, plovers, and American avocets, and summer and autumn bring peregrine falcons, eagles, and osprey. In August, awkward young brown pelicans learn to fish here. Human fishermen flock here, too, casting for spot, blues, trout, flounder, and drum.

Congress established the Pea Island Wildlife Refuge in 1938. It encompasses 5,915 island acres, plus 25,700 acres of Pamlico Sound. Its wildlife "buffet" took root during the Depression, when the Civilian Conservation Corps planted the dunes with sea oats and the marshes with winter food for migrating birds. Blinds overlooking the buffet line attract birders, photographers, and biologists. *14500 Hwy. 12, milepost 31; 252/987–2394.*

CHICAMACOMICO LIFE-SAVING STATION   *map page 45, middle*

South of the refuge lies the village of Rodanthe. Follow the signs beyond the village to the **Chicamacomico Life-Saving Station** (NC 12, milepost 39.5; 252/987–1552), now a museum honoring the men who risked their lives to snatch strangers from the sea. Each Thursday during the summer the staff reenacts the breeches buoy drill on the beach.

Today, the Chicamacomico Life-Saving Station is a museum.

As shipping increased off these shores in the 19th century, shipwrecks increased, too. In the late 1800s the government built lifesaving stations every 7 miles along the coast. Surfmen patrolled the beaches and maintained a 24-hour watch from the stations' towers. They built a reputation for dedication, daring, and skill. Their motto said it all: "You have to go out." No one said they'd come back in.

When possible, they worked from the beach. Fastening a line to a cannon shot and firing over the sinking ship, they dropped the line on deck. Then they towed passengers and crewmen ashore one-by-one in a breeches buoy—a lifesaving ring with a seat in it. But when the ship was far from shore, the surfmen honored their motto. They went out.

Continuing south, beach accesses lead through the dunes to wide, golden beaches noted for open spaces, surf fishing, pelicans, and laughing gulls. (Swim only in areas supervised by lifeguards.)

Windsurfers love Canadian Hole, sound-side a half-mile north of Buxton, for its wide expanse of shallow water. French Canadian windsurfers drift down in fall—which explains the name. You can rent windsurfing equipment at Avon or Buxton.

★ CAPE HATTERAS LIGHTHOUSE   map page 45, middle

The Cape Hatteras Lighthouse, with its distinctive black-and-white, barber-pole stripes, has dominated the shoreline near Buxton since 1870. This 208-foot lighthouse originally stood about 1,600 feet from the surf, but by 1999 the eroding beach was so narrow that the ocean threatened to topple the nation's tallest brick lighthouse and sweep it out to sea.

Although pessimists swore it couldn't be done, the National Park Service had the historic, 2,800-ton lighthouse moved along a portable track system to a new

KEEPER OF THE LIGHT

When it comes to the Hatteras Lighthouse, Rany Jennette saw it all.

Jennette, the son of the lighthouse's last keeper, was born in the keeper's house on this strip of sand in 1921.

Unaka Jennette, his father, joined the Lighthouse Service in 1904, serving as captain of the Hatteras Lightship at Diamond Shoals, a deadly bank of shifting sand ridges 12 miles offshore. "Lightships did the same thing, basically, as lighthouses," Rany Jennette once said. "Only they were out in the water, of course."

When Unaka moved to the Hatteras Lighthouse in 1919, he brought his wife, Jenny Luanna, and their young children, who grew up in a sun-baked Eden.

The Hatteras Lighthouse employed three keepers who worked long hours. "The three keepers had duty every 72 hours," Jennette said. "They had 24-hour duty. They had to light the lamp a half-hour before sunset, and extinguish it at sunrise."

A Fresnel lens magnified and concentrated light from a kerosene mantle lamp. The lens system, made of over 1,000 glass pieces, stood about 12 feet high and 6 feet in diameter. "Of course,

they also had to do maintenance on the houses and also on the lighthouse," he said.

That included painting the lighthouse's candy-cane stripe. Unaka used to tell children he painted vertical stripes on the tower, and then gave it a quick twist to create its famous swirl.

As a boy, Rany Jennette spent happy hours in the lighthouse, polishing the brass works, and watching ships sail the indigo Gulf Stream. Hurricanes, he adored. "You don't have sense enough to be scared at that age," he said.

Ironically a series of hurricanes, one of which sent ocean waters swirling up into the lighthouse, convinced Unaka to take his family inland. The Coast Guard decommissioned the lighthouse in 1935. When the Seashore restored it in 1992, Rany Jennette came home to a new season of guests, welcoming them to his childhood home until 1998. In 1999, when the National Park Service moved the lighthouse to save it from a ravenous sea, Jennette, like many others, watched his historic home's painstaking trek inland, where it again stands guard over the treacherous Graveyard of the Atlantic.

Cape Hatteras Lighthouse, pictured here at its former location, was moved 1,600 feet farther inland in 1999 in order to salvage it from the encroaching sea.

spot once again about 1,600 feet from the sea. The keeper's quarters, cisterns, and oil house made the trip, too. You can climb the lighthouse stairs for the view from Good Friday until Columbus Day. *46375 Lighthouse Rd.; 252/995–4474.*

The beach just southeast of the old lighthouse parking lot, at Cape Point, remains a first-class spot for surf fishermen.

BUXTON WOODS   *map page 45, middle*

NC 12 continues through **Buxton Woods**, a serene maritime forest that includes the graves of seven Nazi spies whose arrival on these shores was poorly timed. In 1942, when U-boats were nearly as plentiful as porpoises offshore, islanders swore German sailors came ashore for Saturday night movies. Maybe, maybe not. But one evening around dusk seven Germans did walk into the village of Avon. Their graves, which no one recalls digging, were located decades later in Buxton Woods.

VILLAGE OF HATTERAS   *map page 45, middle*

A few miles down from Buxton Woods, the busy village of Hatteras is known for its fishing charters, shops, restaurants, vendors, and the free ferry to Ocracoke Island. The ferries pull away every 30 minutes during the day from April 15 through October 15, and every hour otherwise. You can't make reservations; bring some good will and a book. The ride takes about a half-hour. You'll skirt the shoals as the water's tones change from gray-green, to turquoise, to deep blue.

If you like shipwrecks, the **Graveyard of the Atlantic Museum**, next door to the ferry, is the place for you. Here you'll find artifacts from a number of famously lost ships, including the *Huron,* which went down in 1878 with catastrophic loss of life. The *Huron*'s porthole, a few utensils, coins, a shoe—all found a new home here.

The famous ghost ship, the *Carroll A. Deering,* which was found floating near here with sails billowing and not a soul on board, has contributed a few artifacts, too, after wrecking on Diamond Shoals. You'll see the ship's bell here, and small pieces of her wreckage.

Not all of these waters' 2,000-plus shipwrecks are that old, of course. The *U-85,* a German sub that prowled these waters during World War II, contributed an enigma machine, a top-secret decoding device that let German subs communicate with each other.

This museum is in the process of creating itself. A galley of shipwreck artifacts is slated to open in 2009. *59158 Coast Guard Rd.; 252/986–2995.*

Rumbling off the ferry from Hatteras, you're on Ocracoke Island. Sixteen miles long, it supports a population of fewer than 1,000 permanent residents. In summer the village of Ocracoke bustles. Off-season you'll have much of the island to yourself.

You're still in the Cape Hatteras National Seashore on Ocracoke. From Highway 12, access roads cross the dunes to popular fishing beaches, whose relatively gentle waves and low, gradual strands create some good shelling, especially in the off-season.

Ocracoke Island's 16-mile, undeveloped white-sand beach also calls out to water lovers, beach strollers, and sun worshipers. (Look for a lifeguarded section if you like to swim. These waters can be dangerous.)

Ocracoke's famous wild ponies, descendants of Spanish mustangs, once grazed in the low dunes and grass flats to the south and freely roamed Ocracoke Island. Today 25 to 30 wild ponies live in a 170-acre pasture about 5 miles north of the village of Ocracoke. Look for the signs. You have the best chance of seeing the ponies at feeding times: 8:30 AM and 6 PM.

Deep-sea fishing boats such as these may be rented at
various marinas along the Outer Banks.

Feeding black-faced laughing gulls from the Ocracoke-Hatteras ferry.

★ OCRACOKE VILLAGE

If you arrive at Ocracoke Village in summer, you abruptly enter a bustling world of small groceries, sandwich shops, and restaurants. But as you turn south off of NC 12 and head into the old village, you'll find a community of unpretentious little houses set along shaded drives.

The Island Inn, a white, two-story hotel built in the early 1900s, was once the only place to stay in Ocracoke. (*See* Local Favorite Places to Stay, at the end of this chapter.) It's still a helpful landmark.

From the inn's grassy side yard you can follow the faint scent of cedar away from NC 12, into an early-morning community of small, white cottages. Pale pink hydrangeas lounge by the front steps, and snaggle-toothed picket fences yawn as the joggers pass by.

Many of these old houses, which rest beneath the arms of broad shade trees, are summerhouses now, rented out by local realtors. They didn't begin that way. Some have family graveyards tucked in the corner of the yards. Others still have silvery-gray fishing nets piled by driveways, ready to go.

A few blocks down from the inn a boardwalk leads to the **Ocracoke Lighthouse.** Built in 1823, this is the state's oldest continually operating light.

The 75-foot-tall tower, closed to visitors, still guides ships between Ocracoke and Portsmouth Island.

The 1920 general store down the street now stocks gifts and pottery. Farther down, a sleepy-eyed gentleman sells watermelons in his yard, and around the corner his neighbor weeds a garden, while his rooster welcomes the day.

Ocracoke is best seen on foot or by bike. Rent a bicycle down on Silver Lake, the jetty-protected harbor where the ferries dock (locals call it The Creek). You can also rent a kayak from a waterside vendor, and explore the nearby estuaries with a guide or on your own.

It's an easy paddle across Silver Lake's gentle swells. Time your exit to scoot out between ferries if you can, hook a left and paddle down along the cottage-lined waterfront to **Teach's Hole.** In these tidal creeks oysters spit water at terrapins, while black skimmers plummet from the sky, hunting small fish. Life here is peaceful and slow. You'd never guess this was where Blackbeard made his last stand.

Wilmington artist Claude Howell's *Loading the Nets* echoes North Carolina's ties to the sea. (Courtesy Cameron Art Museum, Wilmington)

Fishing nets and a wooden skiff stand at the ready by Parker's Creek, Ocracoke Island.

RISING WIND ON THE BANKS

Mr. Jack's weather forecast proved accurate. In the predawn hours of Friday, the usual breeze that eddied casually from the Sound, playing about in the low-lying shrubs around the cottage, suddenly increased its intensity and changed its mood; it whipped rather than caressed the aspen, causing the leaves to set up an incessant, clattering protest; it hissed through the stunted cedars; it nosed its way importunately under the eaves of the cottage, drummed on windowpanes, and sent a small, unidentified object—plastic, from the sound of it—skittering across the cement floor of the Stricklands' screened porch. The shallows sprouted small breakers, which dashed themselves against the stones of the narrow strip of beach, making an urgent, gulping sound, like a thirsty animal drinking.

The noise woke Nell briefly. Those must be Mr. Jack's "hoigh winds," she thought, then drowsed off again, having identified the natural causes of the disturbance.

The winds did not completely wake Cate, but they infiltrated her sleep. She dreamed agitatedly of bashed ships' timbers and sailors' cries . . . .

—**Gail Godwin**, *A Mother and Two Daughters*, 1982

Cape Lookout National Seashore, a 55-mile strip of golden islands, begins at Portsmouth Island and etches south. Villages once thrived here, but the islands are wild today. No bridges, no highways, no drinking water. To visit Portsmouth Island from Ocracoke, you need a private ferry. For information, call the Ocracoke visitors center (252/928–4531).

Small **ferry services** from Ocracoke, Beaufort, Harker's Island, and other coastal towns allow you to boat across to deserted beaches, peaceful marshlands, a lighthouse, and lost towns. You can reach **Cape Lookout** and the southern end of the seashore by ferry from Beaufort on the mainland. Some ferry services maintain island cottages and jeep taxis on the island.

PORTSMOUTH   *map page 45, lower*

Walking along the inlet's edge, across the flats, up the white-sand hills to Portsmouth, you enter a silent, sun-bleached village of homes, churches, and stores. Listed on the National Register of Historic Places, the town was inhabited

After picking up its cargo from tall ships docked at Portsmouth in the Outer Banks, a lightboat is unloaded at a wharf in Washington, NC, around 1910. (East Carolina Manuscript Collection, East Carolina University, Greenville)

UNDERWATER CAROLINA

The Graveyard of the Atlantic is noted for four centuries of shipwrecks, and for its wreck diving. Certified scuba divers will find some of the best wreck diving on the East Coast. Shipwrecks along these shoals lie in waters ranging from 25 to over 200 feet deep.

The currents off the NC shore can be dangerous, but the sealife can be very abundant. Be careful in these waters. Never dive alone.

Check with the **Outer Banks Visitors Bureau** (800/446–6262) for dive outfitters.

until 1971. Today, of its 21 well-preserved buildings, only one house (a visitors center), and the Methodist Church are open to visitors.

Two centuries ago tall ships from England and the West Indies docked along this waterfront. Seamen loaded ships' cargoes into lightboats, to be "lightered" to mainland ports. In the taverns on the waterfront bartenders improved on yarns spun by sailors a half-world from home.

Portsmouth boomed. Wharves and warehouses lined the deepest inlet in the islands. Stores, churches, schools, a post office, a customs house, and a hospital lined the streets. Green-shuttered houses sat on lush lawns, kitchens built out back to keep the fish smell out of the parlor curtains.

In 1848 a fierce hurricane partially filled the inlet, but the Civil War dealt Portsmouth her deathblow. People fled as Federal forces approached. By the war's end most had new lives on the mainland. A few came home, but with the marine traffic heading for new, deeper inlets, Portsmouth's life ebbed away.

You can ferry to Portsmouth for day trips or overnight. There's no camping in the historic district, though.

SHACKLEFORD BANKS *map page 45, bottom*

From the mainland, the deserted Shackleford Banks seem to hover on the horizon, a sandy mirage between water and sky. Standing on Shackleford Banks today, it's difficult to imagine this as a booming whaling hub, but the stretch of sand three miles northwest of Cape Lookout was the heart of an industry.

No one knows when **Diamond City** tumbled ashore, but it must have been here when New England whalers passed through in 1726. The whalers headed north, to colder waters, but not before the islanders netted a few ideas and took up whaling themselves, substituting their island for a ship, and trees for a crow's nest.

Six crews kept 25-foot boats onshore from February to May, when old men climbed the trees and scanned the horizon. When they spotted a whale, the men rushed to sea. They beached the whale at high tide, and went to work. Men and children cut the blubber while the women melted it in vats, running the oil through reed strainers into old molasses barrels buried in the cool sand.

The oil and whalebone fetched a pretty penny in Beaufort. Diamond City's 500 citizens landed four whales a year; the $18,000 windfall sent the economy into overdrive. The town claimed three stores, a porpoise-processing plant, oyster house, and crab-packing house. They even built a school.

Then the hurricane of 1899 slammed ashore, drowning gardens, flooding forests, floating coffins, and lifting homes from foundations. Worse, ravenous currents gnawed the beach away, leaving the city vulnerable and exposed. A sad exodus began. Families dismantled homes and floated them across the sound to Harker's Island, Marshallberg, or Morehead City's "promised land." By 1903 all that remained were traces of curving streets in the shifting sands.

If you want a ride to Shackleford's Banks, get a ferry from the Beaufort waterfront.

CAPE LOOKOUT LIGHTHOUSE   *map page 45, bottom*

This diamond-patterned lighthouse blinked to life in 1859, and still helps sailors skirt Cape Lookout shoals. From the lighthouse grounds you may see small boats bobbing on the choppy waters off the island curve known as The Hook. If the reels are spinning, the blues are running.

This park's shore is a popular beach destination. The lighthouse is reached via ferry, water taxi, or private or chartered boat. Beaufort's waterfront offers plenty of rides across the sound.

RACHEL CARSON ESTUARY

Boating between Beaufort and Shackleford Banks, you pass through the Rachel Carson Component of the North Carolina National Estuarine Research Reserve—quite a mouthful, which is why most folks just say, "I'm going to Rachel Carson." Naturalist Rachel Carson researched her book *At the Edge of the Sea* here in the 1940s. Today the reserve is best known for the 30 or so wild ponies that live on Carrot Island, across from Beaufort's yacht-lined waterfront.

Cape Lookout Lighthouse.

A GREAT DRIVE ON THE OUTER BANKS

Begin on the mainland, at the Cedar Island Ferry, which loads by a rambling, white visitors center. The 22-mile trip across the Pamlico Sound to Ocracoke takes a little over two hours. Catch an early ferry so that you'll be there before 10 AM. (Be sure to make reservations with the NC Ferry System: 800/BY-FERRY.)

As the ferry glides away from shore, the waters lose the earth's green-gray colors and grab the azure tones of the sky. An hour into the trip, sky meets water in every direction. After threading restless shoals marked with sun-bleached posts, the ferry squeaks through the narrow entrance between stone jetties into Ocracoke Village's saltwater lake.

Start exploring Ocracoke by renting a kayak or checking out the lighthouse. You can grab lunch in any of the cafés in town, or pick up a picnic and head for the beach.

Drive up to the wild pony pens 5 miles out of town, on Highway 12. (Look for the signs.) From there, continue on Highway 12 to any beach access. Tromp across to Ocracoke's undeveloped beach for a picnic or to hunt shells. These waters are great for fishing, wading and, if there's a lifeguard nearby, for swimming. Please remember, the ocean here can be treacherous. Swim only in lifeguarded areas.

Highway 12 takes you north to the next ferry landing, and a half-hour ferry takes you to the village of Hatteras, with its restaurants, motels, museums, shops, and famed lighthouse.

Ocracoke's light has guided and comforted mariners since 1823.

You'll find a remarkable diversity of life in this complex of salt marshes, tidal mudflats, sand flats, eelgrass beds, and upland islands. If you go over at low tide (the best time), you'll find fiddler crabs in their burrows along the creek. The short seaweed-encrusted tubes sticking out of the wet sand are escape hatches for iridescent, plumed worms. They peek out at high tide, and filter meals from the sea.

Farther along you'll cross a salt marsh covered in cord grass. The pony trail leads to the top of a sand berm overlooking Beaufort Inlet, which is crucial to the estuary. Its tides move nutrients into the reserve, and flush pollutants out.

Along the mudflat, where humans forage for clams, birds probe the mud banks. The eelgrass in the shallow waters conceals marine life, including fish, scallops, crabs, and snails. The brackish ponds host long-legged waders, while raccoons and gray fox live in the nearby thicket.

The **North Carolina Maritime Museum** in Beaufort offers tours of "Rachel Carson." *252/728–7317.*

GETTING AROUND

Since the barrier islands covered here stretch along the North Carolina coast, there are many ways to reach them.

From Raleigh, US 64 leads to Manteo. You can drive across to the Outer Banks from Manteo. From Raleigh again, US 70 heads through Morehead City to NC 12, which takes you to the Cedar Island Ferry. The Cedar Island Ferry, in turn, takes you across to Ocracoke, and NC 12.

NC 12, along with the occasional ferry, stitches the northern islands together, making travel simple once you reach the islands.

The southern islands in this chapter are most easily reached by boat from Beaufort. US 70 takes you east from Raleigh to Morehead City and Beaufort.

LOCAL FAVORITE PLACES TO EAT

Back Porch Restaurant. 110 Back Rd., Ocracoke, 252/928–6401. $$$

If the weather is good, consider a table on the screened-in back porch of this casual restaurant. (The tables in the air-conditioned dining room are pleasant, too.) Unique seafood dishes include fillet of a local catch in Vietnamese lime sauce with a julienne vegetable slaw, or deep-fried crab beignets, a longtime favorite. They also serve homemade breads, freshly ground coffees, and homemade desserts. The cicadas and tree frogs in the flower garden provide the background music. No lunch.

The Lifesaving Station. Sanderling Resort and Spa, 1461 Duck Rd., Duck; 252/449–6654. $$$$

This restaurant occupies the old Caffey's Inlet US Life Saving Station No. 5, an 1899 station refurnished with nautical memorabilia. The menu leans toward the nautical as well: shrimp, crab, and corn chowder and daily seafood specials. The restaurant is also known for its excellent wine list, its fresh-baked breads, and its white-chocolate raspberry crème brûlée. They crank their own ice cream, too. Reserve at least three days in advance. No lunch.

Owens' Restaurant. 7114 South Virginia Dare Trail, Nags Head, 252/441–7309. $$$–$$$$

This Outer Banks standard has been dishing up the shrimp since 1946, and it's still operated by the family that got the enterprise rolling. The seafood comes straight from local seafood markets, and you'll find a museum's worth of historic artifacts from the US Lifesaving Service on the walls. Dress is casual and the menu varied, but if you like the tried and true, order the Seafood Outer Banks: fillet of local fish, jumbo shrimp, sea scallops, and jumbo lump crab cake, all fried golden, with salad, fries, or sea breeze potatoes (a potato-and-cheese dish), hush puppies, and a veggie. The Godiva chocolate mousse is the most popular dessert. Closed Jan–mid-March.

Sam & Omie's. Milepost 16.5, near Whalebone Junction; 252/441–7366. $–$$$

They've been pouring cold ones and serving meals for more than 70 years. Fisherfolk, sunbathers, and locals keep this casual eatery bustling. If you've a taste for seafood, try the large shrimp platter: golden-fried shrimp with fries and either coleslaw, fried veggies, or the vegetable of the day. The wood-paneled bar is a popular gathering place in the evening.

LOCAL FAVORITE PLACES TO STAY

For information on the many realtors handling cottage rentals, call the Outer Banks Visitors Bureau (800/446–6262).

The National Parks Service maintains several very popular campgrounds (800/365–CAMP; www.recreation.gov) along the Outer Banks. Bring sunscreen, long tent stakes, and serious mosquito and gnat repellent. Be sure to make reservations.

The Inn on Pamlico Sound. 49684 Hwy. 12, Buxton, 252/995–7030. $$$$

This inn's decks, docks, and porches offer a view of the vast Pamlico Sound, and the view only gets better at sunset. This relaxed, 12-room inn, noted for its complimentary breakfasts (think raspberry-stuffed French toast), gives you plenty to do on-site, from taking the kayaks out on the sound to biking around Buxton to reading on the porch. It's also wrapped in the arms of the Cape Hatteras National Seashore. Adventure packages, including windsurfing and fishing charters, are available. Each guest room has a different look. The Jasmine room, for instance, has a king-size sleigh bed, a tiled whirlpool bath, and French doors looking westward over the sound.

Island Inn. NC 12, Ocracoke; 252/928-4351 or 877/456–3466. $–$$

If only these walls could talk! This low-key, 16-room historic inn was built in 1901 largely from timbers of wrecked ships. It's the oldest functioning business in Ocracoke. It served as the village's school, a dance parlor, a World War II barracks, and an Odd Fellow's lodge before opening as an inn in the 1940s. Ask for a room on the second floor if you enjoy heirlooms, old quilts, and antiques. If you crave a balcony with a sea view, grab one of the rooms in the third-story crow's nest. There are no room phones; the rooster a few blocks over issues a wake-up call around 7 AM. The inn's newer (and costlier) villas across the street offer waterfront balconies and more up-to-date amenities: Jacuzzi, kitchen, and pool.

The White Doe Inn. 319 Sir Walter Raleigh St., Manteo; 252/473–9851 or 800/473–6091. $$$$

This Queen Anne–style B&B is run by former U.S. Park Service rangers Bob and Bebe Woody, who can definitely get you pointed in the right direction for an Outer Banks vacation. The eight-guest-room inn, listed on the National Register of Historic Places, is a couple of blocks from Manteo's waterfront. Rooms are decorated with antiques and reproductions. The most popular room is the Garden Room, the only first-floor room with a private entrance and garden area.

In this typical coastal plain scene, the trees seem to walk on water in Jones Lake near Elizabethtown.

COASTAL PLAIN

SMALL TOWNS AND WATERFRONTS

North Carolina's broad coastal plain rises, barely, from a mainland coast inlaid with hundreds of tiny harbors, inlets, and bays. The plain stretches west—in most places flat as an ironing board—to the Piedmont's rolling hills. Where the Piedmont's lively rivers slow to a lazy crawl, a coastal plain was built with sediments eroded from western mountains.

The plain's seven broad, shallow sounds make up the largest inland shoreline in the United States—a boon to pirates, moonshine runners, and ne'er-do-wells who have hidden along shores so low that trees seem to walk on water. The 2.2 million acres of estuaries along these shores are also the nurseries for North Carolina's seafood industry.

Today's coastal plain consists of two geographic zones. The shore claims a spattering of fishing villages, a growing number of resort and retirement communities, and miles of undeveloped marshlands overlooking indigo sounds. Inland, the plain is a land of molasses-slow rivers, family farms, and towns so small a wily mayor's apt to park an unmanned police car near the lone traffic light, to create the illusion of a police force.

This is a lush land of ages-old cypress swamps, rich estuaries, and drowsy colonial river towns. It's also a land of trailer parks, ticky-tacky military towns, localized poverty, and burgeoning communities of retirees.

HISTORY

In 1700 a rakish young naturalist named John Lawson became mainland North Carolina's first literate tourist. Happily, he found plenty to write home about.

Lawson set out from Charleston, South Carolina, on December 28, 1700, pressing northwest to the Indians' Occaneechi trade path, known today as I–85. He headed north through Piedmont Indian villages, and then east across the central plain, settling finally in Bath, a tiny English community on Pamlico Sound.

During his travels, Lawson walked from Indian village to Indian village, describing homes, religious rites, and food. Shamans fascinated him. The women did, too. "Amongst Women, it seems impossible to find a Scold," he wrote. "Would some of our European Daughters of Thunder set these Indians for a Pattern." Not that they were perfect, he added. The Wateree, were "as ingenious

Eighteenth-century naturalist John Lawson sketched the "Beasts of Carolina," which included bison (long-since vanished from the region), during his travels through the coastal plain. (North Carolina Collection)

at picking of pockets as any, I believe, the World affords; for they will steal with their feet."

Lawson recorded the cypress, fox grapes, and vegetables; buffalo, wolves, and panthers. He described "new" creatures like the opossum, a rope-tailed, death-defying marsupial often seen scurrying beneath starlit skies. "If a Cat has nine Lives, this Creature surely has nineteen; for if you break every bone in their Skin and mash their Skull leaving them for Dead, you may come an hour after and they will be gone quite away," Lawson wrote.

He reported "insects" called alligators hibernating in the creek banks. "They roar and make a hideous Noise against bad Weather, and before they come out of their nest in the Spring." (Their offspring still roar along the Cape Fear River, and in the Croatan National Forest, on the central coast.)

As for North Carolina settlers, Lawson claimed the men had been made lazy by easy living. The women he deemed industrious and fair, with "brisk, charming eyes." They married young, wove their own cloth, and paddled their own canoes.

Lawson doesn't say where he met these brisk-eyed young women, but by 1710 settlers drifting south from Virginia had established three main ports: Edenton, Bath, and Beaufort. And they had built their one-room log cabins along the creeks and branches from the Virginia line south, almost to the Neuse River.

The southern plain remained, firmly, Indian territory.

Lawson argued for a compassionate partnership with the region's natives. "They are really better to us than we are to them," he wrote. "They always give us Victuals at their Quarters, and take care we are armed against Hunger and Thirst: We not do so by them. . . . We look upon them with Scorn and Disdain, and think them little better than Beasts in Human Shape, though if well examined, we shall find that, for all our Religion and Education, we possess more Moral Deformities and Evils than these Savages do, or are acquainted withal."

And, he warned, the Tuscarora made bitter enemies: "[T]hey strive to invent the most inhuman Butcheries for [their enemies] that the Devils themselves could invent or hammer out of Hell." The Tuscarora soon proved the truth of his words.

TUSCARORA WAR

In 1710 John Lawson, now Surveyor-General of North Carolina, parceled off around 18,000 acres of alligator-infested land at the confluence of the Neuse and Trent Rivers to a Swiss playboy, Baron Christoph von Graffenreid, for a Palatine colony in the New World. It was a deadly mistake.

A 19th-century drawing depicting the capture of John Lawson, his black servant, and Baron von Graffenreid by Tuscarora warriors in 1710. (North Carolina Collection)

With invaders on their doorstep, the Tuscarora united the coastal tribes and prepared for war. When Lawson headed up the Neuse River with Baron Von Graffenreid, Tuscarora warriors marched the trespassers to Catechna, near present-day Grifton, for trial. The Baron wrote:

> In the middle of this great space we sat bound side by side, sitting [upon] the ground, the Surveyor-General and I, coats off and bare headed . . . before us was a great fire and around about the fire the conjurer, that is, an old gray Indian, a priest among them, who is commonly a magician, yes even conjures up the devil himself. He made two rings either of meal or very white sand, I do not know which. Right before our feet lay a wolf skin. A little farther in front stood an Indian in the most dignified and terrible posture that can be imagined. . . . Ax in hand, he looked to be the executioner.

Von Graffenreid addressed the crowd, claiming ties to a powerful king. The Tuscarora spared him but not Lawson, who another witness said they stuck "full of fine small splinters of torchwood, like hogs' bristles, and so set them gradually on fire."

At dawn a few days later, the Indians attacked European settlements and homesteads, killing 210 settlers during the first hours of the three-day massacre. Bodies of women were left kneeling, as in prayer. Men were scalped. Unborn babies were ripped from their mothers' bodies and hurled into trees.

War raged for three years until, only a few miles from the place Lawson met his death, several hundred Tuscarora men, women, and children crowded into a palisade. Colonial troops and the Tuscarora's hereditary native enemies surrounded the fort and opened fire. When the smoke cleared three bloody days later, the Tuscarora had been annihilated.

PLANTATION ERA

With the Tuscarora in ruins, the southern plain opened to European settlers.

Wealthy South Carolina planters quickly moved in, creating vast low-country rice plantations along the Cape Fear as affluent planters from Edenton moved in alongside. When North Carolina governor Gabriel Johnston invited his Scots countrymen to Carolina, they came lock, stock, and bagpipe.

A scan of colonial records proves that early Tar Heels were average folks up to the usual misdeeds. They filed separation papers and prenuptial agreements, weaseled out of shoplifting charges, apologized when caught swimming nude in the Chowan River.

Wealth remained in a very few, very well-manicured hands. Most early settlers lived in dirt-floored log cabins, but once sawyers rolled up their sleeves, frame houses with shake roofs sprang up across the countryside. Farmers planted the land cleared by sawyers, raising tobacco, corn, and rice. Women cared for children and homes, whether those homes were rough cabins or "mansion houses"—typically two-story houses, four rooms up and four down, with free-standing kitchens. Generous porches became the sitting rooms of choice.

By the time of the Revolution, about half of North Carolina's adult slaves were "new" slaves—Guinean, Angolan, Ibo, Mandingo, or Coramentee people of West Africa. Many were rice farmers "special ordered" by plantation owners who needed their skill and expertise. The few free blacks congregated around Halifax, near the Virginia border. Small colonies of escaped slaves lived deep in the Dismal Swamp's bamboo mazes near Edenton until the end of the Civil War.

CIVIL WAR

To hear Tar Heels talk, you might think that white, 19th-century North Carolinians were born swaddled in Confederate gray. In reality, political sympathies were initially split. But once North Carolina cast its lot with the South, thousands of young men flooded the military training camps, bringing along violins, slaves, and bedsteads. Almost as soon as they could salute, North Carolina's soldiers were sent to Richmond to defend the Confederacy's capital. By the time Union strategists caught their breath and invaded eastern North Carolina to cut Lee's supply lines, only green recruits remained. They were too few, and too new.

As North Carolina's barrier islands fell and federal troops closed in on the mainland, slave owners herded thousands of slaves west. As Union soldiers marched into Elizabeth City, New Bern, Washington, and Plymouth, wealthy planters "refugeed" inland. Others took a deep breath and hoped for the best. The best was bad enough.

Even Edward Stanly, whom Lincoln had appointed military governor of North Carolina, was horrified at the destruction wreaked by occupying forces. "Thousands and thousands of dollars' worth of property was conveyed North," he wrote. "Libraries, pianos, carpets, mirrors, family portraits, everything in short, that could be removed, was stolen by men abusing slave holders and preaching liberty, justice, and civilization."

As Union soldiers liberated slaves plantation by plantation, around 7,000 black North Carolinians enlisted in Union regiments and 10,000 moved to refugee communities. Thousands more rejoiced and stayed put.

With all ports except Wilmington blockaded and occupied, the war became a series of raids and blunders. In New Bern and Plymouth, wartime romances flourished. Near Kinston a Confederate soldier wrote novellas between raids. Panicked Confederates near Greenville fled one dark, desperate night, terrified by a troop of cows relentlessly munching its way across the countryside.

As the war raged on and Southern ports fell, Wilmington's blockade runners became critical to the South's survival. Wilmington finally toppled in February 1865. Although the Battle of Bentonville lay dead ahead, the outcome of the war was now certain. Gen. Robert E. Lee surrendered at Appomattox Courthouse on April 8, 1865.

For North Carolina the loss of life was staggering. Of 125,000 men who marched off to war, 40,000 died. Across the coastal plain homes, businesses, and towns stood vacant or in ruins, and the region's economy lay in shreds.

FROM ASHES TO TOBACCO

A new cash crop, flue-cured tobacco, paved the way for the coastal plain's recovery. Ex-slaves became sharecroppers, splitting profits with landowners, who provided capital for their joint venture.

Mullet Haul by Wilmington artist Claude Howell, 1947. (Cameron Art Museum, Wilmington)

World War II brought massive military bases to the plain, jump-starting economies in Jacksonville, Havelock, and Goldsboro. Wilmington's shipyards sent hundreds of vessels to war, and thousands of dollars into local pockets.

Around the same time, refrigeration helped turn quiet fishing villages into commercial fishing centers. Fleets of blunt-faced shrimp boats soon churned regularly to sea, pulling tons of shrimp and fish from the waters and shipping them inland. Crab and oyster houses proliferated, and dockside restaurants opened, scooping fresh seafood from boat to kitchen to plates.

SMALL-TOWN LIFE ON THE PLAIN

As you drive across the plain you'll find that small towns don't work like little cities. In small towns people still stop when the traffic light turns yellow, inquire after everyone's well-being, and say "good morning" to strangers.

Conversation remains an art, especially among older people. Strangers may serenely ask your mother's name, where your home is, exactly why you left, and when you're going back. If you are not a lucky person, they may also explain their medical concerns.

If you answer politely, they'll invite you to their town festival, church supper, or community fish fry. This is their way of passing the time, fueling conversations that will take place long after you've left, and creating a history that includes you.

You can guess a small town's age by looking through its eyes. The oldest look across water—usually a river, but occasionally a sound. Most colonial-era towns have a Front Street or Water Street lined with its oldest, grandest architecture.

Decoy carver in his workshop in the Core Sound
area of Harkers Island.

DOWN-HOME COOKING, 1930S STYLE

In the late eighteenth century a traveler, lost in the wilds of North Carolina, was hospitably received at a farmhouse. "Here," he records in his diary, "I found a large table loaded with fat roasted turkeys, geese and ducks, boiled fowls, large hams, hung-beef, barbecued pig etc. enough for five-and-twenty men."

[Even today] chicken salad, chicken pie, chicken and dumplings, chicken hash, and smothered chicken delight the Southern palate.

Every North Carolinian thinks, too, that country-cured hams are among the finest foods. They are fried and served with red gravy; or they are boiled or baked. The fat pork that is fried or used for seasoning boiled vegetables is called fat back, salt pork, side meat, middlin' meat, or sowbelly.

Dear to the heart and the health of every Southerner are the greens or "sallet," turnip, mustard, poke, and water cress, or "creases" according to the section from which one comes. A "mess of turnip sallet" boiled with hog jowl or fat meat is a common dish. It is always considered best when cooked in an iron kettle. The "pot likker," made famous in plantation days, is the juice left in the pot after the greens have been removed.

Corn meal dumplings, generally called "dodgers," are some times cooked in the pot liquor....

••• ● · ● · ● •••

Barbecues, so popular and common throughout the State, are a relic of the old open-fire cooking. Whole pigs and often lambs, chickens, and cuts of beef are cooked over live coals. They are basted frequently with a special highly seasoned sauce, called barbecue sauce. Brunswick stew, often cooked out-of-doors to serve community groups, is a thick stew usually made of chicken, butter beans, onion, corn, and tomatoes, and seasoned with salt pork. Fish muddle, a typical eastern Carolina dish, is made by putting several kinds of fish in a kettle with layers of onions and potatoes, seasoning with fried fat meat, adding water to cover, and cooking to a stew. "Brush roasts," or oysters cooked on a wire netting over an open wood fire, are a popular out-of-doors shore meal. The oysters are served with bowls of melted butter, chow-chow, and plain corn bread.

—*WPA Guide to*
North Carolina, 1930s.

Here sea captains' and merchants' towering old homes sport widow's walks and shady porches. Moss-gentled brick churches wrap protective, wrought-iron arms around the cemetery and churchyard, and old wharves dream of tall ships.

Away from the rivers, the small trade towns founded in the late 1700s or early 1800s face a Main Street. The older neighborhoods, the homes of tobacco families and merchants, will be a block or so off Main Street, whose business has probably slunk away to an ugly little mall at the edge of town.

Finally, towns that sat up and dusted themselves off in the mid-19th century tend to be railroad towns. Often, the railroad bisects Main Street, which may be called Railroad Street. These towns have a curious Old West feel, thanks to their low, blocky, up-in-a-heartbeat architecture. The town depot may now be a museum, or meeting hall. The town's largest houses will tell you who owned the hardware store, and who profited from the railroad.

Almost every town's main street includes a hardware store and café. Café patrons arrive in shifts. Early risers bounce in at 7 AM to bond over ham biscuits; the Rotary Club saunters in for coffee at 8; the bridge club sashays in at 10, etc.

If you order coffee, you have two choices: decaf or regular. By the standards of much of America, they are weakly brewed. Tea is syrup-sweet and iced if you don't say otherwise. If it's midday, try the lunch or dinner special. If it's dark outside, say, "what's for supper?"

These small-town cafés are the most direct route to small-town life. In many cases they're also the easiest way to find out who's got the key to the local museum.

ALL THOSE CHURCHES

First-time visitors to eastern Carolina are always bowled over by the number of churches. It's not unusual to find towns of 5,000 souls with access to 15 or 20 area churches, all of them Protestant. This wasn't always so.

Anglican missionaries visited North Carolina in the early 1700s, hoping to save the colony's collective soul if they could find it. They couldn't.

Reverend John Blair proclaimed the colony "the most barbarous place on the Continent," and fled. Over the next few decades Anglican ministers looked forward to a stint in Carolina like they looked forward to a season in hell. Eventually, independent-minded Tar Heels aligned themselves with "dissenting sects"—Quakers, Methodists, and Baptists. Anglican missionaries heaved a sigh of relief and sallied forth to other continents in search of cannibals.

Today churches dating from the 1700s onward dot the countryside. Some are imposing redbrick structures, built to claim a New World. Some are light, graceful

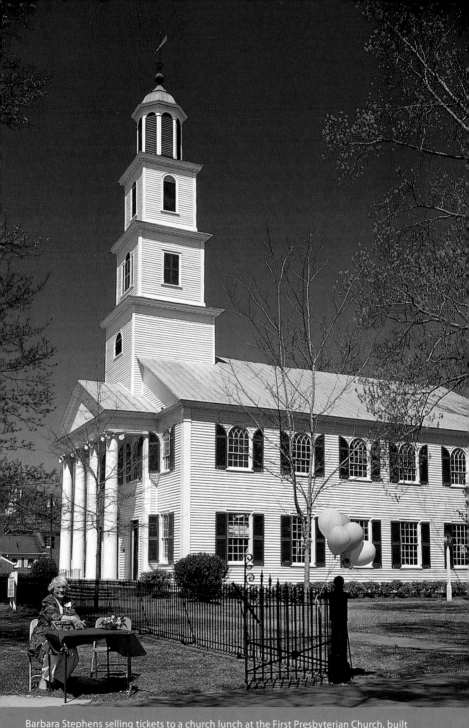

Barbara Stephens selling tickets to a church lunch at the First Presbyterian Church, built in 1822, in New Bern.

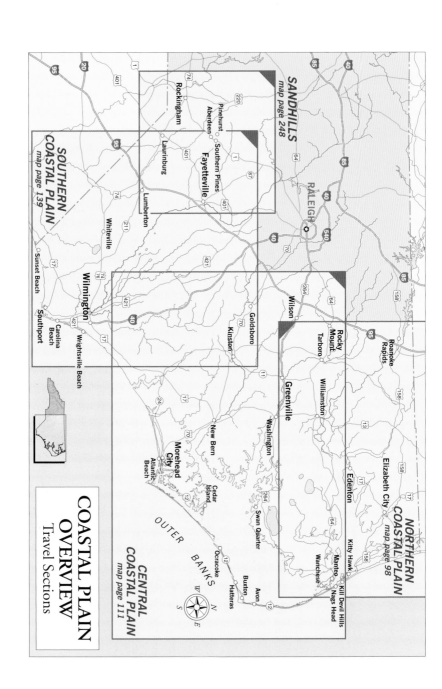

COASTAL PLAIN
OVERVIEW
Travel Sections

SANDHILLS
map page 248

SOUTHERN
COASTAL PLAIN
map page 139

NORTHERN
COASTAL PLAIN
map page 98

CENTRAL
COASTAL PLAIN
map page 111

OUTER BANKS

RALEIGH

Rockingham
Pinehurst
Aberdeen
Southern Pines
Fayetteville
Laurinburg
Lumberton
Whiteville
Sunset Beach
Wilmington
Southport
Carolina Beach
Wrightsville Beach
Goldsboro
Kinston
Wilson
Rocky Mount
Tarboro
Roanoke Rapids
Greenville
Williamston
Washington
New Bern
Morehead City
Atlantic Beach
Cedar Island
Swan Quarter
Ocracoke
Hatteras
Buxton
Avon
Edenton
Elizabeth City
Kitty Hawk
Manteo
Wanchese
Kill Devil Hills
Nags Head

creatures with wooden steeples singing to the sky. Others are as plain-faced and determined as cinderblocks.

Churches remain the social heart of this conservative region, with Baptists filling a quarter of their pews.

Every small town has a Church Street lined with old, established churches. On it, you'll find a Baptist church (or two), a Methodist church, and perhaps a Presbyterian, Disciples of Christ, or Episcopalian church as well. (If not, they'll be on nearby side streets.) The newer evangelistic and Pentecostal churches, where the "amens" can go on for hours, tend to dwell on the outskirts of town.

The Baptist and the African Methodist Episcopalian Zion church (AME Zion) are particularly powerful influences within the African-American community. In general, Baptist churches, which split and reform faster than the Red Sea, stretch like a string of glistening pearls across the countryside.

Regardless of denomination, folks take their churchgoing seriously. Although some churches are now more casual, in many of them children dress in their Sunday best and men wear the ties they opened on Father's Day. Women plot covered-dish suppers, Wednesday night means choir rehearsal, and everybody shakes hands with the preacher after the Sunday service is done.

The churches welcome visitors and offer a clear sense of life on the coastal plain. Country churches, especially, provide wonderful music, from full-throttle gospel to tinny, shape-note harmonies first sung here centuries ago.

If your timing verges on the miraculous, you'll visit a church way out in the country on a Sunday set aside for "dinner on the grounds." After church, the men will prop up a chicken-wire table under the pines and the women will drape tablecloths over it—white linen, red-and-white plastic, faded blue cotton.

Next come plates piled high with fried chicken, chicken stew, potato salad, corn bread, ham biscuits, corn cut off the cob just this morning, tomatoes and cucumbers, collards, turnips, and mustard greens. The Mississippi Mud cakes, sweet potato pies, and banana pudding loll at the end of the table, next to cups of iced tea so sweet that bees alight on them.

It's not heaven, but if you like Southern cooking, it's pretty darned close.

NORTHERN COASTAL PLAIN

 The northern plain gave rise to North Carolina's earliest river ports and political centers, and to massive plantations wrested from the Great Dismal Swamp's slippery grip. Today this region is noted for river towns where 18th-century sea captains' white houses face each other across shady streets. It's also known for its natural areas—and the occasional red wolf and moonshiner.

★ *EDENTON*   *map page 98, B-2*

Edenton's character reflects Tidewater, Virginia's, thanks both to proximity and family ties. With its generous houses, cannon-guarded courthouse greens, wharves, and access to English and West Indies trade items, colonial Edenton quickly became the most graceful town in the region.

It still is. Thanks to a strong sense of survival, a penchant for diplomacy, and historically strong social and economic ties to shipping and business partners in the North, Edenton survived the Civil War unscathed. As a result, it retains one

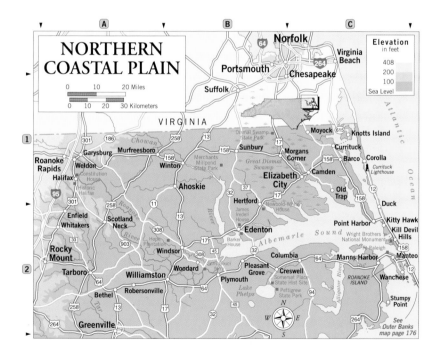

Penelope Barker's house in Edenton.

of the coastal plains' most graceful and complete historic districts—one noted for
its West Indies–influenced architecture.

As North Carolina's first seat of government, Edenton has been home to governors, revolutionaries, a Supreme Court justice, and more lawyers than you could
pound a gavel at.

As you drive into this small town (pop. around 5,500) near the intersection
of US 17 and NC 32, head south on Broad Street and park down by the water
beneath the trees. Before you will be Edenton Bay at the outlet of the Chowan
River into the Albemarle Sound—a broad body of water whose expression is as
changeable as a three-year-old's. Here in 1774, at the white-clapboard, green-
shuttered **Barker House** (505 S. Broad St.; 252/482–7800), facing the water,
Penelope Barker and friends drew up a petition supporting the Continental
Congress and swearing off British tea. Around four dozen women signed the
document; some two or three times.

From Penelope's, where the mallards preen at water's edge, you can walk
around the corner and along the bay to the grassy, cannon-guarded town green.
At the far end, facing down toward the water is the stately **Chowan County
Courthouse,** built in 1767. A number of Edenton's glistening white historic

PENELOPE'S LETTER

Penelope Barker

In the mid-1700s, as revolutionary fervor ran high in the American colonies, provincial deputies in North Carolina voiced their displeasure at British taxes. One sent the following letter to England.

The Provincial Deputies of North Carolina having resolved *not* to drink any more *tea,* nor wear any more British cloth, etc. many ladies of this Province have determined to give a memorable proof of their patriotism, and have accordingly entered into the following honourable and spirited association. I send it to you, to shew your fair countrywomen, how zealously and faithfully American ladies follow the laudable example of their husbands, and what opposition your Ministers may expect to receive from a people thus firmly united against them.

(The association referred to was that formed at the home of Mrs. Penelope Barker of Edenton, when she and a group of women signed a document supporting the deputies' position.)

EDENTON, NORTH CAROLINA, OCTOBER 25, 1774

As we cannot be indifferent on any occasion that appears nearly to affect the peace and happiness of our country…it is a duty which we owe, not only to our near and dear connections who have concurred in them, but to ourselves who are essentially interested in their welfare, to do everything as far as lies in our power to testify our sincere adherence to the same; and we do therefore accordingly subscribe this paper, as a witness of our fixed intention and solemn determination to do so.

—**[signed by Penelope Barker and her guests]**

British papers—getting wind of the patriotism of Edenton ladies, satirized them. In this caricature, two women guzzle a bowl of booze, Penelope flirts shamelessly, and a mother ignores her child.

A century later patriots sanitized the illustration and published a drawing more appropriate for Victorian sensibilities. In this picture, the child sits dutifully under the table, and the women around the table appear more refined, in dress, hair, and posture.

(All illustrations courtesy of North Carolina Collection)

Restored kitchen in the Newbold-White House.

houses, with their porches and porticos, face each other across the wide, sycamore-shaded green.

Edenton's old neighborhoods tend to cluster near the waterfront, and places of historic interest are clearly marked. On Broad Street a block above Penelope Barker's home sits the **Cupola House,** built in 1758. It's the nation's best example of Jacobean architecture. A few blocks farther up Broad is **St. Paul's Episcopal Church,** chartered in 1701. Across the street at the **visitors center** you can pick up a self-guided walking tour. *108 North Broad St.; 252/482-2637.*

Today Edenton is a comfortable, hospitable town well situated for people who want to explore the countryside. Several old homes on Queen Street and Broad Street have become B&Bs; several offer cruises onto the Chowan River and Albemarle Sound, and beyond.

HERTFORD   *map page 98, B-1/2*

Hertford is one river town you can see at its best from the highway—if you choose the right highway. Come in on NC 37, which snakes across the broad Perquimans River and over the Iron Bridge. The town's white houses with their roses and pink azaleas stand at ease along the river.

Founded in 1758, Hertford is as placid as the river whose bank it occupies. Where trade ships once unloaded, fishermen now row flat-bottomed boats among old pilings, idly wetting a line in Perquimans River. (The women here swear Perquimans means "land of beautiful women." It's best to agree.)

Pick up information on Hertford's walking tour at the visitors center, on Front Street. It includes 25 in-town sites, among them a pale yellow 1825 county courthouse.

Front Street's public pier, where water lilies crowd the shore, makes a good reading spot. An even better idea for a lazy afternoon: bring along a picnic and a boat.

Hertford is home to the late Catfish Hunter, who pitched the Oakland As and New York Yankees to World Series titles in the 1970s.

The 1685 **Newbold-White House** is about a mile south of Hertford on US 17. She may not look like much, but history has her back to you. The state's oldest dwelling faces the river. Joseph Scott, a Quaker, built this medieval hall–style house to outlast time. Its 18-inch walls contain many original bricks. Inside, the restored, furnished house wears the same cypress paneling and floorboards the colony's earliest Assembly members knew. Until 1704 this house doubled as the colony's Assembly House.

The guided tour is recommended. It includes the house, several outbuildings, a 17th-century Quaker graveyard, and a seasonal kitchen garden. *151 Newbold White Rd.; 252/426–7567.*

GREAT DISMAL SWAMP   *map page 98, B-1*

Today US 17 runs along the eastern edge of the Great Dismal Swamp—a lonely stretch of road that traces a canal initiated in part by George Washington. Dug by slaves, it drained the swampland and linked North Carolina and Virginia markets.

Virginia aristocrat William Byrd II visited the Great Dismal Swamp in 1728, labeling it a "vast Body of mire and Nastiness." George Washington saw it with different eyes, describing the half-million-acre lowland as a paradise.

Since the 1600s the Great Dismal has served as a haven for runaway slaves, outlaws, and moonshiners. Now it's a haven of another type, welcoming birders, hikers, bicyclists, fishermen, and canoeists. In summer black bears go berrying along the old timber access roads. Deer, bobcat, mink, river otter, raccoons, and gray and red foxes frequent the park's waterways, boardwalks, and paths. Over 200 bird species frequent the refuge, but birding is most popular in April and May, when 35 species of warblers wing in from points south.

The Dismal has seen its share of human wildlife, too, thanks to the infamous Lake Drummond Hotel, which once straddled the North Carolina–Virginia border.

In this canal-side "Halfway House," Virginians honeymooned on the North Carolina side of the hotel, where marriage laws were lax, while Carolinians dueled on the Virginia side of the house. "Fugitives from justice in Virginia reposed as

Paddling through the Great Dismal Swamp.

contentedly in the North Carolina end of the building as did North Carolina fugitives on the Virginia side," one visitor wrote.

The place appealed to Edgar Allan Poe, who is said to have penned his poem "The Raven" there. Poet Robert Frost never stayed in the hotel, but as a heart-broken young man jilted by his first love, he did visit the Dismal, determined to hurl himself into an early grave. (Fortunately, the future poet laureate got roaring drunk in Elizabeth City instead.)

The Lake Drummond Hotel is long gone, along with many of the canals that once made the swamp accessible to loggers. But the main Dismal Swamp Canal, America's oldest man-made waterway, lives on as part of the Intracoastal Waterway.

Excluding runaway slaves and moonshiners, who loved this dizzying wilderness for the cover it provided, and loggers who loved it for its giant cypress trees, most people historically avoided the Great Dismal Swamp. Not so today. These days birders, hikers, cyclists, and canoeists value this lush wildness. And the **Dismal Swamp State Park** (2294 US 17N, South Mills; 252/771–6592), 3 miles south of the Virginia border on Highway 17, offers easy access.

Outfitters have yet to discover the Great Dismal, so for now it's BYOB: Bring Your Own Boat. Bring the rest of your gear, too, including bicycles, hiking gear, etc.

You can drop a canoe or a kayak at the ramp by the parking area or, if you're not a paddler, head for the 80-foot barge-bridge floating across the Dismal Swamp Canal. The bridge puts you at eye level with the swamp as you bike or walk across to the visitors center. There you'll find exhibits on both the nature and history of the area.

The 14,344-acre Dismal Swamp State Park has 17 miles of hiking and mountain-biking trails, most of which follow old logging trails, and an easily accessed 300-foot boardwalk. Call ahead to sign up for frequent birders' hikes and other guided outings. Be forewarned: the wildlife here includes impressive biting insects and ticks, so bring along plenty of repellent.

★ *MERCHANTS MILLPOND STATE PARK*   *map page 98, B-1*

What did the Great Dismal look like before the canals? From US 17, if you head west on US 158 at Morgan's Corner and drive through **Sunbury,** you'll see the signs for Merchants Millpond State Park. Here buoy-marked canoe trails enter a cypress swamp in its prime.

Canoeing on Merchant's Millpond.

Canoes (which you can rent in the park) glide across this cypress-dark water into a world where troupes of tupelo-gum stand like dancers frozen in mid-pirouette, their arms trailing stoles of Spanish moss. Millions of water lilies float delicate armadas of yellow, white, and pale pink blooms across the obsidian water. As evening falls, the tree frogs and crickets spiral their serenade through the growing darkness.

Deep in this park lies a rare, virgin tupelo–bald cypress swamp. The five-mile paddle in is worth every stroke. This ancient place, where gnarled cypress knees rise from mirror-still water and owls hunt at noon beneath a canopy of deep shade, hasn't changed since the Algonquin people paddled through in fire-hollowed canoes a thousand years ago.

Come in early spring, when the water's high and the ticks and snakes are dozing. (This section is closed in summer, when the moccasins are moody and the ticks fierce.)

Canoeists, hikers, and campers usually spot deer, otter, heron, and owls in this park. Black bears, who once lived here in shaggy throngs, shy away from humans. Likewise bobcats and mink. *71 US Highway 158E, Gatesville; 252/357–1191.*

HOPE PLANTATION, NEAR WINDSOR   *map page 98, A/B-2*

This Federal-style plantation house, home of former North Carolina governor David Stone, was almost spirited away by time, neglect, and weather. Fortunately, history-minded locals rescued it, making Hope Plantation one of the finest surprises in eastern North Carolina—once for the quality of its architecture, and once for the unusually complete collection of furnishings made by North Carolina craftsmen.

Stone finished his Princeton studies in 1778, and came home to Windsor to marry Hannah Turner. Stone, who would write four books on architecture, designed their home and built it from native pine and cypress. It eventually sheltered Mr. and Mrs. Stone and their 11 children. Over 100 slaves worked in the plantation's corn, wheat, and cotton fields.

Stone was elected to the North Carolina House of Commons seven times and the U.S. Congress twice. He served two terms as North Carolina Governor, two as a U.S. Senator. But Hannah's death in 1816 brought him to his knees. On a bookcase wall the grieving widower scribbled, "O for the past gone days when I could gaze at my wife."

Their home has been refurbished from a meticulous inventory made at Stone's sudden death two years later, at age 47. (Ask about furniture made by area

THE CABLE FERRY

To reach the **Sans Souci ferry** (which you can, unless the river's flooded), head south on US 17 and turn east on Woodard Road, which meanders through the countryside to the ferry landing. If the ferry's on the other side of the river, honk.

The ferry, which transports two cars at a time during rush hour, creaks across the glass-smooth water, depositing short-cut artists on the opposite shore, where a one-lane drive bordered by cypress, ferns, and wild orchids leads to NC 308.

Hang a right on NC 308, turn right at the T intersection, and you'll cross the river again as you head toward Plymouth.

Ferries have been part of the North Carolina landscape for hundreds of years. The San Souci was taken over by the state's Department of Transportation in the 1930s after having been maintained by local operators for decades. While small ferries were once common, the San Souci is now North Carolina's only cable ferry. *Intersection of Woodard Rd. and Sans Souci Rd.; 252/794–4277.*

Travelers must honk their car horns to get the boatman's attention at the Sans Souci ferry.

cabinetmakers.) The grounds include a kitchen, gardens, orchard, nature trails, and picnic grounds, and the 1763 King-Bazemore House.

Take NC 308 west of Windsor 4 miles, and follow the signs. *132 Hope House Rd.; 252/794–3140.*

HISTORIC HALIFAX   *map page 98, A-1*

Today historic Halifax is a ghost town, its growth stifled long ago when trade began to move by railroad, and the tracks went elsewhere. But this former hotbed of Revolutionary activity is worth a stop for the expectant feel that lingers in the air, and for its growing collection of restored buildings.

In 1776, when Halifax was an important political center, ships' passengers on the upper Roanoke River made their way up the long hill, past the print shop and jail, past the marketplace where free-black and white farmers sold their produce, to a hilltop tavern where they sipped a draft and soothed the travel from their bones. At the same time, in an attorney's office on the edge of town, revolutionists worked on a draft of the "Halifax Resolves," giving North Carolina's delegates to the Continental Congress the power to declare independence from Britain and to create a new government.

Plymouth in 1863 as painted by Merrill G. Wheelock. (North Carolina Museum of Art, Raleigh, purchased with funds from the American Legion Auxiliary, NC chapter, and the State of North Carolina.)

Scheduled guided tours take you into the restored home of an 18th-century merchant, a 19th-century law office, and a 19th-century planter's home. You can also arrange to visit several other historic buildings: a clerk's office, a historic tavern and tavern museum, and a jail—only temporarily, with any luck.

Stop by the **visitors center** for a tour schedule. *25 St. David St.; 252/583–7191.*

Modern Halifax's main avenue includes a few antiques and crafts shops, and a plastic-tablecloth café. The library's genealogy room is well used by people tracking ancestors who headed west through Halifax in the 18th and 19th centuries.

TARBORO   *map page 98, A-2*

On Tarboro's 1760 town common, the state's oldest, an art nouveau fountain salutes 18-year-old Henry Wyatt Lawson, a Tarboro carpenter who claimed the dubious honor of being the first Confederate soldier to die in battle, inspiring half of North Carolina's Civil War slogan, "First at Bethel, Last at Appomattox."

As you enter town, persevere through newer development and turn toward the main business district. Tarboro's 45-block historic district (roughly between Battle Avenue and St. James Street) has been the beneficiary of a thriving trade economy, a post–Civil War business boom, and a few generations of complacency. The wharves are gone, but restored homes from the 1700s to early 1900s line Tarboro's streets. Even Main Street has reclaimed its early-20th-century charm.

The historic district's National Recreation Trail begins at the **Blount-Bridgers House and visitors center.** Free guided tours run every other Saturday, spring through autumn; self-guided tours run year-round. The house displays a large collection of paintings by Hobson Pittman, who spent a harrowing childhood in the area. His work also hangs in the Metropolitan Museum of Art in New York, the Corcoran Gallery in Washington, D.C., and the North Carolina Museum of Art in Raleigh. *130 Bridgers St., at St. Andrews St.; 252/823–4159.*

PLYMOUTH   *map page 98, B-2*

On Water Street, piers and a boardwalk line the west side of Plymouth's three-block business district, where on warm weekends the public parking lot looks like a showroom for boat trailers. Over on Plywood Road old men fish from a pier, casting into the Roanoke, whose tranquil surface belies strong currents below.

Plymouth, which armies took turns burning during the Civil War, is known for its post-war buildings and Civil War history. **Port O' Plymouth Museum** resides in the old depot in a waterfront park (turn north on Washington Street, then right on Water Street). Its exhibits include artifacts from the CSS *Albemarle.* Confederates built the ironclad in an upriver cornfield near Halifax. Gilbert Elliott, a 19-year-old from Elizabeth City, supervised the job of collecting pots, pans, rails, and bolts to melt into iron sides for his warship.

In April 1864 General Hoke of the Confederacy called the *Albemarle* to battle, hoping to retake Plymouth from the Union. One sailor recalled that bullets hitting her sides sounded like "pebbles against an empty barrel." The *Albemarle* wreaked havoc on Federal forces for months, but was torpedoed on October 27, 1864. Today her bullet-riddled smokestack is displayed at the North Carolina Museum of History in Raleigh. Her nemesis, the USS *Southfield,* rests on the river bottom. *302 East Water St.; 252/793–1377.*

CENTRAL COASTAL PLAIN

 North Carolina's central coastal plain is a place of small towns, farming communities, and fields of tobacco, soybeans, and corn. It's also home to dwindling family-owned fishing and shrimping operations, restored Civil War forts, and huge expanses of protected wetlands. Along leisurely waterways lie drowsy towns with eighteenth- and nineteenth-century historic districts at heart. More often than not you'll now find modern retirement and vacation homes lining waterways on the outskirts of those towns.

Along the coast a recent explosion of development is changing the coastline at a breakneck pace as condos, vacation houses, gift shops, and eateries shoulder in along white-sand beaches.

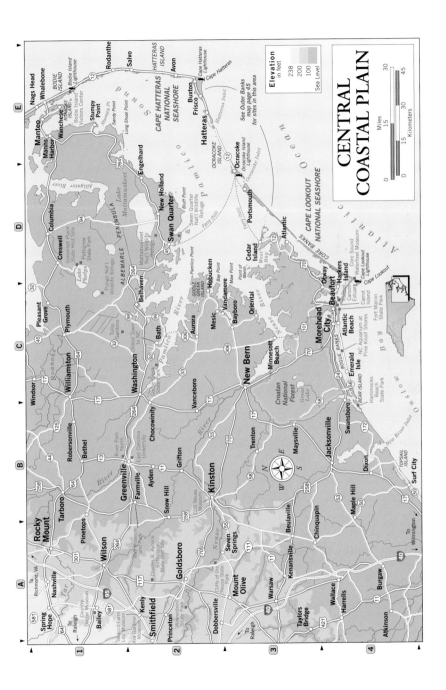

CENTRAL COASTAL PLAIN

Inland, the coastal plain marks the beginning of North Carolina's famous "Tobacco Road." Despite a decline in tobacco cultivation, North Carolina still produces more tobacco than any other state in the union. In the western part of the state farmers grow burley tobacco, which is harvested on the stalk, and hung to air dry.

Here in the East, farmers produce golden-leaf or bright-leaf tobacco. In summer huge, green tobacco leaves are broken from their rubbery stalks, baked golden in heated barns, and shipped to market. In fact, those unapologetically hideous aluminum-colored, RV-size contraptions squatting around the countryside are the "bulk barns" farmers now use to bake, or "cure," their tobacco. The more poetic, tall, windowless barns falling into disrepair are the old-style barns they've replaced.

GREENVILLE *map page 111, B-1/2*

If you travel into the coastal plain from Raleigh, you'll probably drive through Greenville, the home of **East Carolina University** and a regional educational and medical center. It's also the seat of Pitt County, which historically grew more bright-leaf tobacco than any other comparable region in the world.

How quickly are things changing for tobacco farmers in Eastern Carolina? The second edition of this book, released in 2000, said, "In late summer, tobacco's warm, rich odor still blankets parts of this small, fast-growing city.... Inside the warehouses on market days, a procession of farmers with sun-creased faces and tobacco buyers in perma-creased slacks edge up aisles lined with mounds of tobacco, settling on a per-pound price for each pile. That staccato sound—the one that sounds like a cross between a distressed bagpipe and machine gun fire—is the auctioneer."

Today, thanks to changes within the tobacco industry, those auctions are going, going, gone.

Farmers still plant and harvest tobacco (for now, anyway), but they contract their crops directly to the big tobacco companies, eliminating the traditional warehouses and auctioneers. Sprawling tobacco warehouses in the heart of Greenville, Farmville, Kinston, Robersonville, Smithfield, and other eastern towns are being renovated, or have simply closed their massive doors.

In Greenville you may want to visit **River Park North,** with its 10,000-gallon freshwater aquarium and touch tank, and local wildlife displays. *1000 Mumford Rd.; 252/329–4562.*

In western North Carolina farmers hang stalks of burley tobacco in open-air sheds to dry. In eastern North Carolina, where farmers raise golden-leaf tobacco, workers harvest only the tobacco leaves, placing them in tight, heated barns and baking them to a rich, golden brown.

TOBACCO FARMS IN CENTRAL COASTAL PLAIN

In eastern North Carolina thousands of lives still move in cadence with the tobacco seasons. In late February or early March—as soon as the fields dry from winter's gray rains—farmers shrug into heavy jackets, hitch up their discing plows, climb onto their tractors, and rumble toward slumbering fields.

If you happen to see them making their first long, patient sweeps across the earth's arched back, roll your window down. The newly broken earth fills the air with a smell as rich and full of life as December's dream of spring.

In early April, when the dogwoods bloom and the maples and sweet gums begin to hint at leaves, farmers hitch up their plows. You'll know a tobacco field when you see it, even before the plants go in. Grain fields are smooth. Corn, soybeans, and cotton like gentle rows, not too far apart. For tobacco, farmers plow the way the old Sunday School song says: deep and wide. They plow the furrows about a foot deep, because tobacco can't tolerate wet feet, and space the rows three feet apart to give the plants plenty of elbow room.

Farmers transplant tobacco seedlings from greenhouses or the long tobacco beds near their homes. (Some visitors mistake these plastic-covered beds for patches of ice.)

Not long ago, "setting out 'bacca'" was backbreaking work. Workers carried baskets of seedlings up each row, bending to set each plant. Today they ride tractor-pulled transplanters. As the tractor putters along, workers shove the plants into the earth and tamp them down, assembly-line style.

Tobacco seedlings look like young lettuce plants, and taste like bile.

They shoot skyward as the temperature rises and the rains fall in great, ragged curtains. Summer temperatures, which routinely hover in the 90s, spike to 100-plus degrees; the humidity makes the air thick enough to lean against. The coastal plain becomes a natural greenhouse. By early June the tobacco's waist high. By late June it tickles the chin.

Once families spent endless summer days hoeing tobacco rows, snapping suckers out of the plants, and breaking the delicate pink and white trumpet-shaped flowers that sap a plant's weight. Today you may see a few farmers doing these chores by hand, but mostly you'll see them tooling through the fields on tractors, spraying chemicals that kill grass, reduce suckers, and stunt flowers' growth.

Around July 4, armies of local and migrant workers swarm into the fields to harvest the crop, the green leaves swishing closed behind them like living doors.

And if you stop by a country store during the gray winter months, you're sure to find a farmer who's cruised over in his new king-cab pickup truck to drink a "Co-cola" and lament the weather, crops, and luck that have brought him to the brink of ruin. These winter lamentations make "putting in a crop of tobacco" a year-round endeavor.

HOMEPLACE

You won't talk long to tobacco farmers without finding out where they're from. They might say, "down home," "up home," "over home," "home," "the homeplace," or even "yonder home." No matter how they say it, they're talking about the place their family first owned or tended land.

Some farmers own thousands of acres of land, but most tobacco farms are small—300 acres or less. A farmer may have moved his family to town, but old clapboard homeplaces still stand scattered across the countryside. Some are stately old houses crafted by artists. Some are rambling, wisteria-draped affairs. Some are solid, no-nonsense places, remodeled generation by generation to reflect changing fortunes and needs.

All were built to withstand summers that send heat ghosts shimmying along highways and across fields. Builders designed these houses' high ceilings, tall windows, and cool plaster walls to outlast August's dense, breathtaking heat.

Golden-leaf tobacco plants in flower.

Most old houses sport wide front porches.

Once the front porch was the most popular summer room in the house. Young people fell in love there; mothers rocked new babies. Children played hide-and-seek in the yard, freezing statue-still behind gardenias; men sat in stiff-backed chairs and drank glasses of sugary iced tea.

Air conditioners have made porches obsolete. But in the cool of the evening, when the oak leaves rustle like crinolines and the tree frogs break out in their wild, spiraling song, "Come up on the porch," remains the friendliest greeting along Tobacco Road.

Over in Farmville, the **May Museum and Park,** in a restored 1870s home, is best known for its 19th- and 20th-century quilt collection. *213 S. Main St.; 252/753–6725.*

The **Greenville-Pitt County Convention and Visitors Bureau** can direct you to area festivals and events. *303 SW Greenville Blvd.; 252/329–4200.*

SOUTHERN SHORE OF ALBEMARLE SOUND   *map page 111, C/D-1*

US 64 runs east from Plymouth through Scuppernong and Creswell, where brown state signs point toward a majestic, cypress-lined lane that follows an old canal to **Somerset Place.** The state now preserves this vast plantation, once tended by more than 300 slaves, as a historic site. Retired site manager Dorothy Redford, herself a descendant of Somerset slaves, deserves much of the credit for bringing these old brick walkways, a massive canal system, and sprawling plantation house back to life and for reuniting the descendants of people once enslaved here through a series of reunions. The reunions have fallen by the wayside, but the plantation is open year-round. *2572 Lake Shore Rd.; 252/797–4560.*

Pettigrew State Park, next door to Somerset on the southern Albemarle Peninsula, is North Carolina's largest state park, covering 17,376 acres. Lake Phelps, which lazes over most of those acres, has been popular with boatmen for

The low-lying coastal areas of North Carolina have a serene, wild beauty.

millennia. Researchers have found 30 Native American canoes in Lake Phelps, one more than 4,000 years old. The park, known for gentle hiking trails, is named for CSA General James Pettigrew, whose plantation embraced many of these acres. *2252 Lake Shore Rd.; 252/797–4475.*

SCENIC DRIVE ALONG US 264   *map page 111, C/D-1/2*

At Mann's Harbor US 264 drifts south and then west along southern Albemarle Peninsula on one of the least-developed drives in eastern North Carolina.

If you walk along these shores with gulls and terns reeling overhead and fiddler crabs scurrying at your feet, the mapmaker's neat distinction between land and water fades away, blurred by the ripple of a salty breeze across fields of green bulrushes, and marshlands that breathe in and out with the tides.

Once these sounds provided fish, oysters, and shrimp for tiny Native American communities tucked along the shores. In the late 1600s the complexion of those scattered communities changed as English settlers moved from the islands to protected harbors.

For generations, "Down East" settlers planned their days by the mood of the sea and the sky, building modest houses in the shade of oaks, and boats that danced across the water. They worked hand-tied nets, hunted ducks and geese, and—between hurricanes and nor'easters—farmed sandy fields.

Excluding a few lonely ribbons of highway connecting a spattering of tiny towns, the face of this area remained unchanged for generations. But North Carolina's sleepy coastal towns and once wild coastlines have become high-dollar real estate as retirees from "up north" and from the state's urban areas have moved in to settle down, bringing new ideas, new accents, and new dollars for small-town economies.

Away from the development, life remains essentially unchanged. Even the most dilapidated house trailers have a boat in the yard. Occasionally you'll see a man weaving what appears to be a tapestry of sunlight between two pines. Actually, it's a fishing net of clear filament.

Red wolves, which once freely roamed eastern North Carolina, were exterminated by government-paid bounty hunters in the 18th and 19th centuries. In the last century the government paid big to reintroduce the wolves to the wild. You may see one of these protected animals loping along the highway as you edge along the peninsula and head inland toward Lake Mattamuskeet.

The **Mattamuskeet National Wildlife Refuge** centers around North Carolina's largest natural lake. Having survived man's attempts to drain it for farmland and

Eel pots, crab pots, everything for the fisherman at Belhaven Commercial Fishing Supplies.

mine it for peat, the lake still echoes in winter with the cries of trumpeter swans. In February huge flocks of migrating geese plummet from the gray sky to ski crazily along the water's surface, first on one orange foot, and then on the other, wings extended. A massive wildfire here in 2008 blanketed parts of eastern North Carolina in smoke for weeks; the effect of that wildfire on migrating geese has yet to be seen. *38 Mattamuskeet Rd., Swan Quarter; 252/926–4021.*

Waterfowl also winter at nearby **Pocosin Lakes National Wildlife Refuge** (205 S. Ludington Dr., Columbia; 252/796–3004) and at **Swan Quarter National Wildlife Refuge** (38 Mattamuskeet Rd., Swan Quarter; 252/926-4021), in Hyde County.

Belhaven, farther along US 264, is home to the hands-down most eccentric museum in North Carolina.

The **Belhaven Memorial Museum** came to life thanks to Miss Eva Blount, who in the early 1900s was both town matriarch and a prodigious snake killer. (You can see a few of her kills on display in the museum today.) Having decided that Belhaven needed a museum, Miss Eva charged her fellow townsfolk to venture forth, collect anything of interest, and send it home.

The results are fascinating. You'll find a collection of over 30,000 buttons, a flea circus complete with fleas dressed in tiny wedding clothes, antique underclothes, farm tools, eerie medical oddities contributed by the local doctor, eerier biological curiosities contributed by local farmers, strikingly gigantic boots taken off of a German soldier who no longer had apparent use for them, and much, much more. *211 E Main St.; 252/943–6817.*

BATH   *map page 111, C-2*

The Pamtico people abandoned their home on the tip of this peninsula in the late 1600s, bequeathing their name to the Pamlico River and Sound (a corruption of Pamtico), and stepping aside for Europeans who soon made this an English port. Naturalist John Lawson helped plan the town of Bath in 1705, making it North Carolina's oldest town.

Bath's historic structures occupy a couple of shaded blocks between US 264 and the bay. The Craven Street lot Lawson earmarked for a church is home to **St. Thomas's Church.** The brick church, which rests behind a wall made of ballast stones, was built in 1734 and is the state's oldest.

Folks still stroll down to the commons John Lawson designed to watch the sun set on the bay. Bath has become a popular retirement and vacation spot; area waterfront lots now boast houses that would set even the pirate Blackbeard's head reeling. But the heart of Bath hasn't changed much over the centuries.

The log cabins Lawson knew have been replaced by grander structures now restored, open to the public, and clearly marked: the **Palmer-Marsh House** (1744), the **Van Der Veer House** (1790), and the 1830 **Bonner House**—which Lawson might not fully appreciate, since it sits on his lot. If he plunked himself down on its wide front porch, though, he'd enjoy the view he no doubt shared with his lover Hannah and their daughter. You can tour all three houses, which are clustered together near the waterfront.

Bath was Blackbeard's stomping ground for a while, too. His house, which sat out on the point away from his ashen-faced neighbors, has been swallowed by storms and time. Rumors of a secret tunnel and buried treasure are timeless.

When you get to Bath, stop by the **visitors center** at Main and Carteret streets. Their tour includes everything worth seeing. The extremely well-informed guides, who are townsfolk, will tell you about Lawson, Blackbeard, a bored actress who wrote a Broadway smash while stuck here on a riverboat, and the Methodist minister who hexed Bath as he was being run out of town. *207 Carteret St.; 252/923–3971.*

BLACKBEARD THE PIRATE

Blackbeard, aka Edward Teach, was one of the most infamous pirates on the East Coast. After a profitable, blood-chilling career that included taking the city of Charleston hostage, Blackbeard accepted a pardon from North Carolina Governor Eden and retired to North Carolina.

He bought a little place in Bath, on the mainland, and wooed a local girl. Mr. and Mrs. Blackbeard settled down to the good life, visiting and occasionally robbing terrified neighbors. With help from the governor's secretary, Blackbeard soon returned to piracy, setting up camp on Ocracoke.

News travels. Blackbeard's friends dropped by: Charles Vane, Calico Jack Rackham, Ann Bonney, Mary Reed, Israel Hands, Robert Deal, and an army of lesser pirates. The buccaneers "boucaned" a few pigs, uncorked a few kegs of rum, and cranked up the band.

As the pirates cavorted, Virginia's governor developed a bad case of the jitters. On November 21, 1720–long after the party fizzled, his navy struck. Lt. Robert Maynard slipped two ships into the inlet as Blackbeard drank the night away.

Maynard approached at dawn. Blackbeard toasted his damnation, and Maynard attacked. Blackbeard crippled one ship, and blasted the other.

Before the smoke could clear, Maynard sent his crew below. As Blackbeard and his pirates swarmed the gunwales, Maynard's men burst on deck, firing. Blackbeard and Maynard met face-to-face, pistols drawn. They fired; Blackbeard staggered. They drew their swords; Maynard's snapped. As Blackbeard raised his cutlass for the final blow, he was ambushed.

The *Boston News-Letter* reported: "One of Maynard's men, being a Highlander, ingaged Teach with his broadsword, who gave Teach a cut of the Neck, Teach saying well done, Lad, the Highlander reply'd, if it be not well done, I'll do it better, and with that he gave him a second stroke, which cut off his head, laying it flat on his shoulder."

Maynard sailed home with Blackbeard's head swinging from his bowsprit.

The sandy beaches and marshlands of **Goose Creek State Park** provide a haven for wildlife. Broad and lazy, Goose Creek feeds into the Pamlico River at the park's western boundary, offering excellent freshwater and saltwater fishing. *2190 Camp Leach Rd.; 252/923–2191.*

Highway 92/264 continues west to **Washington,** whose historic riverfront district along the Pamlico River was occupied during the Civil War. In fact, at least one house still has cannonballs lodged in its exterior walls.

Cecil B. DeMille's hometown, which has seen a recent upswing in restoration efforts, also includes a host of 18th- and 19th-century homes, a rare prefab mail-order house (ordered from the Sears catalog), several B&Bs, and the restored **Turnage Theater,** which began life as a vaudeville theater. You'll find a cluster of good sandwich-and-salad restaurants on its leisurely Main Street, near the Turnage. *150 W. Main St.; 252/975–1191.*

If you stroll along Washington's waterfront, where you'll see everything from huge yachts to kayaks on the water, you'll eventually run into the **North Carolina Estuarium.** This facility includes over 200 exhibits on the ecology of North Carolina's vast wetlands and estuaries. *223 E. Water St.; 252/948–0000.*

AURORA AND ORIENTAL   *map page 111, C-2*

From just east of Bath NC 306 leads to a small free ferry, which putters across the tree-lined Pamlico River to the **Aurora Fossil Museum.** Since the coastal plain spent eons underwater, it's no surprise that marine creatures contributed most of this museum's fossils. The highlights of this small museum's collection include the business end of a 35-foot great white shark and a mountain of fossils out back—most around 22 million years old. The fossils are dredged up, literally, by a local phosphate mining company. Feel free to pocket your finds. *400 Main St.; 252/322–4238.*

From Aurora, NC 33 takes on different names as it loops along the undeveloped coast, heading through tiny fishing towns that are rapidly becoming upscale retirement communities: Hobucken, Mesic, Vandamere. At Bayboro, NC 55 heads south to **Oriental,** a village named for a ship that sank off the coast. Citizens who have taken the town's name to heart celebrate the New Year by parading a snorting, prancing dragon through town. The town also hosts the Oriental Regatta.

Tulips stage their perennial uprising at Tryon Palace in New Bern.

NEW BERN
map page 111, C-2

Founded by Swiss settlers, New Bern played a leading role in Coastal Carolina back when this busy little port town was home to the colony's Royal Governors. Over the years the town's narrow, two-story houses and office buildings, which stand shoulder-to-shoulder along quiet streets, declined, and the governor's palace fell prey to fire, time, and neglect.

Thanks to a mid-20th-century restoration movement, though, New Bern has pulled herself up by her historic bootstraps. Today beautifully restored house-museums, homes, offices, and antiques shops line quiet streets. In the heart of town, old buildings have come back to life as cafés, shops, and restaurants.

As in colonial times, the focal point here is ★New Bern's Tryon Palace, the centerpiece of the town's historic district. Walking through the double wrought-iron gates and up the shaded brick walkway leading to Tryon Palace, you can almost hear the hollow clap of horses' hooves and the creaking carriage that brought Royal Governor William Tryon and his family to this riverside palace in 1770. (To get there, follow the signs.)

Tryon's architect placed the 38-room brick palace on a rounded point of land overlooking the Trent and Neuse rivers. Digging deep into the colony's coffers, Tryon supplied his new home with statuary, furniture, and paintings from

A gateway into the palace's formal gardens—reminders of Royal governors, ambitious colonists, and history's changing tides.

The Craven County
Courthouse in New Bern.

Europe. His wife Margaret (the brains of the family) read in the garden while their daughter played hoops on wide lawns descending to the river's edge. On the waterfront, ships pulled into the harbor, ferrying goods in and out of the prosperous town.

Tryon and his wife—charmers, both—enjoyed the support of eastern Carolina's wealthy leaders. But Tryon faced stiff opposition and then open rebellion from irate citizens in the Piedmont, who didn't fancy putting a governor in a palace when they could barely put bread on their own tables.

After battling the "Regulators" into submission, Governor Tryon wisely moved his family to New York. Now a new governor, Governor Martin, propped his feet on the palace's brocade footstools. In the eastern part of the state Britain's popularity plunged as taxes rose.

In August 1774 colonial leaders met a few blocks from the palace to form North Carolina's First Provincial Congress. When they called a second meeting, a furious Governor Martin tried to upstage them by calling his Assembly to order. To his horror, he found his Assembly was the Provincial Congress: the colony's leadership had changed sides. Martin packed his wig and fled, making surprised North Carolinians the first to give a royal ruler the boot.

Flowering azaleas and dogwoods are a hallmark of spring throughout the South.

After the Revolution, North Carolina's capital moved west to Raleigh, leaving behind a site that is today known for its palace (rebuilt and refurbished in the 1950s), English gardens, and the thousands of tulips that bloom here each May.

A palace ticket includes admission to several historic homes. The Academy Museum (next door) provides the best history overview. The palace's reconstruction in the 1950s set off a wave of restoration throughout this town which, along with the palace, promotes a full slate of festivals, Revolutionary War reenactments, regattas, gardening workshops, antiques shows, even a good-natured Fourth of July celebration. *610 Pollock St.; 252/514–4900.*

CROATAN NATIONAL FOREST   *map page 111, C-3*

North Carolina's most famous naturalist, John Lawson, lived here in the early 1700s. Today it offers visitors, who generally come in among the pines along Highway 70, pretty much what it offered Lawson: hiking, boating, birding, and primitive camping. Several endangered species live in this 159,000-acre forest, including Lawson's friend, the alligator.

Visiting photographers should check out the White Oak River blind, where they'll see snow-white egrets flying with measured wing-beats through the sky and Swansboro's fishing boats heading out to sea. *141 E. Fisher Ave.; 252/638–5628.*

MOREHEAD CITY   *map page 111, C-4*

US 70 plows straight through Morehead City, where everyone on the street may be bald. Don't let it rattle you.

Each summer, thousands of the hair-impaired from around the world flock here for the Bald is Beautiful Convention. First choice for their annual meeting site was Bald Head Island south of Wilmington, but PR people for the upscale resort nixed the notion. Morehead—"more head"—came in second.

From Morehead's main thoroughfare, Arendell Street, take a right on Morehead Avenue to bridge Bogue Sound and visit Atlantic Beach, Fort Macon, the N.C. Aquarium at Pine Knolls Shore, etc. (*See* From Crystal Coast to Cape Fear, *below.*) The best way to find out what's going on at all of these sites is *This Week,* a free tabloid available in most restaurants and shops.

As you continue along Arendell instead of heading for the ocean, the Morehead City waterfront lies a block to your right. Here you can charter a boat for deep-sea fishing or a party cruise, or catch a meal at a waterfront restaurant. **Sanitary Fish Market,** founded in 1938, is the oldest of the waterfront restaurants. The decor is 1940s chic: pine chairs, sun-darkened pine paneling, mounted barracudas and

John Capps, head of the Bald Headed Men of America Association.

marlins on the walls. Beyond the plate-glass windows, the view is softer: a sailboat glides by on sparkling water, its white sails unfurled. An egret settles on the dining room's sun-bleached pier. The market is closed in December and January. *501 Evans St.; 252/247–3111.*

North Carolina's seafood restaurants originally served everything fried: fried seafood, fried potatoes, fried bread, and slaw. Anyone who asked for a baked potato was suspect. Today the same restaurants may specialize in fried seafood, but in deference to an influx of new tastes, most also serve seafood broiled, steamed, grilled, blackened, or gumboed. The humble hush puppy—a golden, deep-fat-fried corn bread often flavored with onions—still occupies a lofty position on most menus.

BEAUFORT   *map page 111, C-4*

Crossing the bridge from Morehead on US 70, you enter the old fishing village of Beaufort, pronounced *Boh*-furt. (*Byü*-furt is in South Carolina.)

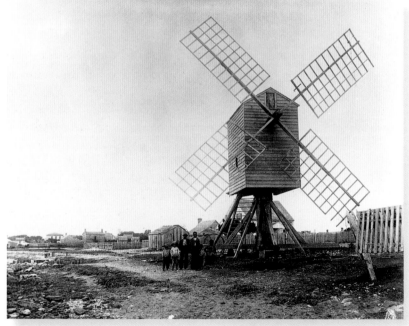

In the 19th century windmills provided power at many locations along the coast, including Beaufort, where this one was photographed in 1890. (NC State Dept. of Archives & History)

The main display hall at the North Carolina Maritime Museum.

Taking an immediate right, you'll meander through a quiet neighborhood of 18th-century cottages and antiques shops. Park on Front Street, which faces Bogue Sound, and walk a while through this town of white, New England–style cottages with broad, West Indies–inspired front porches. Today Beaufort is a popular stop on the Intracoastal Waterway. Sailboats bob in the harbor or dock at the marinas. Anne Street's old homes include several B&Bs.

The sea smells warm and close here, but as you walk down the waterfront past touristy shops and restaurants, the sharp, sweet smell of cedar slices the air. It drifts from the **North Carolina Maritime Museum's Watercraft Center,** a cypress-sided barn where the museum boatbuilder restores old sailing craft, and builds new ones as visitors watch from the balcony. *300 block of Front St.; 252/728–6673.*

For generations, shipbuilding has been a critical skill on the coast. Not long ago it wasn't unusual to find ships-in-progress tucked away in backyards, their massive rib cages and sides materializing piece by piece as time permitted. (You might still see them on Harker's Island, which lies in the sound just off Beaufort's shore.)

Shipwrights, who traditionally scorned levels and squares, also turned their creative hands to home construction, a fact confirmed by the seaworthy angles

The Life-Car on exhibit at the North Carolina Maritime Museum was an enclosed boat formed of copper or iron in which passengers would be conveyed to the shore. When the passengers were put in, the door was bolted shut and the car was then drawn to the land, suspended by rings from a hawser which had previously been stretched from the ship to the shore.

inside many of Beaufort's old homes. The **Beaufort Historic Association's tour** (252/728–5225) includes 18th- and 19th-century homes, the 1796 courthouse, an herb garden and herb cottage, and an 1858 apothecary shop and doctor's office.

The **North Carolina Maritime Museum,** across from the shipwright's shop, displays small boats, shells, and a spine-tingling exhibit of old-timey equipment used to rescue passengers from sinking ships. The life car on exhibit, for instance, was an enclosed boat formed of copper or iron in which passengers were conveyed to shore. Desperate rescuers sometimes sent the life cars to sinking ships in rough seas. Passengers were locked inside the metal cases, and the car was then drawn to the land, suspended by rings from a hawser, which had previously been stretched from the ship to the shore.

Some of this museum's best activities take place outdoors: field trips to estuaries and barrier islands, wildflower hunts, seining expeditions, workshops on wood-carving, boatbuilding, oar-making, etc.

You might be able to get in on a pirate-related adventure here, too. In the early 1700s pirates prowled Beaufort's waters, coming ashore to take on supplies and create bedlam. Blackbeard is rumored to have arranged the murder of one of his young wives here. Divers think they've found his flagship, the *Queen Anne's Revenge,* in 20 feet of water, 3 miles off Beaufort Inlet. Ask about related activities. All museum outings require reservations. *315 Front Street; 252/728–7317.*

Although Blackbeard stranded hundreds of his crewmen here, stealing their share of the loot, no known pirates rest in the **Old Burying Ground** in the heart of town. Ancient live oaks veiled in Spanish moss watch over the graves of priva-teers, sea captains, naval heroes, and shipwrecked sailors.

A most pleasant way to view the area, including **Carrot Island,** with its wild ponies, is to take to the sea. Tour boats depart the waterfront several times daily; other boats cater to fisherfolk, dolphin lovers, birders, and divers. You can also rent a kayak on the waterfront and explore the estuaries on your own. If you're thinking of boarding Blackbeard's sunken ship, the *Queen Anne's Revenge,* forget it. It's off-limits and well patrolled.

From Beaufort, US 70 meanders north across the rivers, tidal creeks, and saltwater marshes separating tiny coastal towns—Bettie, Otway, Williston, Sea-level—and, via NC 12, to the Cedar Island Ferry. A two-and-a-half-hour toll ferry across the Pamlico Sound takes you to Ocracoke Island (*see* Outer Banks chapter)—if you have reservations. *Call 800-BY FERRY.*

A right at Otway leads to **Harker's Island** and the **Core Sound Waterfowl Museum** (1785 Island Rd.; 252/728–1500). The island, famous for its genera-tions of boatbuilders, once made its life from the sea. The Core Sound Waterfowl Museum, at the tip of the island, preserves the traditions of island life, highlight-ing decoy carving, boatbuilding, and the commercial fishing industry.

Often as not, you'll find an islander on hand to demonstrate a local tradition—carving or net making, for instance. Take time to talk to them. You'll certainly learn something, and you'll hear a sound that's fading fast along our coast: a genuine high tide accent.

The Core Sound Decoy Carver's Festival, held early each December, is eastern Carolina's best winter festival.

FROM CRYSTAL COAST TO CAPE FEAR

Atlantic Beach, Salter Path, and Emerald Isle were once isolated villages on a sandy strip of land known as Bogue Banks. Today they have a catchier name: the Crystal Coast. They've almost fused into a vast, overdeveloped avenue of shops, restaurants, high-rise hotels, motels, cottages, and arcades that cater to summer visitors and seasonal fishermen. The shore of the sound and the oceanfront both are lined with cottages usually rented by the week, but public accesses allow easy access for non-renters, too.

ATLANTIC BEACH *map page 111, C-4*

Atlantic Beach is known for arcades, amusements, restless youth, nightclubs, and its thin public beach. In its dance clubs you'll often see men in penny loafers (no socks), chinos, and neat sports shirts dancing with women in full skirts. Women repeat a set of simple but fairly slinky steps as the men whirl around them like

The Bogue Fishing Pier catches the rays of sunrise in Emerald Isle, on Bogue Banks.

demon-possessed Ricky Nelsons, showing off fancy footwork while nonchalantly sipping cold beers.

This is the shag. Ultra-cool beach bums of the 1940s invented this slowed-down, slinked-up version of the Lindy so they could dance to the new music being recorded by African-American artists. (In a pathetic bid for attention, Myrtle Beach, South Carolina, claims to be the birthplace of the shag. People here and at Carolina Beach, near Wilmington, can set you straight.)

If you like to dance, this is the place to learn. Sadly, you must shag to Beach Music—monotonous, depthless tunes that inspire shagging and nothing more. To give the shag a whirl, stop by any of the dance clubs in Atlantic Beach. **Memories Beach and Shag Club** offers lessons for beginners. *128 East Ft. Macon Rd.; 252/240–7424.*

Atlantic Beach likes fast food. The best seafood is found across the bridge, in Morehead City.

An interior hallway in Fort Macon, a Civil War fort.

★ FORT MACON STATE PARK *map page 111, C-4*

This is the most-visited park in the state, partly because of its public bathhouse and beach. But don't overlook the elegant old fort—the best-preserved of North Carolina's Civil War forts.

Fort Macon, a pentagonal fort completed by civilian and slave laborers in 1834, was one of 37 forts built to protect the U.S. from a European invasion. Ironically, she never fired on foreign troops. Southern troops took the fort early in the Civil War, and Union forces reclaimed it a few weeks later.

Tours of this intricately restored fort take you over a moat and through cool, shaded tunnels to a parade yard. Gracefully curving stone stairs lead to walls overlooking what was once a cratered battle scene—now a peaceful beach.

The fort's restorations reflect the Civil War and World War II, when African-American troops served here.

Fort Macon's 389-acre preserve includes a nature trail and public beach. There's a snack bar by the bathhouse, and free picnic tables on the grounds. *2300 E. Ft. Macon Rd.; 252/726-3775.*

NORTH CAROLINA AQUARIUM AT PINE KNOLL SHORES
map page 111, C-4

If you double back on NC 58, you'll find the North Carolina Aquarium at Pine Knoll Shores near Salter Path.

What clued researchers in that they'd found Blackbeard's ship, the *Queen Anne's Revenge,* lolling on the bottom of Beaufort Inlet? Who patrols the final resting place of the German U-352, sunk off of Cape Lookout in World War II? Step inside the NC Aquarium at Pine Knolls Shores and see.

This 93,000-square-foot aquarium frames aquatic life in five eco-galleries: mountain, Piedmont, coastal plain, tidal waters, and ocean. But the 306,000-gallon Living Shipwreck tank—where tiger sharks, nurse sharks, and fin bar sharks patrol a three-quarter-scale German U-boat replica—grabs the most attention.

Despite the allure of the sharks, if Blackbeard were to visit he might zero in on the sandy floor of a nearby 50,000-gallon tank: a replica of his long-lost cannon. The *Queen Anne's Revenge,* which he had sunk when he decided to downsize his ship and crew, has a new crew, too, including bonnet-head sharks.

In all, the aquarium's 40 exhibits are home to 3,000 aquatic creatures, including popular river otters Pungo, Neuse, and Eno. Outside, you can hike two nature trails or explore the marshes from a boardwalk. *1 Roosevelt Blvd. (marker 7 on NC 58); 252/247-4003.*

Three fishermen display a loggerhead turtle caught near Cape Lookout in 1908. Turtles were captured for their meat in the late 19th century, although the loggerhead was not favored for eating. Now endangered, they continue to nest in small numbers on the Outer Banks. Hatchlings may be observed in the North Carolina Aquarium at Pine Knoll Shores near Atlantic Beach. (North Carolina Maritime Museum)

Sunrise over Wright Beach south of Topsail Island.

Toward the middle of Bogue Banks, NC 58 passes through several old fishing villages newly fitted up with beach cottages, condominiums, Jet Ski rentals, etc. A regional beach access near Indian Beach leads through tall oat-covered dunes to a shell-strewn beach where fiddler crabs and sandpipers dance along the shore. These are family beaches. Toddlers chase the waves out and shriek as the waves roll back in. Young people parade along the beach, studiously ignoring the fishermen who roll their pants legs up to wade into the surf, cast, and back up toward listing lawn chairs.

Most of the beach access is private (and the cottages rentable), but public accesses are scattered along the shore.

Heading south toward Cape Fear, irregularly shaped islands cluster along the mainland shore south of Emerald Isle like strewn pieces of a giant jigsaw puzzle. No island highway stitches these islands together. Some are accessible by mainland bridges, some only by boat. Many are privately owned.

You can reach **Hammocks Beach State Park** (1572 Hammocks Beach Rd.; 910/326–4881), which includes Bear Island, from Swansboro, a still-quiet fishing village at the mouth of the White Oak River. Signs lead the way from town. The Gourmet Cafe, at 99 West Church Street, in Swansboro, is a good place for lunch.

One of the most peaceful, unaltered islands in the state, Bear Island, which is accessible by ferry from within the park, is a paradise for swimmers and waders, who come for the shells. Campers pitch tents on primitive sites for 14 days at a stretch. There are, by the way, no bears on Bear Island. The island took its name from the Bear River, which exits mainland Onslow County near here. Historically, bruins were plentiful in Onslow County's lowlands.

South of Bear Island, on islands owned by the Camp Lejeune Marine Base, the term "shelling" takes on a whole new meaning. Avoid these islands: Some are used for live-fire drills.

TOPSAIL ISLAND   *map page 111, B-4*

Southwest of Camp Lejeune lies 20-mile-long Topsail Island. For years the island had a past so secret it had no history at all. All it had was rumors of a secret rocket project and unexplained buildings: squat cement towers, a blast-proof warehouse, and the Jolly Roger Motel, whose linen closet looked suspiciously like a bomb shelter and whose patio could double for a launchpad. Inquiries concerning the rocket project received a curt reply from the National Archives: "There is no evidence any such rocket program ever existed."

Recently declassified documents reveal that the island was part of the Navy's secret program to develop a supersonic, jet-powered missile. In 1947 and 1948 some 200 two-stage experimental rockets were built there and blasted into the sky as technicians tracked them from the island's towers. Today the Navy's "explosion-proof assembly shop" is a museum dedicated to "Operation Bumblebee," which led to the creation of jet engines and the Navy's first guided missiles.

A couple of blocks away, the 1950s-style rooms, pier, and launchpad/patio at the **Jolly Roger** (*see* Local Favorite Places to Stay at the end of this chapter) are popular with those who appreciate a cheerfully unfashionable beach with an uncluttered beachfront and gentle waves.

SOUTHERN COASTAL PLAIN

 This area has only one true city, Wilmington, which sits low on the banks of the Cape Fear River, about 28 miles from the river's mouth. For the most part, though, the southern coastal plain is a place of vacation beaches, tiny farming communities, retirement communities, swamps, and "mysterious" Carolina bays.

Most people traveling to this region from the Raleigh area take I–40 straight to Wilmington, but the country roads are worth traveling if you have the time.

★ WILMINGTON   *map page 139*

As river cities go, Wilmington is a latecomer. Europeans first sailed up the Cape Fear River in 1524, recording a fair climate, fruitful countryside, teeming waters, and friendly natives. After several settlements failed, including one by Barbadoans (who retreated to found Charleston, South Carolina), the lowlands along this powerful red-brown river remained Indian territory for almost another 200 years. The Waccamaw and other native people fled after the Tuscarora War, and rice planters moved in.

Wealthy planters founded Brunswick Town in 1725 near the mouth of the river. Hurricanes and marauding Spaniards soon sent merchants upriver to a more protected site, today's Wilmington.

From the beginning, rice cultivation suited the Cape Fear's landscape. Planters used sprawling natural lakes and lagoons to flood vast rice fields, and built docks and warehouses, turning creeping, reed-edged waterways into highways of commerce as they transported rice to Wilmington's wharves and beyond.

Rice cultivation was backbreaking work. In 100-degree temperatures and 98-percent humidity, it was probably heartbreaking as well. Slaves tilled the fields, sowed the crop by hand, harvested it with sickles, threshed it, and polished the rice with mortars and pestles. Janet Schaw, who visited in 1775, wrote, "the labor required for [rice] is only for slaves, and I think the hardest work I have seen them engaged in." As fortunes along the Cape Fear grew, so did the need for strong backs. By 1860, 60 percent of the area's population was enslaved; Wilmington's slave market was one of the state's largest.

As rice plantations prospered, Wilmington flourished. The railroad gave the city a second boost in the mid-1800s. Until the early 1900s Wilmington was North Carolina's largest city.

During the Civil War, Wilmington became a critical Confederate port. Six forts guarded the 28-mile channel into the city, creating a deadly gauntlet for Federal ships, which blockaded the city in July of 1861. Thanks to Frying Pan Shoals, a lethal kaleidoscope of sandbars curving seaward from the Cape Fear River, Union ships were forced to patrol a 50-mile arc into the ocean, allowing blockade-runners a chance to slip into the darkened port.

During the war, blockade-runners snuck $65 million worth of goods into the city. Most went to the military, but in true Rhett Butler style, blockade-runners also risked their lives to sneak parasols, hoopskirts, silks, and calicos past Federal

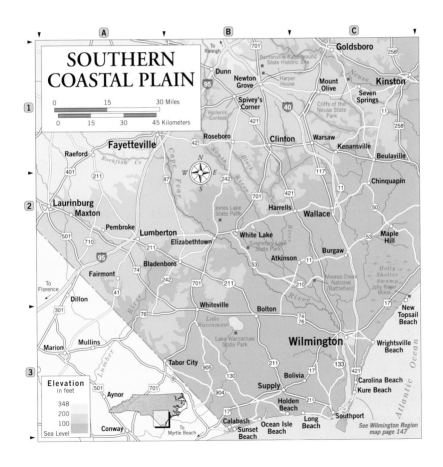

A ferry transports a carriage across the Cape Fear River in the port of Wilmington, probably around the turn of the 19th century. (Special Collections Library, Duke University)

ships. According to one witness, 260 blockade-runners visited Wilmington between May 1863 and December 1864.

By 1864 the city was the only Southern port that hadn't been shelled into submission. Now half the food for Lee's army came through Wilmington, and Lee warned that if the forts protecting Wilmington fell, he would have to abandon Richmond.

Union forces struck on Christmas Eve, 1864. Fort Fisher fell on January 15, 1865, during the largest land-sea battle ever fought in the United States. The tide had turned. Wilmington's protectors toppled one by one. On February 22, 1865, Mayor John Dawson surrendered the city, saving it from total destruction. Still, Union soldiers torched the 60-some-odd plantations along the river. Only Orton Plantation, which the Union used as a hospital, survived.

After the war, the rise of the textile and tobacco cities in the Piedmont signaled Wilmington's fall from the ranks of North Carolina's most populous cities. The city is still an important international port. Once tall-masted sailing rigs and schooners glided up the channel to Wilmington's docks. Today modern container ships nudge the 6,000-foot concrete wharf, and giant cranes dominate the landscape.

Modern Wilmington is noted for white-sand beaches, historic sites, and a restored waterfront of restaurants, clubs, shops, and museums. The city's 200-block National Register historic district, one of the state's largest, includes the

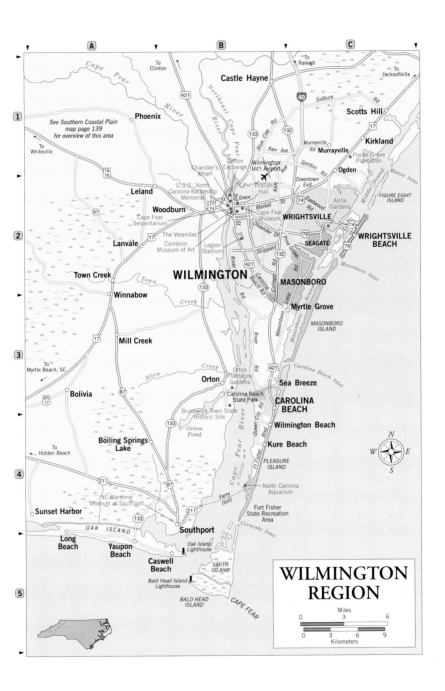

A **B** **C**

1

Cape Fear

To Clinton

To Raleigh

To Jacksonville

Northeast Cape Fear River

Castle Hayne

40 Sidbury Rd

Scotts Hill

See Southern Coastal Plain map page 139 for overview of this area

Phoenix

River

421

Blue Clay Rd

133 132

Kerr Ave Murrayville Rd

Murrayville

Kirkland

Poplar Grove Plantation

Mason Sound

To Whiteville

74 76

Chandler's Wharf

Cotton Exchange

Wilmington Int'l Airport

Gordon Rd

Ogden

Kerr Ave

Downtown Exit

Airlie Gardens

FIGURE EIGHT ISLAND

Middle Sound

Leland

U.S.S. North Carolina Battleship Memorial

3rd St Grace

Thalian Hall

74 Eastwood Rd

2

87

Woodburn

17 74

Market St

Cape Fear Museum

WRIGHTSVILLE

76

WRIGHTSVILLE BEACH

74

Lanvale

17

The Verandas

Cameron Museum of Art

Legion Stadium

Oleander Dr

Shipyard

Pine Grove Rd

132

SEAGATE

76

Mason Inlet

Town Creek

Town

421

River

Carolina Beach Rd

College Rd

MASONBORO

Masonboro Inlet

WILMINGTON

133

Creek

Winnabow

Masonboro Loop

Myrtle Grove

Masonboro Sound

MASONBORO ISLAND

3

17

Mill Creek

Allen

Creek

421

River

Carolina Beach Inlet

To Myrtle Beach, SC

BR 17

Bolivia

87

Orton

Orton Plantation Gardens

Carolina Beach Rd

Snow's Cut

Sea Breeze

CAROLINA BEACH

133

Brunswick Town State Historic Site

Carolina Beach State Park

Orton Pond

River Rd

Cape Fear River

Dow Rd

Ft Fisher Blvd

Wilmington Beach

Kure Beach

Boiling Springs Lake

To Holden Beach

211

87

PLEASURE ISLAND

4

NC Maritime Museum at Southport

North Carolina Aquarium

Ferry (toll)

Fort Fisher State Recreation Area

Corncake Inlet

Sunset Harbor

133

OAK ISLAND

Southport

211

N
W E
S

Long Beach

Yaupon Beach

Oak Island Lighthouse

SMITH ISLAND

Caswell Beach

Bald Head Island Lighthouse

WILMINGTON REGION

5

BALD HEAD ISLAND

CAPE FEAR

Miles
0   3   6

0   3   6   9
Kilometers

Feeding pigeons at Riverwalk during the annual Azalea Festival in Wilmington.

Burgwin-Wright House, which was possibly Lord Cornwallis's headquarters during the last gasp of the Revolution; Bellamy Mansion; an 1858 theater called Thalian Hall; and shaded Victorian neighborhoods. (You'll find B&Bs scattered throughout the historic district, too.)

The beaches are the number-one attraction in Michael Jordan's hometown. New Hanover County maintains nearly 100 public access sites along the shoreline. Some have showers, restrooms, and lifeguards; others are dune crossovers. Look for the orange-and-blue signs.

Fishing piers, which hurricanes regularly shorten and owners regularly extend, also dot the coast, providing additional beach access. In spring and fall, when the blues, spots, and king mackerels run, fishermen cast elbow-to-elbow along these rails. Wilmington, home of the North Carolina Azalea Festival, is prettiest in April, when banks of azaleas brighten shady parks and yards.

WILMINGTON HIGHLIGHTS   map page 141

Chandler's Wharf, a two-block restored ship-chandlers' district on Water Street, has shops, and restaurants. Wilmington's diverse chefs often specialize in seafood

Wilmington's historic waterfront, along the Cape Fear River, bustles with shops, cafes, yachts, and tour boats.

dishes, and garden-to-table cuisine. The eight or nine waterfront blocks between Chandler's Wharf and the Cotton Exchange are the place to go for shops, cafés, and nightlife.

The red-and-white tugboats you see a ways upriver are going to the North Carolina State Ports Facility, which links Wilmington with over 200 ports worldwide, exporting tobacco, textiles, and wood products.

If your interests lean toward the cold-blooded, look for the **Cape Fear Serpentarium**, in downtown Wilmington. Within this unassuming building coil, slither, and hiss 100 species of venomous snakes, including green and black mambas, king cobras, and the world's largest collection of bushmasters—the rarest poisonous snake on earth. *20 Orange St.; 910/762–1669.*

The 67 acres of the extravagant post-Victorian, European-style **Airlie Gardens** were built around Cape Fear Coast's natural plants. *300 Airlie Rd., 2 miles west of Wrightsville Beach; 910/798–7700.*

The well-preserved **Cotton Exchange** houses over 30 specialty shops and restaurants, as well as the **visitors center**. *24 N. Third St., at Princess St.; 910/341–4030 visitors center.*

Offering the best overview of area history, the **Cape Fear Museum** maintains a tremendous collection of Civil War artifacts from the old Blockade Runner Museum, including a diorama of the battle fought at nearby Fort Fisher. The Michael Jordan Discovery Room has exhibits designed specifically for children. *814 Market St.; 910/798–4350.*

The likes of Lillian Russell, Oscar Wilde, and Buffalo Bill Cody once performed at **Thalian Hall**, a gilded Victorian opera house. Today, the restored arts center books jazz artists, new plays, and dance companies. *310 Chestnut St.; 910/343–3660.*

The **Cameron Art Museum** opens its doors on 200 years of North Carolinian and American art. Its permanent collections include the works of local artists Claude Howell and Minnie Evans, and a major collection of Mary Cassatt's color prints.

Howell, the first Tar Heel to exhibit work in the Metropolitan Museum of Art, lived and worked in Wilmington most of his life. "Outside artist" Minnie Evans worked as a gatekeeper at Wilmington's Arlie Gardens and came to art late in life. The story is that while working at Arlie she sometimes gave her visionary artwork to passersby. Those who tossed her gifts are probably kicking themselves now. Evans is recognized as one of the major visionary artists of the 20th century. *3201 S. 17th St.; 910/395–5999.*

Costumed guides show visitors around the 1850 **Poplar Grove Plantation**, with its manor house, tenant house, kitchen, smoke house, herb cellar, and gardens. At the Cultural Arts Center a weaver dips a skein of wool into a vat of pea-green dye, lifts it out, and hangs it on a wooden rack, where the wool goes from pea green to dull blue, to brilliant indigo. Craftspeople here make traditional dyes from plants in the dye garden, while weavers keep the looms humming. The plantation is about 15 miles northeast of town. *10200 US 17 N; 910/686–9518.*

Front parlor at Poplar Grove.

The USS *North Carolina* was one of the largest battleships of the American Pacific fleet during the Second World War, and took part in every major naval offensive in the Pacific theater.

RIVER CIRCLE TOUR

Many of the area's most dramatic historic sites and finest beaches lie along a two-hour loop around Wilmington. (That's two hours driving time. The loop, which connects plantation tours, historic sites, nature walks, beaches, and gardens, could take a day or a week.)

From US 17 in Wilmington, US 421 heads north to the USS *North Carolina* **Battleship Memorial**, one of the most-visited historic sites in the state. The sleek World War II dreadnought, painted in the same blue-gray she wore while patrolling the Pacific, looks as fit for duty today as she did when she blasted away at Japanese ships and kamikaze pilots at Okinawa.

Optimistic Japanese radio announcers heralded the USS *North Carolina*'s demise six times during World War II, but despite close calls, including a direct torpedo hit, the battleship took part in every major naval offensive in the Pacific. She carried out nine shore bombardments, sank a Japanese troop ship, shot down 24 aircraft, and earned 15 battle stars.

An excellent two-hour self-guided tour, available year-round, takes you through the restored ship from the laundry to the sick bay to the command center, and puts you behind the giant guns on deck. *1 Battleship Rd.; 910/251–5797.*

ORTON PLANTATION   *map page 141, B-3*

Orton is the only Cape Fear rice plantation that survived the Civil War. In size, it is only a faint echo of the original, but that doesn't make the white-columned Greek Revival home, manicured gardens, and grounds less appealing.

Orton's 20-acre gardens, which welcome visitors, take advantage of nature's backdrop of open fields, marshlands, and Spanish moss. Indigenous trees,

LIGHTS, CAMERAS, ACTION

If you see a number of oddly familiar places and faces as you explore the Wilmington area, don't assume you're experiencing déjà-vu. It could be more of a case of "did-you-view," as in, did you view any of the hundreds of television shows and movies filmed in Wilmington and its surrounds, from *Dawson's Creek* to *Blue Velvet*.

North Carolina is currently the country's third-busiest filming destination, and Wilmington sees her share of lights, cameras, and catering trucks. To get a feel for "Hollywood East," try the **EUE/ Screen Gems Studios** tour. The largest film production studio east of Hollywood offers one-hour guided weekend tours. *1223 N. 23rd St.; 910/343–3433.*

You can also sign up for an independent downtown walking tour of movie and TV locations with **Wilmington Walking Tours**. *910/794-7177.*

especially cypress and live oaks, dominate the gardens, whose brick walkways wind through wisteria, palms, and thousands of annuals.

You'll also find water gardens and a comforting medley of Southern standards here—camellias, azaleas, hydrangeas, and crepe myrtles. The gardens, which lie wrapped in the arms of hundreds of acres of rice fields, welcome visitors from March through November, when winter robs them of their color.

Orton became the first Wilmington location to attract Hollywood's attention, when Frank Capra, Jr., decided to shoot Stephen King's *Firestarter* here in 1982. Orton has also starred in TV shows and scores of movies, including *The Divine Secrets of the Ya-Ya Sisterhood, A Walk to Remember,* and *I Know What You Did Last Summer.*

The plantation house bears little resemblance to "King" Roger Moore's original 1735 home, which has been remodeled over the years. The house itself isn't open to the public, but if you saw Sissy Spacek plug her husband in *Crimes of the Heart,* you've already visited Orton. *9149 Orton Rd. SE; 910/371–6851.*

BRUNSWICK TOWN   *map page 141, B-3/4*

South on NC 133 lies Brunswick Town, once colonial North Carolina's busiest port. As the British fled North Carolina in 1776, Cornwallis shelled the

The Luola Chapel at Orton Plantation.

town, reducing it to rubble. Home and shop foundations remain, while the ruins of St. Philips Church, where royal governors once married (scandalously, at times), watch over Brunswick Town in ghostly splendor. A tour trail explores the town, and crosses the earthworks of Fort Anderson, a Confederate fort. *8884 St. Phillips Rd. SE; 910/371–6613.*

SOUTHPORT
map page 141, B-4

From Brunswick Town, NC 133 continues downriver toward Southport, a retirement town that is the antithesis of Wilmington's bustle. If you want a quiet haven, a Southport B&B is a good bet. This town is known for old sea captains' houses set back from meandering streets, in yards where oaks drip Spanish moss. It's also known for its riverfront restaurants.

SOUTHPORT AREA BEACHES

BALD HEAD ISLAND *map page 141, B-5*

From the Indigo Plantation marina, ferries leave on the hour for Bald Head Island. If explorer Giovanni Verrazano, who discovered Bald Head Island in 1524, could see it now, the changes would make his knees buckle. Chances are, he'd land in a golf cart.

Verrazano found a windswept, heavily wooded island guarded by the hazardous shoals that earned Cape Fear its name. Today he'd find golf courses, croquet greenswards, tennis courts, restaurants, shops, cottages, B&Bs, and condominiums—all designed to stay in step with the island environment.

Bald Head Island Resort, which welcomes day visitors and long-term guests, occupies the southern shore of Bald Head Island, whose jutting chin is Cape Fear. Bald Head is the largest island in the Smith Island complex, which is largely

Since Old Baldy took up his post in 1817, tidelands and salt marshes have replaced ocean swells.

owned by the state. It teems with wildlife. Loggerhead turtles and green sea turtles, both protected species, return to the island every year to lay their eggs. The turtles always have the right-of-way. Across the sound Battery Island is a breeding spot for herons, egrets, and ibises. Alligators creep through the marshlands.

Old Baldy, a restored 1817 lighthouse, is the state's oldest. Shifting shoals have made it obsolete, but you can climb the tower.

OAK ISLAND   *map page 141, A-4/5*

Below Southport the North Carolina coast jogs west toward Oak Island's vacation communities. The family beaches on this south-facing island are known for swimming. Don't let the gentle waves fool you, though: these currents can be very dangerous. **Oak Island Lighthouse,** which replaced Old Baldy, sits on the east end of this island near Fort Caswell, a Civil War fort now owned by the North Carolina Baptist Assembly. Oak Island's best public beach access lies to the west at the point, but 60 public access points dot the island's beach.

BRUNSWICK ISLANDS AND SURROUNDS   *map page 139, B-3*

Golf enthusiasts know this region for its 30-plus championship golf courses, designed by Arnold Palmer, Rees Jones, Dan Maples, Willard Byrd, and others. Standouts include Tiger's Eye Golf Links, ranked in the top 100 public golf courses in the US by *Golf Digest* in 2007, and Leopard's Chase Golf Club, which

A moonrise over Flora's Bluff on South Beach.

Golf Digest and *Golf Magazine* rated one of the 10 best new public courses in the US in 2007. The two courses, designed by Tim Cate, are noted for their secluded feel and scenic landscapes.

Seafood lovers know this region for its fried seafood. At mealtime people heading in this general direction tend to veer toward **Calabash,** a small town just on this side of the South Carolina border, on US 17. Twenty-some seafood restaurants line the village streets. The local seafood, which comes in daily, is cooked Calabash style: deep-fried in a thin batter, and served with hush puppies, potatoes, slaw, and tea.

Like Oak Island, the Brunswick Islands face south, and they all welcome visitors. **Holden Beach** has long been noted for its easy-paced family beaches. **Ocean Isle** places a special emphasis on its wildlife. At **Sunset Beach** a boardwalk at the end of town leads to a beach known for gentle waves.

FERRY RIDES AND SIDE TRIPS

FORT FISHER AREA   *map page 141, B-4*

Take the Southport-Fort Fisher ferry across the Cape Fear River. At the **North Carolina Aquarium** you'll see examples of life from the warm Gulf Stream, notably sharks and tropical fish. *900 Loggerhead Rd.; 910/458-8257.*

Outside the aquarium, the **Fort Fisher State Recreation Area** offers 5 miles of little-used public beach access, restrooms, etc.

Gnarled live oaks shade the trail to Fort Fisher, whose collapse signaled the death of the Confederacy. Fort Fisher fell on January 15, 1865; nature is finishing the job. Two-thirds of the earthwork fort has succumbed to erosion. *1610 Ft. Fisher Blvd. S, Kure Beach; 910/458-5538.*

CAROLINA BEACH   *map page 147, B-3*

From Fort Fisher US 421 heads north to Kure Beach and Carolina Beach on Pleasure Island. Carolina Beach lies about 20 minutes south of Wilmington. This family beach, on the ocean side of the island, offers hotels, cottages, and several public beach accesses. It's also noted for party boats, charter boats, and dinner cruises.

CAROLINA BEACH STATE PARK   *map page 141, B-3*

On the western side of the man-made Pleasure Island overlooking the Cape Fear River is one of the most biologically diverse parks in the state. In this park trails wind among marshes, riverbanks, forests, ponds, and pocosins. But this preserve

A small yacht basin along the Intracoastal Waterway at Wrightsville Beach.

is best known for its carnivorous Venus flytraps—small, bug-eating plants that live near Wilmington and nearly nowhere else on earth. Meat-hungry sundews and pitcher plants live here, too.

WRIGHTSVILLE BEACH   *map page 141, C-2*

North of Carolina Beach, NC 132 intersects with US 76, which cuts east toward Wrightsville Beach. Fishing tournaments and sailing events are popular on all Wilmington's beaches, but surfing is particularly popular at Wrightsville Beach. Several Intracoastal Waterway cruise ships stop at Wrightsville Beach, too. You can also rent canoes, kayaks, and sailboats here; sign up for various tours; or cruise over to Masonboro Island.

INLAND ON THE SOUTHERN COASTAL PLAIN

As you travel inland to Moore's Creek National Battlefield (north on US 421, to NC 210) and beyond, you'll drive through wooded lowlands and still-water swamps, and by geological features known as Carolina bays—unexplained oval-shaped indentations in the earth's surface.

Venus flytraps are one of the botanical oddities found throughout this coastal region of the state.

When settlers rambled ashore on the mainland in the mid-1700s they headed inland along this general route, through thick pine forests surrounding unusual, spring-fed lakes. At one time geologists thought the shallow, crystal "Bay Lakes" were created by meteorite showers millions of years ago, but now most believe the lakes were created by artesian springs and by winds, and are between 5,000 and 60,000 years old. You can swim in some of them today.

MOORE'S CREEK NATIONAL BATTLEFIELD *map page 139, C-2*

When North Carolina's royal governor Josiah Martin fled Tryon Palace on the eve of the Revolution, he called for Loyalist settlers to come to his aid. A troop of 1,600 Scots met near Fayetteville and marched toward their leader, who cowered on a ship off Wilmington's shore. As the Loyalists rumbled east, two Patriot leaders watched with interest. Richard Caswell and Alexander Lillington had only 1,020 men, but they'd enlisted cunning on their side.

Today at Moore's Creek National Battlefield an old stagecoach trail leads to their carefully chosen battle site: the bridge over Widow Moore's Creek. The battle fought there in the wee hours of the morning, on February 27, 1776, decided the course of the Revolution in North Carolina.

The night before the battle, Caswell's men slipped across the bridge, building campfires along the bank nearest the approaching army. Other patriots dug in on the opposite bank. The Loyalists, seeing the campfires, crept near. At dawn they charged. Nobody was home.

The Patriots had crossed the bridge, taking its planks and leaving two logs for the Loyalists to cross. Undaunted, the Loyalists sprinted for the logs, which had been greased with soap and tallow. As the Loyalists plummeted into the frigid creek 20 feet below, the Patriots opened fire.

Three minutes later the Loyalists surrendered, giving up 850 prisoners, 2,000 weapons, and $75,000 in gold. Governor Martin and the Brits, with faces as red as their coats, headed south and stayed there until the last weeks of the war.

Today the site of their defeat includes a museum, a reconstruction of the infamously slick bridge, two trails, and the Heroic Woman Monument, a tribute to Mary Slocum, who tended the wounded at this battle. *20 mi northwest of Wilmington; take US 421 to NC 210, head west, following National Park Service signs. 40 Patriots Hall Dr., Currie; 910/283–5591.*

Getting ready for a Revolutionary War reenactment at Moore's Creek National Battlefield.

Popular for group camping, **Singletary Lake State Park** (6707 NC 53, Kelly; 910/669–2928) offers cabins and mess halls. If that's too primitive, try the town of **White Lake,** a few miles down the road. This privately developed white-sand lake is known for motels, ski shows, glass-bottomed boats, and Ferris wheels. North of White Lake on NC 242, **Jones Lake State Park** (4117 Highway 242 N, Elizabethtown; 910/588–4550) provides camping, swimming, boating, hiking, and nature studies.

SPIVEY'S CORNER   *map page 139, B-1*

Continue north on NC 242 and US 421 to Spivey's Corner, a peaceful little community, unless it's June, in which case the noise can be deafening. With reporters coming in from as far away as Australia, the Spivey's Corner Hollerin' Contest dents eardrums around the world.

Your admission fee buys you a spot in the competition but, says co-founder and spokesman Ermon Godwin, Jr., if you want to win, start practicing now. "All the people that come up here and scream and yell will not be good hollerers," he cautions. "It's not like hog-calling. It's an art. The best way to do it is take an

Singletary Lake State Park

old hymn like 'Amazing Grace.' Hum that tune and keep building up your voice until you can be heard a half-mile away," he advises. "You have to learn to control your voice."

Hollering was once a form of communication for rural Carolinians, whose distinctive hollers let neighbors know if they were okay, or needed help. Other contests include whistling, conch-shell blowing, and fox-horn blowing. Bring a blanket or a chair, and dress for hot weather.

BENTONVILLE BATTLEGROUND   *map page 139, B-1*

Common sense suggests that the Civil War in North Carolina would end with the fall of Wilmington, but her largest land battle lay ahead.

As U.S. Gen. William T. Sherman scorched South Carolina and headed north, North Carolinians despaired. "The tide of the war was rolling in upon us," wrote Chapel Hill resident Cornelia Phillips Spencer in *The Last Ninety Days of the War in North Carolina.* "The smoke of burning Columbia, and of the fair villages and countless plantations that lay in the route…rolled slowly up our sky; and panic-stricken refugees, homeless and penniless, brought every day fresh tales of havoc and ruin."

Sherman torched Fayetteville's arsenal, on the Cape Fear River, and turned east. Meanwhile, Confederate Gen. Joseph Johnston forged a desperate plan to block Sherman's march to Richmond.

As the two armies converged on a small farm near Bentonville, the Harper family fled their two-story farmhouse. Their home, with its neat shutters and portico, sat squarely in the sights of Sherman's 60,000-man army and Johnston's 20,000 troops. For three days the sky over their home rained lead. The Harpers' fields—intended for corn, soybeans, and cotton—became earthworks, killing fields, and mass graves. Their house, intended to nurture a family, became a hospital, with wounded spilling across the front yard. As Sherman's reinforcements arrived, Johnston withdrew to Smithfield. Casualties for both sides numbered over 4,000.

Gen. Robert E. Lee surrendered at Appomattox Courthouse, Virginia, on April 8, 1865. Johnston surrendered to Sherman 17 days later. The war was over.

Today the **Harper House** is restored as a field hospital. (The oft-sighted spirit in floor-length skirts may be Mrs. Harper.) The site includes a small museum and 100 of the 6,000 acres involved in the fray. Beyond the park, 29 historical markers along the road trace the battle. The park stages reenactments each March. *5466 Harper House Rd. Four Oaks; 910/594–0789.*

SMALL-TOWN MUSEUMS ALONG
TOBACCO ROAD EAST

KINSTON: AN IRONCLAD
map page 139, C-1

The *CSS Neuse,* one of three Civil War ironclads on display in the nation, is the best-preserved ironclad of the lot. Not bad for a ship that went to war half-dressed.

The Confederates began the *CSS Neuse* in a tiny town now known as Seven Springs. They floated her wooden hull downstream to Kinston and outfitted her with engines and half the planned–for amount of siding, since iron was very scarce.

When the ship's commander, Joseph Price, received orders to sneak the ship down the Neuse to help retake New Bern, the river was so low the catfish could walk across. He shoved off, and stuck fast. By the time the ship floated free the battle was lost, and he was up the river, literally. Price sank the ship in 1865 to keep her from enemy hands.

Today the ship's skeleton lies in state on US 70 on the west side of town. The museum proper resides on Kinston's main drag. *2612 W. Vernon Ave.; 252/522–2091.*

CHARLES B. AYCOCK BIRTHPLACE   *map page 111, A-2*

One of the state's most famous governors was born on this typical 19th-century "pre-tobacco" farm that nestles comfortably against a slight rise, like a sleepy child against his mother's arm. The Aycock Farm's tiny, unpainted house rests beneath generous, wide-armed oaks, and a bucket hangs over

A Civil War naval battle at Cape Hatteras in 1861, as depicted by Currier & Ives. (North Carolina Collection)

Charles B. Aycock Birthplace

children pitched in, too, raising cotton, food crops, and corn.

North Carolina's future "Education Governor" slept in a closet-size room off the side porch.

Charles took his love of politics and oratory from his dad, a state senator. His mother instilled in him a love of education. Charles and his brothers—but not his sisters—went to school in a schoolhouse like the one on-site: hard seats and dunce's cap included.

Charles, who earned a law degree from The University of North Carolina, was elected governor in 1900. The 1,100 public schools built during his tenure offered all North Carolina children educations, for the first time.

This North Carolina State Historic Site invites guests to pitch in with the chores Charles left behind—plowing, raking, weeding, hoeing, harvesting, canning. If your timing's good, you may even get to shear a sheep.

The Aycocks' home is being renovated at this writing, thanks to arsonists who torched it in 2008. It reopens in summer 2009. *264 Gov. Aycock Rd., Fremont; 919/242–5581.*

KENLY: TOBACCO FARM LIFE MUSEUM *map page 111, A-1/2*

How much difference did a tobacco economy make? This museum answers that question for you, with exhibits that focus on rural farm life from 1880 to World War II.

the well. Within shouting distance, a corncrib holds corn for the livestock, and sheep crowd into a barn where the Aycocks kept horses, mules, and a cow.

Charles B. Aycock was born on this Wayne County farm in 1859 to Serina and Benjamin Aycock—relatively well-to-do planters living in circumstances that would have sent Scarlet O'Hara fumbling for the smelling salts.

Serina Aycock, who couldn't read or write, ran the farm while her husband pursued a political career. Vegetables from the garden helped feed her family. Like their neighbors, the Aycocks made their own cloth and sewed their own clothes.

As many as 13 slaves helped keep the homestead running, but Serina's nine

The museum's restored farmstead includes a farmhouse and kitchen, smokehouse, tobacco barn, milk house, pack house, and a working blacksmith shop. An 1890 one-room schoolhouse stands alongside.

The museum stages demonstrations periodically through the year, but on the last weekend in June you'll see farm history revitalized through demonstrations and entertainment. Visitors can try their hand at "tying" or "looping" tobacco on a long tobacco stick.

With a flick of the wrist, the looper ties the bundle of tobacco on alternating sides of the stick. After 20 or so bundles are in place, the looper ties the end of the stick with a rodeo-style flourish and breaks the twine. The process is slightly

Country Doctor Museum

faster than greased lightning, as you'll see once the tobacco starts flying and the twine starts singing.

This tiring job was once performed by women who worked 10- and 12-hour days beneath tin barn shelters and shade trees. Men worked in sweltering fields, carefully breaking ripe leaves from the plants, packing them in mule-drawn carts, and "trucking" them to the shelter, where the women and children worked. Today, with bulk barns these tasks are obsolete. *US 301 N at the edge of town; 919/284–3431.*

BAILEY: COUNTRY DOCTOR MUSEUM *map page 111, A-1*

At the only museum in the nation dedicated entirely to the country doctor, you can explore a restored 1857 doctor's office and an 1887 examination room—amputation kits included. The museum also exposes the mysteries of a 19th-century apothecary shop, and features an herb garden that grows more than 60 medicinal plants used in eastern North Carolina around 1900.

Tobacco Farm Life Museum

Herbs played an important role in medical practices then. Few doctors' offices included herb gardens, but physicians commonly hired people to collect herbs, and used them to treat everything from heart flutters to lethargy.

Most plants in this garden, which was established by the North Carolina Wildflower Preservation Society, were prescribed or were widely accepted home remedies. *6642 Peele Rd.; 252/235–4165.*

SMITHFIELD: AVA GARDNER MUSEUM *map page 111, A-2*

In 1941 Ava Gardner—who grew up in tiny Brogden, North Carolina, near Smithfield—smoldered her way off of Tobacco Road and into an MGM limousine. But long before Hollywood took note, 12-year-old Tom Banks knew Ava was a star.

In 1939 Banks teased Ava each morning as she walked by on her way to school. One day the future glamour girl snapped. She chased her tormentor around the corner, collared him—and planted a kiss on his red face.

For the next 50 years Tom Banks clipped every Ava Gardner article he laid his hands on. He collected posters from her 60 movies, saved her calendars, and hoarded her magazine covers.

His collection is now the heart of the Ava Gardner Museum in Smithfield. The museum maintains a library of Ava's movies; artifacts include Ava's jewelry, clothes, and movie costumes *.325 E. Market St.; 919/934–5830.*

Ava Gardner Museum

Bald cypress trees emerge like ghosts from the swamp of Lake Waccamaw, 35 miles west of Wilmington.

A GREAT DRIVE ON THE COASTAL PLAIN

For a small-town Main Street tour, head to the inland coast east of Greenville. You may want to pick up a picnic lunch in Greenville, or you can try a main-street café in one of the small towns along your way.

From Greenville, NC 33 South meanders an hour or so east through Grimesland, to Edwards. Cross the railroad tracks just beyond Edwards and hang a left on 33, heading about 3 miles into the sleepy town of Aurora.

You'll find the Aurora Fossil Museum on Main Street. Check out the museum and then cross the street to the park, to look for fossils and shark teeth in the mound of museum-supplied fill. Chances are you'll find plenty of artifacts. If you need help identifying your finds, head back in to the museum. They know their sharks' teeth, and chances are better than average that you'll leave with a pocket full of prehistory.

From Aurora head north 7 miles on NC 33 to NC 306 and to the free ferry across the Pamlico Sound. You'll find picnic tables by the ferry dock, in case you brought that picnic lunch. Leave your car in the ferry line to hold your place. The ferry trip takes only 20 minutes or so, but it offers the joy of being on the water. Once you putter off the ferry, follow NC 99 about 10 miles to beautiful little Belhaven and the charmingly eccentric Belhaven Memorial Museum, on Main Street. (There's also a café on Main Street and an ice-cream parlor around the corner.)

From the Belhaven Museum, return to 99 and drive west 18 miles to historic Bath for their excellent history tour. You can check out North Carolina's first colonial capital and the onetime stomping ground of Blackbeard the Pirate. From Bath, NC 92 will take you 14 miles to Washington (known as "Little Washington" to those who don't live there and "The Original Washington" to those who do). Grab dinner in one of the Main Street restaurants and, perhaps, a show at the Turnage Theater. From Washington you can zip back to Greenville on US 264. It's about 20 miles.

GETTING AROUND

Most people in the East joke that our best highways were designed to get Raleigh lawmakers to the beach as quickly as possible. Looking at a map, you can see why.

US 64 bolts from Raleigh to Mann's Harbor and the Outer Banks, in the north. US 70 goes from Raleigh to Morehead and the Crystal Coast, on the central coast. I–40 zips you from Raleigh down to Wilmington and the southern beaches.

If you're in a north-south state of mind, I–95 is the quickest inland route from Virginia to South Carolina and points between. Along the coast US 17 is your best north-south bet, but it's not a very fast bet.

Beyond that, abandon your need for speed. The coastal

On Wilmington's riverfront: an excursion boat and the Cape Fear Bridge.

plain remains a region of spidery roads and small towns. As you drive our country roads, watch for farmers who drive huge, lumbering machinery . . . very slowly. Also scan roadsides for deer, which are spry and plentiful. If you see one, slow to a crawl. There are usually more deer coming. Of course you don't want to hurt a deer, gentle reader, but the damage to a car in a deer-car collision can be shocking. Neither party wins.

LOCAL FAVORITE PLACES TO EAT

B's Barbecue. 700 B's Barbecue Rd., Greenville; no phone. $

Barbecue cooked over an open fire is hard to come by—unless you park beneath the oak trees at B's and hit the chow line. A plate includes eastern-style barbecue or chicken (if you like your chicken on the juicy side, ask for dark meat), slaw or string beans, potatoes, and pups. The tea's sugar rush staves off post-pig lethargy. B's serves lunch until the food runs out. Come early, especially on Saturdays. You can eat inside at tables and booths or outside at the picnic tables. No dinner.

Dixie Grille. 116 Market St., Wilmington; 910/762–7280. $

The stone-ground grits at this storefront café are world-class. In fact, you'd be hard-pressed to find a better Southern breakfast: eggs, applewood-smoked bacon, biscuits, and grits. Or sweet-potato pancakes, or a fried green tomato BLT.... The lunch menu is stacked with salads and sandwiches. No dinner.

Ella's. 1148 River Rd., Calabash; 910/579–6728. $$

Check out the entryway photo of the late Miss Ella and, over it, the famous words Jimmy Durante used to close his radio and television act: "Good night, Miss Calabash, wherever you are." Ella, one of this restaurant's founders, was one of his two "Miss Calabashes." "He said he was going to make them famous," Ella's granddaughter, Cammie Dodds, says, and he was true to his word. The most popular plate at this casual seafood restaurant? A seafood platter of fish, shrimp, oysters, deviled crabs, and scallops, all cooked Calabash style: lightly battered and fried. Fries, coleslaw, and hush puppies round it out. Local seafood is used when possible.

Port Land Grille. 1908 Eastwood Rd., Wilmington; 910/256–6056. $$$-$$$$

Many dishes at this upscale restaurant use ingredients from NC fisherfolk and farmers. You can't get much more North Carolina than this: chicken-fried, naturally raised catfish (farmed in Ayden, NC) served over Anson Mills heirloom rice; hoppin' john with local, wild-caught shrimp; beer-braised Southern-style collard greens; citrus tartar sauce; and a grainy mustard, tasso ham, roasted garlic sauce. No lunch.

LOCAL FAVORITE PLACES TO STAY

Captain's Quarters Inn. 202 W. Queen St., Edenton; 252/482–8945. $$

This 1907 inn, two blocks from the Albemarle Sound in Edenton's historic district, maintains a cheerfully nautical theme in deference to the owners' interest in sailing. Of its eight rooms, the Blackbeard Room with its framed maps is most popular. Have your coffee on the wraparound porch. Sailing packages are available.

Harmony House Inn. 215 Pollock St., New Bern; 252/636–3810. $$

Once sawed in half by feuding co-owners, this 1850 Greek Revival inn was reunited when it opened as an inn, fittingly named Harmony House. The seven rooms and three suites are furnished with antiques and locally made reproductions. Room 4, a large corner room, is most popular. The William and Emily Suite, with its two-person hot tub, invites romance; the rocking chairs on the front porch woo readers.

The Jolly Roger Motel. 803 Ocean Blvd., Topsail Beach; 910/328–4616. $$

The 65 vintage 1960s-style rooms and efficiency apartments, pier, and launchpad/patio here are popular with those who appreciate a cheerfully unfashionable beach and plenty of World War II history. (Fisherfolk are year-round regulars.) Wartime Navy observers used to hide in what's now the Jolly Roger's linen closet—and what was then a bomb shelter—as researchers blasted top-secret test rockets off from their launchpad, which is the present-day patio.

The Verandas. 202 Nun St., Wilmington; 910/251–2212. $$$

The current owners literally helped this building rise from the ashes. The 1854 house suffered a fire in 1992; after renovation, it emerged as one of North Carolina's finest inns. All eight rooms here are corner units with sitting areas; several open onto verandas. All rooms (and the entrance) are on the second floor. Each room is decorated in a different style: one looks like a small French apartment, another is hung with artwork from the Amazon River Basin, and yet another evokes a tree house.

NORTHERN PIEDMONT
A N D   T O B A C C O   R O A D

 In the soft soil of coastal Carolina, colonists rolled hogsheads of tobacco to river ports and to ships bound for England. The trail those giant barrels pressed into the earth earned the nickname Tobacco Road.

Almost from the beginning, tobacco received mixed reviews. In the 1580s Queen Elizabeth's courtiers tamped it into their pipes as fast as they could lay hands on it. James I, on the other hand, despised tobacco, calling its use a "vile and stinking" custom, "loathsome to the eye, hatefull to the nose, harmfulle to the braine, dangerous to the lungs. . . ."

Modern medicine sides with King James, but that doesn't mean tobacco's hazards make great conversation in North Carolina. Old habits die hard; old economies die harder. Tobacco Road has evolved into a superhighway linking North Carolina farms, sales warehouses, and manufacturers to millions of consumers worldwide.

Tobacco, traditionally raised in 89 to 100 North Carolina counties and processed in Piedmont factories, puts billions of dollars into Tar Heel pockets each year. The tobacco industry fills government coffers, too, coughing up millions of dollars' worth of state and local taxes.

Burley tobacco dries in a hillside field in Yancey County, located in western North Carolina.

Workers planting black burley tobacco seedlings, a variety best suited to the Appalachian region as opposed to the golden leaf common to the lowlands.

In the past, tobacco has provided as many as one in every 11 jobs in North Carolina. As a result of legal actions taken against big tobacco companies and anti-tobacco legislation passed in the 1990s, tobacco's future in North Carolina's economy is less certain than in years past.

For now, at least, anytime you drive along Tobacco Road, which stretches across the central plain and through the big tobacco towns—Durham, Reidsville, and Winston-Salem—you'll witness some part of the tobacco process or some result of tobacco money on North Carolina's culture and history.

This chapter focuses on the region west of I–95. For the tobacco area east of I–95, *see* the Coastal Plain chapter.

HISTORY

The bright-leaf tobacco industry came to life in Caldwell County in 1839, born of desperation and good fortune.

On this particular summer night, the story goes, an 18-year-old slave named Stephen sat up tending a barn of tobacco on the Slade Farm. Every now and

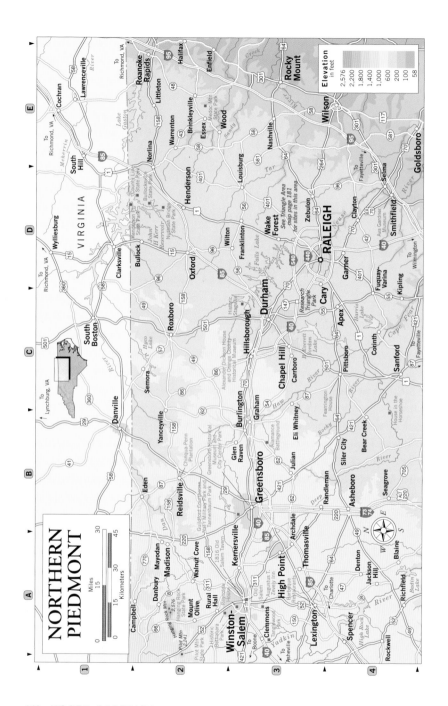

NORTHERN PIEDMONT

then he fed the barn's fires a little wood, pushing steady, smoky heat through the tobacco-filled barn— enough heat to "cure" the tobacco; not enough to set the drying leaves on fire.

As the moon wandered in and out between the clouds, he might have talked with a girl who happened by, or hummed a tune, or shouted across the field to a friend tending another barn.

On this night, they say, he did the unthinkable: he fell asleep. When the crash of thunder jolted him awake, he found his wood soaked, his barn cool, and himself in deep trouble. He grabbed the first dry fuel he could lay hands on—charcoal, from the blacksmith's store—and built a fire hot enough to curl the devil's toenails.

The charcoal's blast baked the cool leaves golden, and replaced their bitterness with a taste smooth as butter. Stephen's accidental bright-leaf sold for 40 cents a pound in a 10-cents-a-pound market, and an industry was born.

Built in the mid-1800s, this one-room barn served as Washington Duke's first tobacco factory. Today the barn is one of several exhibits at the Duke Homestead & Tobacco Museum in Durham.

ASHES TO ASHES

In April 1865, following the Union victory at the Battle of Bentonville, U.S. General William Sherman and CSA General Joseph Johnston met midway between their battle lines to discuss peace.

The two war-weary generals sat together at a small table in the Bennets' home, seven miles from a whistle-stop called Durham Station. A clock on the unpainted wall patiently ticked away the days as the men struggled to find terms acceptable to themselves, to a Congress outraged by the assassination of President Abraham

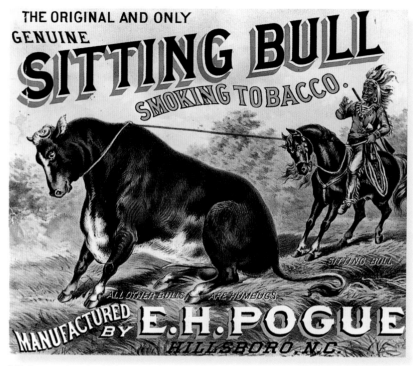

THE ORIGINAL AND ONLY GENUINE
SITTING BULL SMOKING TOBACCO.
ALL OTHER BULLS ARE HUMBUGS.
MANUFACTURED BY E.H.POGUE
HILLSBORO, N.C.

SITTING BULL

E. H. Pogue advertised "the original and only sitting bull" smoking tobacco. This popular brand spurred many imitations in the late 19th century. (New-York Historical Society)

Lincoln, and to Confederate president Jefferson Davis, who soon demanded that Johnston withdraw.

Johnston stayed put. For over a week, as the generals negotiated, their armies milled around Durham Station, joking together, shooting targets, raiding J. R. Green's two-story tobacco shop at Durham Station, and smoking something called bright-leaf tobacco.

When the generals finally shook hands, both armies went home with a little of J. R. Green's tobacco, trailing a taste for bright-leaf tobacco from one end of the country to the other.

"Within a few weeks, letters scrawled by men more accustomed to the trigger than the pen came addressed to the postmaster, the station agent, or other officials," writes Joseph C. Robert, author of *The Story of Tobacco in America*. "They were out of that Durham tobacco and wanted more. From whom could they get it? This was a day of triumph for the new Bright tobacco."

Within a decade, Bull Durham tobacco—sold in small, white cotton pouches cinched with golden threads—was the best-selling tobacco in the world, and Durham was on the map. The Durham Bull's image graced barns, businesses' walls, even the Great Pyramid, in Egypt.

Meanwhile, Washington Duke peddled packets of bright-leaf tobacco from the back of a wagon, and then from a Durham factory. "As for me," his son James B. Duke said when he took over the family business, "I'm going into the cigarette business."

North Carolina went with him.

Duke's cigarette-rolling machines—the industry's first—were ravenous, and eastern North Carolina farmers rushed to feed them. War and slavery's demise had stunned the eastern economy. Or, as country poets put it, "Five-cent cotton and ten-cent meat, How in the world can a poor man eat?"

By planting tobacco, that's how.

For the first time, eastern farmers had a major at-home market. They bought the tiny seeds—a tablespoon to plant six acres—and planted thousands of acres, some almost within earshot of the Atlantic's roar. They sawed pine planks and built tight new barns. They studied temperature charts. They went to the fields, and "put in a crop." It was, wrote the usually unflappable U.S. Census Bureau, "one of the most abnormal developments in agriculture the world has ever known."

Abnormal or not, it worked. Farmers with no bootstraps left to reach for pulled themselves up clinging to filaments of thin, blue tobacco smoke.

WAR BOOMS

When America marched off to the Great War, tobacco fell in alongside. "You ask me what we need to win this war. I answer tobacco as much as bullets," General John Pershing said, and he got it.

World War I entrenched cigarettes in America's lifestyle. The Great Depression concentrated the major tobacco factories in North Carolina, and World War II gave the industry another boost.

North Carolina remains the country's largest producer of tobacco. It grows across the state from Onslow County on the coast, to mountainous Haywood County in the west, where rows of burley tobacco step sideways up tiny, steeple-sharp fields. The Piedmont's tobacco manufacturers—including R. J. Reynolds, which rolls a third of all of the cigarettes sold in the United States—blend those tobaccos with

SONG OF AN AUCTIONEER

The tobacco lies in long lines of lemon yellow piles of varying amounts in shallow baskets on the warehouse floor. The procession moves down the lines. First the warehouseman glances at a pile, cries a suggested price and the auctioneer sings it. To new ears his song, cried out of the side of a scarcely moving mouth, sounds like an idiot making a noise with his finger and his lip. There is rhythm in it but no sense. But sense begins to emerge. He is saying prices in an ascending order and begging for prices above them.

"Twenty-five, six, six, gimme six."

He seems to be talking to himself in the procession which the buyers make behind him in two rows on either side of the line of baskets. Only occasionally do they bid aloud. But the auctioneer sees the signals of their eyes, their thumbs, fingers or lips. He goes on, fancier sometimes in his song:

"Sweet as honey, honey, honey, gimme thirty, gimme thirty."

A buyer winks.

"Thirty, thirty."

No nod, no winks, no thumb lifted.

"'merican thirty." (He says, "Sold American," only on radio programs.)

Behind the principal buyers or in lines beyond them speculators march in the procession which moves fast enough to sell 300 to 360 separate piles in an hour. "Pin hookers" they are called and most of them are little fellows who look for bargains which they may be able to resell. They throw up their arms to bid. Often the warehouse itself buys. Behind all the buying as close as they can crowd, are the farmers. If they don't like what they get they can turn their tags and sell again. Sometimes the same tobacco sold by the auctioneer will bring widely separate prices at separate sales. The average of what they pay for the grades they want is the limit on the buyers. In reaching this average they may be way up and way down on particular piles.

—**Jonathan Daniels,** *Tar Heels: A Portrait of North Carolina,* 1941

Buyers at a tobacco auction make their bids while inspecting the merchandise in Smith's Brightleaf Tobacco warehouse in Farmville. Auctions like these were once a standard part of life on Tobacco Road.

imported leaves, producing cigarettes and other tobacco products.

For over a century, North Carolina and tobacco seemed like a match made in heaven.

TRIANGLE AREA: RALEIGH, DURHAM, AND CHAPEL HILL

The Triangle Area, or the Raleigh-Durham Triangle, refers to the heavily developed urban area between and including three Piedmont cities: Raleigh to the east, Durham to the north, and Chapel Hill to the west.

Participants compete in a tobacco-tying contest at the Golden Leaf Celebration in Wilson.

A few decades ago, red farmland stretched between these small cities. Today most farms have stepped aside to accommodate housing developments and research parks. You'll see an occasional farmhouse tended by a farmer as stubborn as the clay on his boots, but the merger of these cities' outlying development is nearly complete.

Raleigh, the state capital, is a small, progressive city known for its government employees, good museums, and many parks.

Durham, an old tobacco town, is nationally known as the home of Duke University, and a city of medical and research facilities.

Chapel Hill, the smallest city of the three, is widely considered the most liberal town in a historically conservative state. It's home to the University of North Carolina.

In the center of the Triangle Area is another triangle. Research Triangle Park, a place of manicured lawns and buttoned-down research facilities, is one of the largest planned research parks in the world.

Note: **The Triangle Area** refers to the Raleigh, Durham, Chapel Hill area. **The Triangle** refers to the Research Triangle Park between Durham and Raleigh.

RALEIGH *map page 176*

Legislators founded North Carolina's capital city in 1792, slicing a center for their agricultural state from plantation lands. Today this city of 287,000 makes its living from government, education, medicine, and research.

Raleigh is known for its excellent museums and historic government buildings. To visit from the beltway, take Edenton Street downtown to Union Square, and park beneath the North Carolina Museum of History. The most interesting stops—the Capitol, North Carolina Museum of History, North Carolina State Museum of Natural Sciences, City Market, and Executive Mansion—are within walking distance. The Executive Mansion sits on the edge of a 20-block Victorian neighborhood, **Oakwood.**

A local tobacco field, circa 1920.

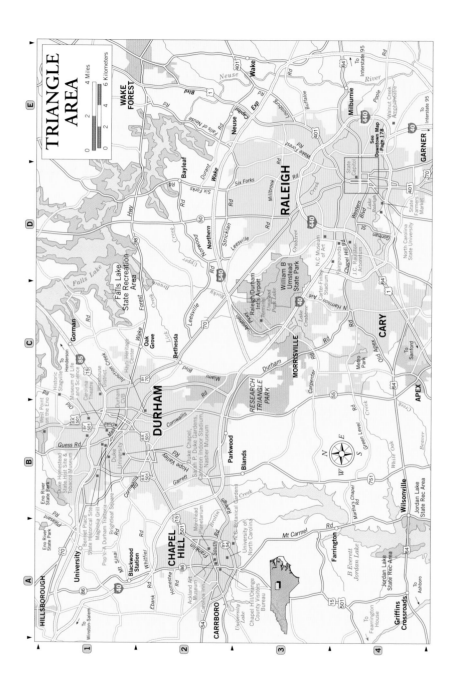

TRIANGLE AREA

0   2   4   4 Miles

0   2   4   6 Kilometers

HILLSBOROUGH
To
Winston-Salem

Eno River
State Park

Eno River
State Park

University

Bennett Place
State Historical Site
Magnolia Grill
Pop's Durham Trattoria
Brightleaf Square

Mt. Sinai Rd

Blackwood
Station

Whitfield Rd

Guess Rd

Duke Homestead
State Hist Site &
Tobacco Museum

Duke
University

Duke Main

Cornwallis Rd

Duke Chapel
Sarah P. Duke Gardens
Cameron Indoor Stadium
Nasher Museum

Garrett

Hope Valley Rd

DURHAM

Carolina Theatre
Durham CVB
Historic Stagville
Museum of Life
and Science
Hayti Heritage
Center

Warehouse
District

Bennett Rd

Gorman

Oak Grove

Bethesda

Carpenter Rd

MORRISVILLE

RESEARCH TRIANGLE PARK

Durham Rd

Miami Blvd

Parkwood

Blands

Leesville Rd

Norwood

RALEIGH

Six Forks Rd

Millbrook Rd

Strickland Rd

Leesville Rd

Northern

Creek

Durant Rd

Wake

Bayleaf

Falls of Neuse Rd

Capital Blvd

Neuse

Neuse River

Wake

WAKE FOREST

Louisburg Rd

Buffalo Rd

Poole Rd

Walnut Creek Amphitheatre

Milburnie

GARNER

To
Interstate 95

State Farmers' Market

State Capitol

See Downtown Map Page 178

Western Blvd

Gorman St

North Carolina State University

J.C. Raulston Arboretum

Chapel Hill Rd

Carter-Finley Stadium
Fairgrounds

N.C Museum of Art

William B Umstead State Park

Aviation Pkwy

Raleigh-Durham Int'l Airport

Umstead
Lake

Crabtree

Crabtree Creek

CARY

Old Apex Rd

To
Sanford

APEX

Green Level Rd

White Oak Creek

Beaver Creek

Metro Park

To
Ashboro

Martha's Chapel Rd

Wilsonville

Jordan Lake
State Rec Area

Jordan Lake
State Rec Area

Griffins Crossroads

To
Fearrington
House

B Everett
Jordan Lake

Farrington Rd

Farrington

Mt Carmel Rd

N.C.S. Botanical Gardens

University of North Carolina

Morehead Planetarium

Franklin St

South Rd

CHAPEL HILL

CARRBORO

Carolina Inn

Ackland Art Museum

Chapel Hill/Orange County Visitors Bureau

University Lake

Homestead Rd

Ebank Rd

Falls Lake

Falls Lake State Recreation Area

Falls Lake

Wake Forest Rd

Rocky Creek

Lick Creek

New Hope Creek

NORTH CAROLINA

176   NORTH CAROLINA

Raleigh, the City of Oaks, suits walkers—especially in spring, when choirs of azaleas and dogwoods bloom; and in autumn, when centuries-old oaks steeple golden branches overhead. Raleigh is often called "a park with a city in it," by its PR people mostly, but they have a point. Raleigh's greenways and 156 public parks keep the city well grounded. For generations, families have visited Pullen Park on Sunday afternoon, called by the 1911 carousel whose gentle stampede of carved horses, ostriches, and pigs moves in rhythm with a Wurlitzer band organ.

Tours, maps, and information are available at the **Raleigh Convention and Visitor's Bureau**, *220 Fayetteville St.; 919/834–5900.*

RALEIGH'S HIGHLIGHTS

State Capitol. North Carolina's first capitol building burned in 1831 as low-bidding workmen tried to fireproof it. Its stately Greek Revival replacement, made of local granite, overlooks walkways and broad, grassy grounds whose many statues include the three North Carolina-born U.S. Presidents—Andrew Johnson, Andrew Jackson, and James Polk.

Inside, governors, legislators, and scurrying aides have worn distinct pathways in the granite stairs and hallways leading to the legislative chambers. Antonio Canova's marble sculpture of a toga-clad George Washington dominates the four-story rotunda.

The west staircase is as chipped as a boxer's front teeth. During Reconstruction, carpetbag legislators put an open bar in an upstairs committee room. According to legend, mishandled whiskey barrels chipped the steps as they bounced downstairs.

The restored 1840 capitol is home to the governor's and lieutenant governor's offices, but the legislature meets in the State Legislative Building across the mall at 16 West Jones Street. *1 E. Edenton St.; 919/733–4994.*

Executive Mansion. Walking east on Jones Street from the Legislative Building, you'll wind up at the Executive Mansion, the state's best Victorian Queen

The state capitol, in the heart of Raleigh.

Anne architecture. Tours are available through the Raleigh CVB (*above*). *200 N. Blount St.; 919/807–7948.*

North Carolina Museum of History. Though beautiful architecturally, the history museum has underwhelming permanent exhibits that trace state history and focus on North Carolina folklife—from shape note singing to quilting, to wailing the blues. It also includes the North Carolina Sports Hall of Fame.

More interesting changing exhibits detail specific topics. For instance, John White's original watercolors of North Carolina's native people recently visited courtesy of the British Museum's exhibit, "Mysteries of the Lost Colony and a New World: England's First View of America." *5 East Edenton St.; 919/807–7900.*

North Carolina Museum of Natural Sciences. "The Terror of the South" has taken up residence in North Carolina's Museum of Natural Sciences, and he shows no signs of leaving. Not that curators want him to go. The meat-eating dinosaur, who predates T. Rex by 45 million years, is the only Acrocanthosaurus

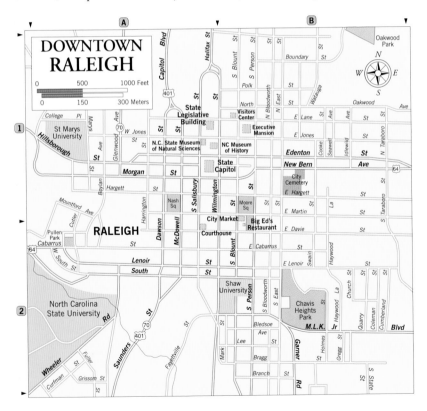

Dinosaurs rule at the very popular NC Museum of Natural Sciences, in Raleigh.

on display in the world. He is not alone here: the museum's 66-million-year-old Thescelosaurus is the first discovered to hold a fossilized heart.

Animals—enough to fill a midsize zoo—buzz, burrow, and browse in the museum's habitats. The "From the Mountains to the Sea" exhibit re-creates five North Carolina environmental habitats, and introduces you to some citizens of each. "Underground" introduces you to the amazing variety of rare gems and minerals found in North Carolina. And over in the fossil lab you can chat with a paleontologist while she reassembles a mammoth's skeleton. *Bicentennial Plaza, 11 W Jones St.; 919/733-7450.*

City Market. City Market's renovated redbrick depot and period buildings house art galleries, artists' studios, a microbrewery, restaurants, and a small farmers' market where third-generation vendors sell their produce. The historic market area occupies a two-block space bordered by East Martin, East Davis, South Person, and South Blount streets. If you're there in time for lunch, try **Big Ed's Restaurant** (220 Wolfe St.; 919/836–9909). It's known for its Southern cooking.

State Farmer's Market. It's 5 AM. Workers in jeans and rolled-up shirtsleeves stride briskly through the predawn light, unloading Mack trucks and pickups, and stocking acres of vegetable and fruit stands. Vendors pat North Carolina-grown tomatoes, cucumbers, cantaloupes, collards, new potatoes, watermelons, squash,

The NC Museum of Art welcomes art exhibits from around the world.

and apples into place, preparing for the shoppers who will visit the state's largest farmer's market later today.

The State Farmer's Market is open every day except Christmas, and has become a weekend tradition for thousands. The Farmer's Market Restaurant does a brisk Southern breakfast trade: scrambled eggs, ham and red-eye gravy, grits, and homemade biscuits. (Order the brains and eggs, and you're on your own.) *1201 Agriculture St.; 919/733–7417 market, 919/755–1550 restaurant.*

North Carolina Museum of Art. Though out of reach from downtown Raleigh, this museum is worth the drive. It's got an outstanding collection of European art from the 13th through 19th centuries, and American art from colonial days to today. The permanent collection includes works by Raphael, Rubens, Van Dyck, Monet, Homer, and Wyeth. The museum hosts outstanding traveling exhibits from around the world. Closed Mondays. *2110 Blue Ridge Rd.; 919/839–6262.*

J. C. Raulston Arboretum at North Carolina State University. This arboretum's more than 5,000 trees and shrubs represent the most diverse collections in the Southeast. The arboretum includes a Japanese Garden and raked-stone Zen garden, a White Garden, and a Rose Garden whose blooms generally peak mid- to late-May. With 200 roses in the garden, though, you can count on catching the hint of rose perfume here until first frost. *4415 Beryl Rd.; 919/515–3132.*

The Lakes. When people in the Triangle head for the water, they're usually heading for Jordan Lake State Recreational Area, west of Raleigh on US 64, or Falls Lake Recreational Area north of Raleigh on NC 50.

You'll need to bring your own boat if you want to boat or ski, but both Jordan Lake and Falls Lake have swimming areas, campgrounds, hiking trails, and mountain-bike trails. These recreational areas encompass thousands of acres each.

THE DELANY SISTERS OF RALEIGH

By the mid 1990s, the 100-plus-year-old Delany sisters of Raleigh had emerged in the American consciousness as symbols of down-home humor and common sense. The quotes below were taken from their autobiography, Having Our Say, *which also inspired a popular play.*

SADIE:

Bessie and I have lived in New York for the last seventy-five years, but Raleigh will always be home. Raleigh is where Mama and Papa met, as students at Saint Augustine's School, which was a school for Negroes. Mama and Papa got married in the campus chapel back in 1886 and raised all ten of us children right there at good old "Saint Aug's." Papa became vice principal and Mama was the matron, which meant she ran things day-to-day at the school.

I don't remember my mother ever calling my father by his first name, Henry. He was always "Mr. Delany" or "Your Pa."

······ ◦ ▪ ◦ ······

Jim Crow was an ugly, complicated business. Fortunately for Bessie and me, our earliest experiences with whites predated Jim Crow. North Carolina was a fairly liberal state, and Raleigh was a center of education as well as the capital. Raleigh was a good place for a Negro of the South to be living, compared to most places at that time. We remember Raleigh when there was still plenty of Confederate veterans hanging around, some lounging on the steps of the Capitol and others at the Old Soldiers' Home. Those veterans were a lonely bunch, and friendly. They always wanted to talk to anybody who walked by.

BESSIE:

Papa used to say, "You catch more flies with molasses than vinegar." He believed you could get further in life by being nice to people. Well, this is easy for Sadie to swallow. Sadie is molasses without even trying! She can sweet-talk the world, or play dumb, or whatever it takes to get by without a fuss. But even as a tiny little child, I wasn't afraid of anything. I'd meet the Devil before day and look him in the eye, no matter what the price. If Sadie is molasses, then I am vinegar!

. . . when I was young nothing could hold me back. No sir! I thought I could change the world. It took me a hundred years to figure out I *can't* change the world. I can only change Bessie. And, honey, that ain't easy, either.

For information on Falls Lake, call 919/676–1027. For information on Jordan Lake, call 919/362–0586.

DURHAM: BULL CITY   *map page 176, B-2*

In 1900 Durham's young streets bustled with farmers' wagons, fast-talking auctioneers, factory workers, and the occasional tobacco tycoon. Today tobacco plays a renovated role in downtown Durham's landscape, as old tobacco facilities are being reborn to house offices, homes, shops, restaurants, and nightspots.

Durham is known today as the City of Medicine USA. Nearly one in four Bull City–ites works in a health-related field, making medicine the city's top industry. Durham's 300-plus health-related companies and practices have a combined annual payroll of more than $1.5 billion. At the heart of Durham's medical and research community are five hospitals, including Duke University Medical Center and Research Triangle Park.

Durham is also home to Duke University, which was started with tobacco money, and to one of the Southeast's top blues festivals.

MOVERS AND SHAKERS

Bull Durham tobacco put Durham on the map, but James B. Duke and the American Tobacco Company kept it there.

James B. Duke founded the American Tobacco Company in 1890. Within a decade the company gobbled up its competitors, and dominated the world tobacco industry.

Duke tobacco money soon built electricity-guzzling textile mills across the Carolinas, and newfangled electric power companies to keep them spinning. In Durham, beaux arts and art deco–style banks and businesses rose shoulder-to-shoulder with showy Italianate and Neoclassical Revival buildings—almost all of them built, directly or indirectly, on tobacco boom money.

Tobacco didn't overlook Uncle Sam's projects, either. Durham's Neoclassical Revival Post Office went up in 1934 at the height of the Great Depression. Taxes levied on Durham tobacco paid for it in 15 minutes the day it opened.

African-American businesses thrived along Durham's "Black Wall Street," too. Activist W. E. B. DuBois said, "there is in this small city a group of 5,000 colored people, whose social and economic development is perhaps more striking than that of any similar group in the nation."

Booker T. Washington just told people, "wait 'til you get to Durham."

The **Mechanics & Farmers Bank** (116 W. Parrish St.) and the **North Carolina Mutual Life Insurance Company** (411 W. Chapel Hill St.) symbolize Black Wall Street today. Founded in 1898 by African-American businessmen, North Carolina Mutual remains one of the world's largest black-owned and managed businesses. Tours of its photo gallery are available.

DUKE UNIVERSITY *map page 176, B-1*

Tobacco money meant more than good jobs and good times. North Carolina's tobacco barons tended to be generous with their home state. In Winston-Salem that generosity came to life in the arts. In Durham James B. Duke established an endowment for a new school—Duke University.

Duke University's grand **West Campus,** with buildings and walkways constructed entirely of blue-gray stone, is one of the nation's most beautiful. Its two most arresting features are Duke Chapel and the Sarah B. Duke Gardens.

The Lucky Strike water tower is a visible reminder of Durham's tobacco boom.

James B. Duke picked the location of **Duke Chapel** in 1925 as he walked along a wooded plateau. "Here's where it oughta be," the tycoon told the president of the new school. And that's where the Neo-Gothic chapel stands today, every line of its being straining toward heaven. With a 210-foot tower and 77 stained-glass windows, the chapel dominates West Campus. The chapel, which features a 5,200-pipe organ, is open most days; nondenominational services are held Sundays at 11 AM. *Duke University West Campus; 919/684-3917.*

Other near-religious rites—Duke basketball games—take place on West Campus at **Cameron Indoor Stadium.** The Duke Blue Devils are consistently ranked among the nation's top teams. *1600 Whitford Dr.; 919/684-2120.*

As you might expect, Duke basketball games are sold out months in advance. If it's any consolation, every TV in every sports bar in the area will be tuned to the game du jour.

The ★**Sarah P. Duke Gardens** spread over 55 landscaped and wooded acres on West Campus. (There's free parking at the Anderson Street entrance.) Italianate terraces designed by Ellen B. Shipman form the gardens' historic core. In April the wisteria-draped pergola at the entryway wraps the upper terraces in perfume. The narrow paths of the Blomquist Garden of Native Plants wind past more than

Washington Duke, James Duke's father, stands in front of his first tobacco production cabin in Durham. (NC State Dept. of Archives & History)

People's Security Insurance is one of several major insurance companies based in North Carolina.

900 varieties of wildflowers. The slate-roofed garden pavilion by the pond may be the garden's most serene spot. The 20-acre Asiatic Arboretum illustrates the close ties between the plants of eastern Asia and the eastern United States. Its 550 Asian species and cultivars include collections of deciduous magnolias and Japanese maples. *426 Anderson St., Duke University West Campus; 919/684–3698.*

DOWNTOWN DURHAM

The best way to see downtown Durham—the first commercial district to be designated a National Historic District—is on foot. Maps for a 2-mile walking tour of the area are available at the **Durham Convention and Visitors Bureau.** *101 Morgan St.; 919/680–8316.*

By day some 14,000 workers head for offices and shops in downtown Durham's renovated tobacco warehouses. By night the bustle finds a different rhythm, as folks head for restaurants, performance centers, art galleries, and clubs—also located in massive, redbrick tobacco facilities refurbished to reflect 21st-century tastes and serve 21st-century interests and needs.

Duke Chapel (above and right) dominates Duke University's West Campus.

Downtown, look for Bright Leaf Square and the American Tobacco Campus. Bright Leaf Square, the city's first reclaimed tobacco warehouses, features shops, restaurants, art galleries, and one-of-a-kind stores. The American Tobacco Campus, a million square feet of renovated historic tobacco warehouses, includes, among other things, restaurants and an amphitheater. The old Ligget-Myers facility will be used for similar purposes.

The Durham Performing Arts Center, opening next door to the American Tobacco Campus, brings in Broadway shows, comedians, and musicians. Nightlife also bustles along Ninth Street, across from Duke University. Ninth Street is noted for its restaurants, bars, and bookstores.

You'll find several nationally reviewed restaurants in Durham, including Another Thyme, Pop's, Magnolia Grill, and Taverna Nikos. The best place to grab a dog, however, is the Durham Bulls' ballpark.

The **Durham Bulls** have been swinging away in Durham since 1924. Their original home, where the movie *Bull Durham* was shot, is now known as the Historic Durham Athletic Park. It's now home to the Bull Durham Blues Festival. The Bulls' current park, the **Durham Bulls Athletic Park**

(409 Blackwell St.; 919/956–2855), or DBAP, which opened in 1995, packs in around 400,000 fans a year.

BULL CITY SCIENCE

Interestingly enough, the city that nurtured North Carolina's blues tradition has also nurtured its research and science potential. The **Research Triangle Park** is the most famous example.

For decades, the Piedmont's universities trained researchers and scientists who earned their prestigious diplomas and then went elsewhere to make their contribution to the world. The Research Triangle Park was created in the 1950s to help put a plug in North Carolina's "brain drain." The largest planned research park in the US, the 7,000-acre Research Triangle Park has given rise to a host of business parks specializing in pharmaceuticals, biotechnology, and related fields. RTP includes facilities for some 160 research and development companies. You can pick up a self-directed driving tour map at the CVB. *12 Davis Dr.; 919/549–8181.*

Another well-known research facility in the area is the **Duke Lemur Center.** This facility, which opened in 1966, is home to 207 primate prosimians including lemurs, lorises, and bush babies. (If you want to see the center's lemurs in an easier-to-access environment, drop by the Museum of Life and Science.)

Researchers here breed these primates, and reintroduce them into a natural home in Madagascar. The primates sometimes do a stint in various US zoos before heading for Madagascar, and often spend time in the natural environment provided here, developing skills for living on their own in the wild before actually giving it a try.

Human primates particularly enjoy the center's outdoor walking tour, but this is not a spur-of-the-moment, glad-you-popped-in destination. Call at least two weeks in advance for tour reservations. You may want to schedule your stroll for the cooler hours of the day, when the animals tend to be more active. It's difficult to find, so call for directions. *3705 Erwin Rd.; 919/489–3364.*

The 65,000 square feet of indoor exhibits and 13 acres of outdoor exhibits at the ★**Museum of Life and Science** include plenty of wildlife native to North Carolina—black bears and red wolves, for instance—but butterflies are the stars of this show. This museum is best known as the home of one of the largest butterfly houses in the world.

You'll find giant owl-eye butterflies, monarchs, blue morphos, blue-spotted purples, and other exotic-winged beauties flitting and drifting around the museum's

30-foot-tall conservatory. Their haven is also home to tropical plants that replicate a rain forest in one area and a "fruit and spice garden" in another.

The butterfly house packs a bonus: it's always 80 degrees, which is a welcome relief at the height of a North Carolina summer. *433 W Murray Ave.; 919/220–5429.*

BULL CITY ARTS

Thanks largely to Duke University, the arts make themselves at home in Durham, whose major festivals include the **American Dance Festival**, one of the largest, most influential modern dance festivals in the world. Held each June and July, it offers audiences a full slate of inspiring performances, premieres of commissioned dance works, and behind-the-scenes tours. *919/684–6402.*

Other big events include the International Jazz Festival (February through April); the Bull Durham Blues Festival (September); Centerfest, North Carolina's oldest street arts festival (September); Festival for the Eno (July 4 weekend); and the Bimbé Cultural Arts Festival (June).

The splendidly renovated Beaux Arts **Carolina Theatre** is now an auditorium for performing arts. Its marquee announces performances by the Durham Symphony and Triangle Opera. The theater's diverse calendar also includes independent films, comedians, and other musicians. *309 West Morgan St.; 919/560–3030.*

At the **Nasher Museum of Art** (formerly the Duke University Museum of Art), you can check out a permanent collection of medieval sculpture, African art, and pre-Columbian art. The museum, housed in a building designed by Rafael Viñoly, is growing its collection of contemporary art, an interest reflected in the traveling exhibits invited to the museum. The museum is on Duke University's East Campus, next to the Sarah P. Duke Gardens. *2001 Campus Dr.; 919/684–5135.*

The restored **St. Joseph's Church,** one of the nation's oldest autonomous African-American churches, is today part of the **Hayti Heritage Center,** which showcases the work of local African-American artists and sponsors the Bull Durham Blues Festival. *804 Old Fayetteville St.; 919/683–1709.*

DURHAM AREA PARKS AND HISTORIC SITES

Durham is home to around 60 parks and recreation areas. The popular **West Point on the Eno** includes a reconstructed 1778 gristmill, a historic home and blacksmith shop, and the Hugh Mangum Museum of Photography, which occupies the restored 1890s-era darkroom Mangum was able to eke out of a corner of his father's tobacco pack house.

Tobacco facilities, once financial
lifelines in the Piedmont, find
new life as restaurants, galleries,
theaters, and shops in Durham's
Brightleaf Historic District.

BULL CITY BLUES

Durham's tobacco markets drew more than farmers and auctioneers. Blues musicians, too, headed for Durham, guitars slung over their shoulders. Their chameleonic art took on the up-and-coming colors of Durham's soul. These African-American musicians sent Durham's hot young energy flowing through their hands and dancing up and down their fret boards. They fingerpicked an energetic, hopeful shade of blue, one that made folks want to get up and dance.

Reverend Gary Davis, Blind Boy Fuller, Sonny Terry, and Brownie McGhee helped put Piedmont Blues on music's map. Modern-day artists like John Dee Holeman, Taj Mahal, and Algia Mae Hinton help keep it there.

Today blues artists from the North Carolina Piedmont and around the world strut their sounds at the **Bull Durham Blues Festival** (919/683–1709), one of the Southeast's largest blues events. There's a blues element in the Festival for the Eno, held in July, and blues artists also keep the downtown clubs hopping.

If you want to check out a couple of popular blues clubs, look for the **Broad Street Café** (1116 Broad St.; 919/416–9707) or the **James Joyce Irish Pub** (912 W. Main St.; 919/683–3022), which features both Irish music and blues.

Mangum, who grew up on this farm, was stricken by wanderlust at an early age and spent much of his life traveling through North Carolina, Virginia, and West Virginia, snapping portraits as he went. A slight man with a gentle smile, Mangum was given to mildly eccentric tastes. He loved to photograph striking people in odd hats, adored capturing beautiful women (including his wife Annie) on his glass negatives, and delighted in photographing vaudeville troupes.

Mangum died in the flu epidemic of 1922, but you can get a sense of the man from the rotating exhibits of his portraits that hang in this museum. And you can look the early 20th century in the eye as it stares back dressed in its finest.

This park is also noted for its picnicking, hiking, rafting, and canoeing, plus the Festival for the Eno held each July. *5101 N. Roxboro Rd.; 919/471–1623.*

At the **Bennett Place State Historic Site,** you'll find a reconstruction of the small farmhouse where Johnston surrendered to Sherman. *4409 Bennett Memorial Rd.; 919/383–4345.*

The **Duke Homestead State Historic Site and Tobacco Museum** is a living-history museum where costumed players demonstrate the early farming techniques and tobacco manufacturing processes Washington Duke's family employed during the 19th century. *2828 Duke Homestead Rd.; 919/477–5498.*

The 18th- and 19th-century buildings of **Historic Stagville,** once one of the largest plantations in the South, include original slave quarters. *5828 Old Oxford Hwy.; 919/620–0120.*

CHAPEL HILL   *map page 176, A-2*

Most university towns, somewhere along the way, fostered universities. Here, a university fostered a town. Chapel Hill, which grew up solely to serve the nation's first state-supported university (founded in 1795), remains eternally young, eternally innovative, and eternally too liberal for many North Carolinians' tastes.

Although Chapel Hill is a city of 55,000 people, its business district, with wide, tree-lined walkways, feels like a village. Franklin Street, which fronts the university,

Demonstration of soap making at the Duke Homestead and Tobacco Museum.

A suspension footbridge crosses the Eno River in the Eno River State Park, just one of many popular parks in the Triangle Area.

RATS AND ROUGE AT CHAPEL HILL?

University of North Carolina, the first state-supported university in the country to open its doors (1795), did not however accept women until more than a hundred years later—and then only if they wore hats and gloves to class and were accompanied by a chaperone. Males backed away in horror and fear; as one pioneer observed, "No matter how crowded the lecture room, a coed always has two benches to herself." In 1901 thirteen female students were not permitted to have their pictures in the yearbook, and years later, women were still not invited to their own graduation ceremonies. When a residence hall for these valiant scholars was being considered, the college newspaper headlines blared, "Shaves and Shines but no Rats and Rouge . . . Chapel Hill is a place inherently for men and men who desire no women around…women would only prove a distracting influence, could do no possible good, and would turn the grand old institution into a semi-effeminate college."

—**Lynn Sherr,** *The American Woman's Gazetteer,* 1976

is lined with bookstores, small shops, restaurants, and clubs. The stone wall in front of the commons is a great perch for people watchers. For free maps and guides, try the **Chapel Hill/Orange County Visitors Bureau** (501 W. Franklin St.; 919/968–2060).

UNC CAMPUS   *map page 176, A-2/3*

University of North Carolina–Chapel Hill's colonial campus, with its planetarium, arboretum, museums, botanical garden, and historic buildings, provides Chapel Hill's main visitor attractions. Borrow a Walkman at the Morehead Planetarium, located on Franklin Street—the main campus drag—and set off on a campus tour, following brick walkways around the grassy commons where Thomas Wolfe once daydreamed and studied. Old East (1795), Person Hall (1797), the 1852 PlayMakers Theatre, and the Old Well are popular on-campus stops. Contact the **UNC at Chapel Hill Visitors Center** (250 E. Franklin St.; 919/962–1630) for information.

GRADUATION DAY

Thomas Wolfe, 1900–1938, is North Carolina's most famous writer. In his first novel, Look Homeward, Angel, *Wolfe's father, a stonecutter, is represented as Old Gant, and his mother, who ran a boarding house, as Eliza. Thomas Wolfe entered The University of North Carolina in 1916.*

Gant and Eliza came to his graduation. He found them lodgings in the town: it was early June—hot, green, fiercely and voluptuously Southern. The campus was a green oven; the old grads went about in greasy pairs; the cool pretty girls, who never sweated, came in to see their young men graduate, and to the dance; the mamas and papas were shown about dumbly and shyly.

The college was charming, half-deserted. Most of the students, except the graduating class, had departed. The air was charged with the fresh sensual heat, the deep green shimmer of heavy leafage, a thousand spermy earth and flower-scents. The young men were touched with sadness, with groping excitement, with glory.

On this rich stage, Gant, who had left his charnel-house of death for three days, saw his son Eugene. He came, gathered to life again, out of his grave. He saw his son enthroned in all the florid sentiment of commencement, and the whole of his heart was lifted out of the dust. Upon the lordly sward, shaded by great trees, and ringed by his solemn classmen and their families, Eugene read the Class Poem ("O Mother Of Our Myriad Hopes"). Then Vergil Weldon spoke, high-husky, deep, and solemn-sad; and Living Truth welled in their hearts. It was a Great Utterance. Be true! Be clean! Be good! Be men! Absorb the Negation! The world has need of. Life was never so worth. Never in history had there been. No other class had shown so great a promise as. Among other achievements, the editor of the paper had lifted the moral and intellectual level of the State two inches. The university spirit! Character! Service! Leadership!

Eugene's face grew dark with pride and joy there in the lovely wilderness. He could not speak. There was a glory in the world: life was panting for his embrace.

—**Thomas Wolfe,**
Look Homeward, Angel, 1929

The University of North Carolina campus in 1861 was depicted by E. Valois in this lithograph. Left to right are New East, Old East, South Building, Old West, and New West bordering the grassy commons where Thomas Wolfe once daydreamed. (North Carolina Collection)

In **Wilson Library** (South Rd.; 919/962–1143) the Sir Walter Raleigh Rooms' rare maps would be familiar to the armchair explorer who misplaced the Lost Colony. The octagonal **Hayes Plantation library,** inside the Wilson library, includes most of the Edenton plantation's 2,000 books and original furnishings. Another exhibit offers the lowdown on Siamese twins Eng and Chang, who settled in Surry County in 1840.

Stargazers easily spend hours at the **Morehead Planetarium and Science Center** (250 E. Franklin St.; 919/962–1236), which once served as a training facility for Mercury, Gemini, Apollo, and Skylab astronauts. The **Coker Arboretum** (Country Club Rd. and Raleigh St.; 919/962–0522), next door, is more down-to-earth. Its collection of native and exotic shrubs and trees has been inter-planted with daylilies and with daffodils, which add a dash of yellow to the landscape by early March.

Ackland Art Museum, on South Columbia, houses works by Rubens, Delacroix, and Degas, plus a collection of Indian art. It's also very strong in Asian and African art. *101 S. Columbia St.; 919/966–5736.*

One of the Southeast's largest natural botanical gardens, with over 600 acres of preserved land, is just southeast of campus. The **North Carolina Botanical Gardens** include trails, carnivorous plants, and herb gardens. You'll also find

North Carolina and regional plants arranged by habitat. *Old Mason Farm Rd. and Fordham Blvd.; follow signs or call for directions; 919/962–0522.*

Basketball—specifically men's basketball—is a passion in North Carolina and especially in the Triangle Area, where Atlantic Coast Conference (ACC) rivalries span generations. The UNC Tar Heels play at the **Dean E. Smith Center,** locally known as the Dean Dome. UNC supports 28 varsity men's and women's sports teams. *300 Skipper Bowles Dr.; 919/962–2296.*

HILLSBOROUGH   *map page 168, C-2/3*

Although tax collector Edmund Fanning may not have thought so in 1770 as he ran shrieking from Hillsborough's courthouse with outraged neighbors cracking a horsewhip at his heels, Hillsborough (just north and west of Chapel Hill and Durham) may be the prettiest town in North Carolina's Piedmont region.

If you drive into Hillsborough from Durham, you may think colonial North Carolina's summer capital took its name from the rolling hills of the countryside. Not so. This town of 5,000, once home to governors and Declaration of Independence signer William Hooper, was named for the Earl of Hillsborough.

Despite visits from British troops during the Revolution and Confederate troops during the Civil War, time has strolled these sleepy avenues unimpeded and unignited since 1754. Colonial, antebellum, Victorian, and modern homes with grassy English lawns settled here side-by-side. Over 100 Hillsborough homes and buildings are on the National Register of Historic Places.

To get your bearings, stop by the **Alexander Dickson House.** At this farmhouse, headquarters of CSA Major Wade Hampton an orientation video prefaces the walking tour with a history of Hillsborough. *150 E. King St.; 919/732–7741.*

Hillsborough is best known for colonial history, but explorer John Lawson visited an Occaneechee Indian village here in 1701. Occaneechee artifacts and a village diorama reside at the **Orange County Historical Museum.** An Occoneechee village being reconstructed downtown is slated to be finished in mid-2009. *201 N. Churchton St.; 919/732–2201.*

In the cupola of the courthouse a 1769 English clock patiently bides Hillsborough's time.

West of Hillsborough (south of Burlington) lies **Alamance Battleground,** where North Carolina's royal governor William Tryon and the Regulators had at it back in 1771, blasting away over taxes. This North Carolina State Historic Site orients visitors with a film and battleground monuments. *5803 NC 62 S.; 336/227–4785.*

Reidsville, an old tobacco town, was once the home of the American Tobacco Company, a remnant of the monopoly James B. Duke created. Former North Carolina governor David Settle Reid's restored home is now the Chamber of Commerce building, downtown (follow the signs). Reidsville's downtown is being revitalized as art shops, galleries, and antiques dealers move into the area.

Reidsville's primary destination, ★**Chinqua-Penn Plantation**, lies outside town. It just may be the most unexpected stop along Tobacco Road.

This Gilded Age mansion is a three-dimensional mosaic of timeless religious icons, brazen folk art, delicate tapestries, Asian knickknacks, French furnishings, priceless paintings, murals, and entire rooms lifted from other countries and other centuries—all of it collected in the 1920s by Betsy and Thomas Jefferson Penn. The 27-room mansion defies description—not for lack of words, but for lack of ink. Anyone with a modicum of curiosity could spend a day touring the living room alone. (The ghost in the dining room, by the way, is Betsy's.)

Chinqua-Penn's 22-acre landscaped gardens, which have been restored to reflect their 1920s charm, are most popular in April, when 10,000 tulips burst into bloom. *2138 Wentworth St.; 336/349–4576.*

The population of Greensboro is 255,000, but its downtown moves with the cadence of a smaller town. The downtown business district, which once reeled from the impact of malls on the outskirts of town, has awakened to the idea of revitalization. Art galleries, nightclubs, upscale restaurants, and museums now populate the area.

At the heart of Greensboro's downtown district lies 1.9-acre **Center City Park**, snatched from the grip of parking lots and turned into a place of lush lawns, dancing fountains, and performance spaces for local artists. *200 N. Elm St.*

Across the street from this gathering place you'll find the **Greensboro Cultural Center** (200 N. Davie St.; 336/373–2712), home to numerous arts groups including the **African American Atelier** (336/333–6885), a gallery of African-American Art. The Guilford Native American Art Gallery (336/273–6605) is in the same building.

The **Eastern Music Festival** (336/333–7450) held each summer, June through August, is this city's most popular event. But Greensboro, which nurtures deep Quaker roots, may be best known for starting the lunch counter sit-ins of the 1960s.

The main entrance to the
Chinqua-Penn Plantation.

On February 1, 1960, four African-American students from the Agricultural and Technical College of North Carolina pushed through the glass doors of F. W. Woolworth Co. on Elm Street, taking seats at the whites-only lunch counter. "We had the confidence of a Mack truck," Franklin McCain later said. "I probably felt better that day than I've ever felt in my life."

In the next days, white and black students from other Greensboro schools—Bennett College, Guilford College, and Greensboro College—joined the protest at great personal and political risk. An anecdote from this period: Bennett College, at this time a school for black women, required its students to wear gloves when they went downtown. When the students requested permission to join the protest, it was granted on the condition that they *not* wear the gloves that identified them with the school. The sit-in began a movement that helped force integration throughout the South.

Part of the lunch counter and its empty stools are the centerpiece of a curiously antiseptic Civil Rights exhibit at the **Greensboro Historical Museum**, downtown. This museum also offers the best Greensboro history overview, including exhibits on Greensboro natives Dolley Madison (wife of President James Madison) and short story writer William Sidney Porter, or O. Henry. *130 Summit Ave.; 336/373–2043.*

If you head south from Greensboro on NC 220B, you can visit the Richard Petty Museum, North Carolina's zoological park, a potters' community, and a Native American temple complex. (*See* the Southern Piedmont chapter.)

In north Greensboro on Battleground Avenue, signs point to **Guilford Courthouse National Military Park**, the site of North Carolina's largest Revolutionary War battle. Today the only red coats here belong to reenactors who storm the area each March, or to joggers and bicyclists who use the network of trails that connect the 220-acre park's grassy meadows, massive oaks, granite monuments, and statuary. *2332 New Garden Rd.; 336/288–1776.*

This early engraving claims to show the British attacking the Americans in the Battle of Guilford Courthouse, the largest Revolutionary War battle in North Carolina. (Anne S. K. Brown Military Collection, Brown University Library, Providence, RI)

This display at the Greensboro Historical Museum memorializes the Woolworth sit-in.

The Old Mill of Guilford on Beaver Creek.

The Battle of Guilford Courthouse pitted Britain's Lord Charles Cornwallis's soldiers against Major General Nathanael Greene's forces, which included 1,000 drafted North Carolina backcountry sharpshooters. To get those sharpshooters to line up behind a skimpy rail fence on the front line, Greene offered them a deal: if they squeezed off two rounds at the British, they could go home. If they didn't, he'd shoot them where they stood.

The British advanced. The sharpshooters fired once, fired twice, and ended their military careers with a heartfelt stampede. "To our infinite distress and mortification, the North Carolina militia took to flight," wrote Lighthorse Harry Lee. "Every effort was made...to stop this unaccountable panic, for not a man of the corps had been killed or even wounded. . . . All was in vain; so thoroughly confounded were these unhappy men that, throwing away arms, knapsacks, and even canteens, they rushed like a headlong torrent through the woods." Still, the battle sent Cornwallis limping to surrender at Yorktown, Virginia.

The park's visitor center features a film on the battle, interactive exhibits, a bookstore, and self-guided auto and bike tours of the park. At nearby **Tannenbaum Park** the cabin Joseph and Hannah Hoskins fled as the battle drew near is the heart of a backcountry farmstead. *2200 New Garden Rd.; 336/545–5315.*

History's hand has scattered Quaker museums and meetinghouses throughout the countryside, but most are open only a few hours each week. Look for brochures at area visitors centers and the **Greensboro Convention and Visitors Bureau** (2200 Pinecroft Rd., Suite 200; 336/274–2282 or 800/344–2282).

Tobacco put Durham and Reidsville on the map, but Winston-Salem was a major point on North Carolina's map long before Joe Camel loped onto the scene. Winston-Salem is now home to numerous artists, including author Maya Angelou.

The city began in 1766 as a Moravian commune on the edge of America's wild western frontier. Today their restored 18th-century village, Old Salem, is one of the nation's most authentic colonial sites.

★ OLD SALEM

Old Salem, the literal and figurative heart of Winston-Salem, hasn't changed much since William Loughton Smith visited in May 1791:

> After traveling through the woods for many days, the sight of this little settlement of Moravians is highly curious and interesting.... The first view of the town is romantic, just as it breaks upon you through the woods; it is pleasantly seated on a rising ground, and is surrounded by beautiful meadows, well-cultivated fields, and shady woods. The antique appearance of the houses, built in the German style, and the trees among which they are placed have a singular and pleasing effect; the whole resembles a beautiful village, and forms a pastoral scene.

Today, over a half-million visitors a year explore **Old Salem**, now a living-history museum where you can talk with costumed interpreters practicing 18th-century trades. You can see exactly what made this town so prosperous. *900 Old Salem Rd.; 336/721–7300.*

In the two-story brick-and-log **Single Brothers House**, guests stroll a stone-paved hallway lined with 18th-century shops. In one a dye-maker explains the natural dyes Salem's craftsmen grew, harvested, and used. In another a tailor holds needle and thread up to the light. Decorated Moravian pottery—the first art in "the City of the Arts"—lines the potter's shop walls. *600 S. Main St.; 336/721–7300.*

Over in the **Old Salem Tavern** (736 S. Main St.; 336/748–8585)—once Salem's link to the outside world—costumed interpreters discuss slavery. At **Winkler Bakery** (525 S. Main St.; 336/721–7302) women in long, dark dresses and chaste white bonnets slide loaves of Swedish rye into the wood-fired oven as visitors line up to buy warm gingerbread and sugar cookies.

Old Salem's guides know their stuff, and like to chat. The *Old Salem Official Guidebook,* available at the visitors center, is jam-packed with detail.

Salem was unique on the Carolina frontier. Moravians, a Protestant group from Germany, settled in Pennsylvania in the early 1700s and looked south for good, cheap land. In 1753 they bought 100,000 acres in the North Carolina backcountry for $35,000, and named it Wachovia.

They chose the Carolina tract for three reasons. First, for religious freedom. Second, for the area's rich natural resources. And third: location, location, location. The tract sat on the Great Wagon Road, which meant they could expect a constant stream of customers eager to buy their products.

Bishop August Spangenberg led a group of 11 men to North Carolina to choose a site for Salem. The bishop must have thought he teetered on the edge of the world. In November of 1752 he wrote to friends in Pennsylvania:

> The land is very rich, and has been much frequented by buffalo, whose tracks are everywhere, and can often be followed with profit. The wolves here give us music every morning, from six corners at once, such music as I have never heard. . . .

The Moravian Book Shop in the restored 18th-century village of Old Salem.

The statue of Richard J. Reynolds in front of the Wachovia Bank Building in downtown Winston-Salem.

Finally, the axes rang out and the brethren began a town—two large dormitories, a store, tavern, pottery, mill, sawmill, barn, four shops, and meeting hall.

Happily for historians, the Moravians recorded everything—dewfall, lovers' spats, slaves' behavior, religious rites—and socked their notes away in the church archives. Today historians mine those archives, turning up nuggets of truth more precious than emeralds mined in the Appalachians.

Thanks to yesterday's note-takers and today's historians, Salem's 100 historic buildings and 30-some gardens rank among the most authentic restorations in the country. And we know some of Salem's early residents—white, slave, and free blacks—almost as well as we know Salem's quiet streets.

Even the 1816 Old Salem Tavern profits from the colonial Moravians' love for detail. Some of their recipes survive from the 1700s.

OTHER WINSTON-SALEM HIGHLIGHTS

The **Museum of Early Southern Decorative Arts** (MESDA), a collage of historic Southern rooms, is North Carolina's most interesting, most immediate history and art museum. On the edge of Old Salem, the museum has 24 fascinating rooms dismantled in Maryland, Virginia, North Carolina, South Carolina, Georgia, Kentucky, and Tennessee and reassembled here—woodwork, portraits,

Reynolda House Museum of American Art.

needlepoint, silverware, et al. Visitors walk from historic site to historic site, all within the space of the museum. *924 S. Main St.; 336/721–7300.*

R. J. Reynolds, his wife Katherine Smith Reynolds, and their children once lived in **Reynolda House**, a 64-room mansion designed by Charles Barton Keen. The museum's permanent collection, which spans three centuries, includes works by Mary Cassatt, Andrew Wyeth, Georgia O'Keeffe, Thomas Hart Benton, John Singleton Copley, Frederic E. Church, Gilbert Stuart, Thomas Eakins, and Jacob Lawrence. It was begun by the Reynolds family, and continues to expand.

Built in 1917, Reynolda also retains many original furnishings and family memorabilia. In the basement you can almost hear the Reynolds children playing handball, splashing in the pool, or sending a gutter ball rocketing down a lane in the bowling alley. (Listen closely as you walk through the upstairs rooms, and you can almost hear them shooting the bulbs out of the chandeliers during less idyllic times.)

Reynolda Gardens—129 acres of wooded paths, vegetable gardens, and formal flower gardens—surround the home. The estate's servant quarters, stables, and outbuildings have been converted into specialty shops and restaurants. From I–40, take Silas Creek Parkway north to the Wake Forest University exit. *2250 Reynolda Rd.; 336/758–5150.*

Secca, the English-style manor house across the street from Reynolda House was the home of the late industrialist James G. Hanes, who put America in skivvies. Today his mansion is the Southeastern Center for Contemporary Art, known for ever-changing exhibits by nationally known artists. *750 Marguerite Dr.; 336/725–1904.*

Hit the **Piedmont Craftsmen Gallery and Shop** for quality crafts made by Southeastern craftspeople—many from North Carolina. Its Crafts Fair, the third weekend in November, touts the work of around 130 artists. *601 N. Trade St.; 336/725–1516.*

Produced by the North Carolina Black Repertory Company, the biannual **National Black Theater Festival** is held in early August in odd-numbered years. Theaters across Winston-Salem showcase original dramatic productions with widely varied African-American themes. *610 Collesium Dr.; 336/723–7907.*

Winston-Salem test-markets Broadway performances, which makes the Stevens Center, at the **North Carolina School of the Arts,** a good place to see the big shows before they're the big shows. The Stevens Center also hosts productions by the NCSA, one of the foremost arts conservatories in the country, and the Winston-Salem Piedmont Triad Symphony. *1533 S. Main St.; 336/770–3399.*

The Moravians at Bethabara palisaded their settlement for protection from Indians. (Moravian Archives, Bethlehem)

Tanglewood Park, 9 miles west of Winston-Salem in the town of Clemmons, was a gift from the Reynolds family to Forsyth County. The 1,300-acre park—home of the Manor House B&B—provides three golf courses, a steeplechase each May, tennis, swimming, equestrian trails, paddle boats, and ducks waiting at this moment for a crust of bread. *Off US 158; 336/778–6300.*

On the outskirts of Winston-Salem, **Historic Bethabara Park** contains two of the most important colonial gardens in the United States. The community gardens are the only known, well-documented colonial community gardens in America, says director Ellen Kutcher.

For that we can thank Moravian surveyor Christian Reuter, who dropped by with pens and ink in 1759 and 1761 to map the gardens row-by-row. Using his maps, archaeologists relocated the gardens in 1985. The gardens have been reconstructed from actual garden maps that list what was planted in each one of the rows.

Planted in the spring of 1754, the brethren's vegetable garden soon fed 300 people a day—the Moravians, plus refugees from the French and Indian War who fled into the palisade.

Today this is a community garden of a different stripe. Around 30 Winston-Salem gardeners lease plots here each year, planting from Christian Reuter's 1759 plant list. One bed grows heirloom vegetables, but most gardeners cultivate hybrid descendants of the Moravians' crops.

The Medicinal Garden, which includes medicinal herbs plus various vitamin-rich plants, wasn't difficult to relocate: the fennel still held its original ground. The garden is being restored, again using Reuter's map and plant list.

Today visitors stroll through these gardens, chatting with gardeners about colonial gardening techniques and the gardens' history. They rest in the cool, vine-covered arbor as martins swoop overhead, or explore the Medicinal Garden, which in June offers the hypnotic scent of roses. They explore the small museum, the restored Gemeinhaus (1788), the Potter's House (1782), the Brewer's House (1803), and the reconstructed 1756 palisade fort. Gardeners sharpen their hoes around mid-April. *2147 Bethabara Rd.; 336/924–8191.*

YADKIN VALLEY WINERIES

Grapes have long played a role in North Carolina history, wowing early explorers with their abundance. North Carolina settlers began making Scuppernong wine here in the 1700s, using the pulp of sweet, bronze-colored grapes that grew easily and produced abundantly. For centuries Scuppernong grape vines were beloved fixtures behind many traditional Carolina homes.

A GREAT DRIVE IN NORTHERN PIEDMONT

Once you exit the Piedmont's main highways and urban centers, just about any drive is scenic. The Piedmont is a place of gentle curves: in the hillsides, in the boulder-strewn streambeds, in the flow of country roads.

To add a scenic drive to a Winston-Salem trip, think northwest. Meander north on 311 through the little town of Walnut Grove; then take 89 to Meadows and head toward Hanging Rock State Park.

This park offers hilly but easy hikes, plenty of picnic ops, and the enticing option of sitting still and listening to the wind in the oaks, maples, hickories, and pines.

NC 89 continues to Mt. Airy, actor Andy Griffith's hometown, where the Main Street pays homage to Mayberry. Drop by Floyd's City Barber Shop on Main Street, tour the town in a 1962 patrol car, or see the old city jail.

The Snappy Lunch (125 N. Main St.; 336/786–4931) predates the *Andy Griffith Show*. As a boy, Griffith used to grab a hot dog and a pop here for 15 cents. Today a hot dog sets you back $1.30—or you can splurge with a pork chop sandwich.

At sunset you might want to catch a double feature at the Bright Leaf Drive-In (150 N. Andy Griffith Pkwy.; 336/786—5494), on the edge of town. Pop a speaker in your window and settle back with some concession-stand cuisine. From here it's a 40-minute drive back to Winston-Salem along Route 52.

* * *

That tradition is expanding today, as vineyards take root across the state. Case in point: the Yadkin Valley, a fertile, 1.4 million-acre valley west of Winston-Salem, is currently home to 13 vineyards and wineries, most of which offer tours and tastings. You may find traditional Scuppernongs growing in some of these vineyards, but you'll also find Chardonnay, Cabernet Sauvignon, Riesling, Merlot, and Sauvignon Blanc thriving here as well.

Each vineyard offers visitors a glimpse of its own character and history. In addition to tours and tastings, they also provide picnic spots, art galleries, gift shops, music, and outstanding scenery. Contact the **Winston-Salem Convention and Visitors Bureau** (336/728–4200) for information on their driving tour, Wine Trails of the Yadkin Valley.

GETTING AROUND

The Piedmont claims more highways than any other region of the state. I–95 runs roughly north–south along the region's eastern border, slicing in at a slight southward slant.

I–85 and I–40 are the area's lifelines. I–85 runs north to south from Virginia as far as Durham, and then turns west to link the largest urban centers of the northern Piedmont: Durham, Burlington, Greensboro, High Point. From there it zigzags south, toward Charlotte.

I–40 unites Raleigh, Chapel Hill, Durham, Greensboro, Winston-Salem, and Hickory before it heads west.

These major thoroughfares generally get you there in a hurry, wherever you're headed. But between them is a much more leisurely (and usually much more pleasant) interlacing of roads that often travel pretty much the way horse-drawn carts did. When time allows, opt for those less hectic routes. You'll meet more of Carolina that way.

Westbend Vineyards in Lewisville, at the head of the Yadkin Valley.

SPECIALTY SHOPPING IN THE PIEDMONT

You'll find a host of Piedmont outlets offering attractively priced North Carolina–made furniture and textiles, as well as specialty venues worth looking into. Here are a few to get you started.

REPLACEMENTS, LTD. (GREENSBORO)

Replacements' showroom and warehouse just north of Greensboro on I-85/40 make up a never-never land of lost crystal, china, jelly glasses—even those eerily blank-faced plates and saucers that snuck into America's cupboards via laundry detergent boxes in the 1960s.

The massive facilities, which include a 225,000-square-foot showroom, are home to 12 million pieces of tableware in 290,000 patterns. If you broke it, they can replace it. And, indeed, shoppers with chipped pasts come here by the busload. Hollywood stars, royalty, and first ladies phone in, too. (Their patterns are displayed along a back wall.) Take the Mt. Hope Church Road exit off I-85, turn left at the stop sign, and left again on Knox Road. *1089 Knox Rd.; 336/697-3000.*

HIGH POINT FURNITURE

High Point craftsmen, who began making furniture in 1880, carved a multimillion-dollar industry out of the region's hardwood forests. Today the city of High Point is home to 64 furniture-manufacturing facilities plus a number of furniture distributors. Over 40 area stores, showrooms, and outlets sell everything from discontinued furniture lines to crystal chandeliers handmade in Eden, North Carolina.

HICKORY FURNITURE

The town of Hickory has been a major furniture producer since the 1800s, and Highway 321 between Hickory and Blowing Rock is known nationally for its furniture showrooms and outlets. The **Hickory Furniture Mart** (2220 Hwy. 70 SE; 828/322–3510) gathers together more than 100 outlets, stores, and furniture galleries, representing manufacturers from North Carolina and beyond.

Fine furniture making has been a North Carolinian tradition for over a century. This Farm Security Administration photo from the 1930s shows a man crafting rocking chairs. (Library of Congress)

LOCAL FAVORITE PLACES TO EAT

Big Ed's Restaurant. 220 Wolfe St., Raleigh; 919/836–9909. $

More artifacts dangle from the ceiling here than any tasteful museum curator would allow. This is down-home cooking with fresh ingredients—very good, very casual. Top-selling plates include chicken with molasses-flavored barbecue sauce and sliced barbecue. Or consider the chicken pastry, served with the usual Southern suspects: collards, yams, okra.

The 1816 Old Salem Tavern. 736 South Main St., Winston-Salem; 336/748–8585. $$

Tasty dishes from historic Moravian recipes—chicken pie, gingerbread, and fresh-baked bread, that haven't changed since the day George Washington dropped by—are served in an 1816 dining room whose rustic tables, hearths, and plank floors were inspired by descriptions in early Moravian documents.

Fearrington House. 2000 Fearrington Village, Pittsboro; 919/542–2121. $$$$

Well regarded for its New Southern/ contemporary American cuisine, this softly lit, formal dining room prepares its dishes, such as seared scallops with cauliflower puree, using local, organic produce. Consider the hot chocolate soufflé, a constant on the menu since the restaurant opened. No lunch.

Lexington BBQ #1. 10 Hwy. 29-70 S.; 336/249–9814. $

This is a popular pick, but the entire town of Lexington is a dining destination, known for western-style barbecue made from pork shoulders and dressed in a sweet tomato-vinegar sauce. Twenty or so restaurants stand cheek-by-jowl along the main drags. Many slow-roast their barbecue out back.

Magnolia Grill. 1002 Ninth St., Durham; 919/286–3609. $$-$$$

In a one-time corner grocery in downtown Durham, the Magnolia Grill has wowed diners since it opened some 20-odd years ago with seasonal menus that reflect locally available produce. You might find Carolina lump crab and fingerling potato hash with apple-smoked bacon, local farm eggs sunny-side up, and béarnaise aioli; or twice-baked grits soufflé with wild and exotic mushroom ragout.

Pop's: A Durham Trattoria. 810 W. Peabody St., Durham; 919/956–7677. $-$$$

Fresh, local ingredients are the rule in this popular northern Italian restaurant. Try a wood-oven-fired pizza with Granny Smith apples, Brie, ricotta, and white truffle. Or forego pizza for the crispy "chicken cooked under a brick," served with potato gnocchi, proscuitto, pine nuts, and garlic jus.

LOCAL FAVORITE PLACES TO STAY

Augustus T. Zevely Inn. 803 S. Main St., Winston-Salem; 336/748–9299. $$

Once the home of a mid-19th-century physician, this is the only inn in the Old Salem Historic District. It's been restored and largely furnished with Old Salem Collection furniture and accessories— reproductions based on historic pieces in Old Salem. The Summer Kitchen Room, for example, has a working, raised-hearth cooking fireplace and oven. Downstairs rooms have radiant-heated floors. The dining room and parlor have corner fireplaces characteristic of Moravian architecture. The porch out back is a great place to enjoy the heirloom flower garden and the sprawling magnolia tree. Breakfast includes Moravian baked goods.

The Carolina Inn. 211 Pittsboro St., Chapel Hill; 919/933-2001. $$$

This elegant old inn at the edge of the UNC campus was built in 1924 by UNC grad John Sprunt Hill, who soon gave it to the university to use as "a cheerful inn for visitors." It is exactly that. Restored in 1996, the inn blends Georgian and neoclassical features with elements of Southern plantation houses. Fronted by massive white columns, it echoes the design of Mt. Vernon, and the 184 guest rooms and suites are furnished with antiques and reproductions. The inn has an excellent restaurant, the Carolina Crossroads, which is noted for its inventive New American cuisine. The inn is listed on the National Register of Historic Places; profits help fund the UNC library system.

Proximity Hotel. 704 Green Valley Rd., Greensboro; 336/379–8200. $$$$

The first LEED Platinum Hotel in the country, the sleek Proximity uses 40% less energy and 30% less water than a comparable structure. Green enhancements are deliberately unobtrusive at this luxury property, but peek up on the roof and you'll spot the 100 solar panels that heat your water and you'll certainly notice the oversize windows that let light and fresh air into your room. The overall design echoes that of a historic Greensboro textile mill—the Proximity Cotton Mill. The open expanses of the public areas and the huge windows recall the feel and design of an old industrial space, while the 147 oversize guest rooms and 10 suites have a sleek, contemporary feel.

SOUTHERN PIEDMONT

 "Piedmont" means, literally, "foot of the mountains." North Carolina's mountains have size-12 EEE feet.

The Piedmont plateau covers about 40 percent of the state, about the same amount as the coastal plain, and extends from the fall line in the east to the Appalachians in the west. "Soil" in the Piedmont means bright red clay.

In general, the Piedmont rises from about 500 feet above sea level in the east to 1,500 feet in the west. Its stooped mountains, now protected in several state parks and a national forest, are the cores of North America's most ancient ranges.

Those ranges have melted away over the millennia, softened by time, winds, and rains. Today remnant peeks overlook small towns set in a patchwork of cornfields and dairy farms, the state's largest cities, and quiet communities of traditional potters who have found a time-honored use for the Piedmont's generous supply of clay.

The Piedmont is the most industrial and urban section of the state. The tobacco, textile, and furniture industries helped shape this region, and the influence of the tobacco and furniture industries, in particular, remains strong. Pharmaceuticals, medicine, research, government, education, and banking also help shape the human landscape of the Piedmont today.

Charlotte, the "Queen City," is the center of one of the largest urban areas in the nation. Other cities lie to her north: Raleigh, Durham, Burlington, Greensboro, Winston-Salem. Malls often ring Piedmont cities. Along I–85 and I–40 furniture outlets are so popular that tour buses hover in the parking lots. (*See* the Northern Piedmont chapter.)

In smaller, more typical Piedmont towns and cities you'll find a couple of museums downtown and a pleasant historic district nearby. You may also find a small district of cafés, shops, and coffeehouses near one of the Piedmont's many colleges or universities.

To get a true sense of the region, venture off the major highways from time to time, onto twisting lanes laid out by streams and jostling wagons. In sight of metro skylines and asphalt arteries, traditional Piedmont Carolina lives wrapped in the smell of Moravian wheat bread, the hum of a potter's wheel, the sigh of a long-leaf pine.

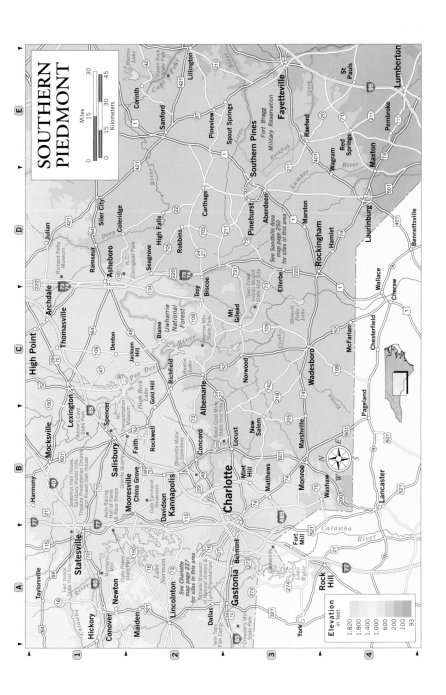

SOUTHERN PIEDMONT

Miles
0   15   30

Kilometers
0   15   30   45

Elevation
in feet

1,820
1,800
1,400
1,000
600
200
100
93

Beginning in the 19th century, textile manufacture became one of North Carolina's biggest industries. Here children in rags make whole cloth. (University of Maryland)

SETTLEMENT

Unlike the coastal plain, where civilization seeped inland along languid rivers and streams, the Piedmont was settled by Germans and Scots who barreled into the area in the mid-1700s. European diseases had decimated the Catawba and other native peoples, leaving the clay hills ripe for the taking.

Settlers came first on foot and horseback, following the Indian Trade Path from eastern Virginia and the Great Wagon Road from Pennsylvania. Soon they rumbled along in Conestoga wagons, pushing south along what is today I-85. They came singly, in families, and as entire communities, searching for religious freedom, cheap land, and water that could irrigate a crop and spin a mill wheel.

Moravians from Germany became the first tradesmen. Their bustling mission towns included Salem, the heart of Winston-Salem, once a major tobacco center in the northern Piedmont. Quakers settled the hills around Greensboro, which became the home of North Carolina's Underground Railroad and the sit-ins of the early Civil Rights movement. To the south, Salisbury, Charlotte, and other backcountry towns sputtered to life as trade centers.

In 1770 backcountry Regulators traded lead with royal governor William Tryon's militia over unfair taxes. But the Revolution largely bypassed the

Piedmont, not out of respect for its large, pacifist Quaker and Moravian populations, but because Piedmont clay held little military value. The only major battle fought here—at Guilford County Courthouse near Greensboro—was more than enough for the reluctant sharpshooters drafted to fight it.

After the Revolution the state legislature stepped off a new capital city, Raleigh, and a university at Chapel Hill (*see* the Northern Piedmont chapter).

Immigrants still rattled down the Wagon Road—though many followed Salisbury's son, Daniel Boone, west to Kentucky. Hessian soldiers, who came to America courtesy of King George, hung up their red coats and settled down. One of those soldiers was John Reed, whose boy Conrad stumbled across a 17-pound gold nugget near Charlotte in 1799, setting off America's first gold rush.

North Carolina seceded from the Union in 1861. Textile mills shifted gears, churning out oceans of gray material for uniforms. Men who'd never owned a slave enlisted to defend states' rights and their homes.

No major Civil War battles took place on this red soil, but industries and homes went up in smoke as Sherman's forces swarmed across the state in 1864. Following the Battle of Bentonville, to the east, Sherman accepted the surrender of CSA General Joe Johnston's troops at Bennet House, near Durham, ending North Carolina's war.

Now the state built new economic muscles around the railroad's iron skeleton. In Burlington, Kannapolis, Charlotte, and Gastonia, streams were collared to fuel textile mills, putting entire families to work. In High Point, Hickory, and Lenoir furniture-makers carved an industry out of sprawling hardwood forests.

A Carolina gold dollar from the 1830s. (Courtesy NCDA&H)

CHARLOTTE   *map page 223*

If you're visiting Charlotte, you're probably in town on business. You're not alone. Most of Charlotte is in town on business.

With a population of 640,000, Charlotte is the geographic center of one of the largest urban areas in the U.S.—a midsize city in a web of small towns. Nearly 1.6 million people live in the metro area. Charlotte claims North Carolina's most dramatic man-made skyline and one of the nation's largest banking communities.

The Charlotte skyline is the most dramatic in the state.

SHOPPING IN THE CHARLOTTE AREA

Charlotte shops. The 200 or so retailers, outlets, and restaurants at **Concord Mills** (8111 Concord Mills Blvd., Concord; 704/979–3000) pull in a cool 2 million shoppers each year, many of whom head to Off 5th Saks Fifth Avenue, Sun & Ski Sports, and Bass Pro Shops Outdoor World, a 150,000-square-foot sportsman's smorgasbord.

SouthPark Mall (440 Sharon Rd.; 704/364–4411) draws luxury shoppers with its more than 150 upscale retailers, including Nordstrom, Nieman Marcus, Tiffany, and Louis Vuitton.

You'll find a number of boutiques in the **SouthPark Mall area,** too. If you're interested in upscale boutiques, these open-air shopping plazas are good bets: Phillips Place (Fairview Rd. and Cameron Valley Parkway) or Morrison (Sharon and Colony Rds.).

Over 300 Fortune 500 businesses maintain offices in Charlotte, the largest city between Washington, D.C. and Atlanta.

Charlotte may wear more white-collar shirts than most of North Carolina, but those collars do come unbuttoned. North Carolina's Queen City dishes up nightlife with the best of them, from "New Southern" restaurants to blues clubs to gallery crawls.

Charlotte's downtown area, Center City, is a great place to scout evening entertainment. The intersection of Trade and Tryon, once two Indian trading paths, marks the town center. Jazz bars along Tryon Street and nearby College Street pack them in. The Jazz Café on Brevard, one block over from College, is one of the city's most popular jazz clubs. Also hot: the Blue Restaurant and Bar on the corner of 5th and Gallery streets. (*See* Local Favorite Places to Eat at the end of this chapter.)

From Center City you can access Charlotte's historic South End, a reborn cotton-mill district, by trolley or light rail. A once-a-month South End gallery crawl introduces folks to the local arts scene. Call 704/332–9587 for information. If you miss the crawls, you might want to focus your efforts around Camden Street, which is known for its galleries.

If martinis are more your style, try Tutto Mondo (1820 South Blvd.; 704/332–8149), a popular uptown gathering place. South End flows into Dilworth historic district, known for its cafés, clubs, and shops.

Charlotte's NoDa neighborhood, another historic mill area, might also pique your curiosity. This arts community is known for its galleries, funky performance venues, and casual dining. NoDa stands for North Davidson, and rhymes with "soda."

CHARLOTTE HIGHLIGHTS

More than a half-million people a year visit **Discovery Place,** Charlotte's hands-on science and technology museum. Some come to watch the rat basketball. Some come to check out the East Coast's largest eyeball. Others come to stroll a three-story rain forest complete with waterfall and tropical birds, mosey about the butterfly room, check out the aquarium, or line up for the OMNIMAX Theater. The museum's Kelly Space Voyager Planetarium honors North Carolina Astronaut Michael J. Smith, pilot of the fallen *Challenger* space shuttle. *301 North Tryon St.; 704/372–6261.*

Charlotte's **Mint Museum of Art**, one of the state's best art museums, takes its name from a little-known chapter of NC history.

Gold put Charlotte on the map during the North Carolina gold rush, with the first branch mint in the U.S. opening its doors here in 1836. The Charlotte Mint stamped raw Carolina gold into $5 million worth of coins, jump-starting the city's huge banking industry, which is today one of the nation's largest. (In Charlotte's Myers Park, known for its Victorian architecture, you walk along shady streets originally paved with fill from Charlotte's early mines.)

The Charlotte Mint closed in 1861, and preservationists moved it to its current address to save it from the wrecking ball. It reopened in 1936 as the Mint Museum of Art.

The Mint Museum of Art is home to American and European paintings, Victorian silver, pre-Columbian and African art, historic costumes, one of the nation's outstanding pottery and porcelain collections—and, as you might expect, a complete set of Charlotte-minted gold coins.

The Mint Museum of Craft & Design, in a separate facility over in Center City, houses the museum's American Crafts Collection. It showcases NC crafts, including woodworking, ceramics, and furniture making, but includes crafts from all over the world. *2730 Randolph Rd.; 704/337–2000.*

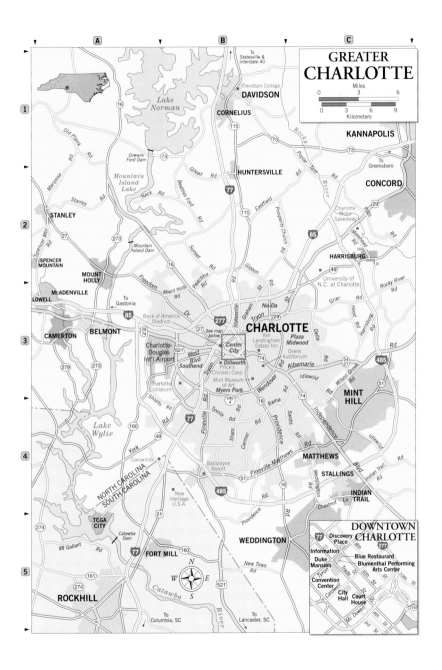

GREATER
CHARLOTTE

Miles
0 — 3 — 6

Kilometers
0 — 3 — 6 — 9

To Statesville & Interstate 40

Davidson College
DAVIDSON

CORNELIUS

KANNAPOLIS

To Greensboro

CONCORD

Lake Norman

Old Plank Rd

Cowans Ford Dam

HUNTERSVILLE

Mountain Island Lake

Charlotte Motor Speedway

STANLEY

Spencer Mtn Rd

SPENCER MOUNTAIN

Mountain Island Dam

HARRISBURG

University of N.C. at Charlotte

MOUNT HOLLY

Freedom

Mount Holly Rd

Peachtree Rd

Rocky River Rd

McADENVILLE

LOWELL

To Gastonia

No-Da

Grier Rd

Hood Rd

Bank of America Stadium

CHARLOTTE

Van Landingham Estate Inn

Plaza Midwood

CAMERTON

BELMONT

Charlotte-Douglas Int'l Airport

West Blvd

Center City

Ovens Auditorium

Dilworth

Southend

Price's Chicken Coop

MINT HILL

Charlotte Coliseum

Mint Museum of Art

Myers Park

City 4

Rama Rd

Wendover Rd

Albemarle Rd

Idlewild Rd

Lake Wylie

Pineville Rd

Sharon Rd

Carmel Rd

Providence Rd

Sardis Rd

Independence Blvd

York Rd

Carowinds

MATTHEWS

NORTH CAROLINA
SOUTH CAROLINA

New Heritage U.S.A.

Ballantyne Resort

Pineville-Matthews Rd

STALLINGS

Weddington Rd

INDIAN TRAIL

Indian Trail Rd

Chestnut Ln

TEGA CITY

Catawba Dam

Mt Gallant Rd

FORT MILL

WEDDINGTON

New Town Rd

Providence Rd

ROCKHILL

Catawba River

To Columbia, SC

To Lancaster, SC

DOWNTOWN CHARLOTTE

Discovery Place

Information

Blue Restaurant

Duke Mansion

Blumenthal Performing Arts Center

Convention Center

City Hall

Court House

The **Blumenthal Performing Arts Center** (130 N. Tryon St.) brings Broadway shows to Charlotte and presents performances by the Charlotte Symphony Orchestra, among others. **Spirit Square** (345 N. College St.) is the place to go for community theatre. You can get information on both at the **Charlotte Information Center** (800/231–4636).

The Carolina Panthers football team calls Charlotte home, too. They play at the **Bank of America Stadium** (800 S. Mint St.; 704/358–7800), downtown.

GASTONIA   *map page 217, A-2/3*

Landlocked Gastonia, which lies west of Charlotte on I–85, is home to some of the best fish camps in the state—an unexpected spinoff of the textile mills that kept this area in money from the mid-1800s until late in the 20th century, when many of North Carolina's textile mills packed up shop.

The camps got their start during the Depression. In the 1930s, cooks boiled up kettles of Catawba River fish over open fires, spooning out fish stew to patrons who ate in sawdust-floored open-air eateries called "camps."

Over the years the camps evolved into restaurants, and the Catawba River fish gave way to fresh seafood trucked in from the coast. Today folks still head for the fish camps' heaping plates of fried fish, shrimp, and oysters. Most camps welcome guests seven days a week, and a few are open for lunch.

The rule here is "good food and plenty of it."

A local favorite among the many Gastonia fish camps is Twin Tops Fish Camp on New Hope Road. (*See* Local Favorite Places to Eat, at the end of this chapter.)

After lunch, head for the **Schiele Museum of Natural History and Lynn Planetarium,** one of the state's most-visited museums. Exhibits include one of the Southeast's largest mounted land mammal collections, as well as geology, pale-ontology, archaeology, and anthropology exhibits and a planetarium. Outdoors, nature trails lead to a reconstructed Catawba Indian village, an 18th-century backcountry farm, and a wildlife garden designed to attract butterflies and hum-mingbirds. Take the New Hope Road exit off I–85 and follow the brown signs to the museum. *1500 E. Garrison Blvd.; 704/866–6908.*

CROWDER'S MOUNTAIN STATE PARK   *map page 217, A-3*

Crowder's Mountain and Kings Pinnacle, which rise only 800 feet from the park floor—are remnants of an Appalachian chain that towered thousands of feet above sea level millions of years ago. Their quartzite-rich cores stood strong while their neighbors melted away.

When buffalo roamed these prairies, these mountains marked the boundary between Catawba and Cherokee hunting grounds. The buffalo are long gone, but possums, foxes, raccoons, chipmunks, salamanders, and 160 bird species scurry among the red maples, pines, rhododendrons, laurels, and oaks. The namesake state park was created in the early 1970s to keep these two wizened old mountains out of the hands of kyanite-hungry strip miners.

You can backpack into these secluded campgrounds or picnic near the lake. You can also canoe the shoreline or cast for bream and bass. Hikes range from easy to strenuous; Crowder's Mountain's sheer 150-foot vertical cliffs challenge even experienced climbers. No pitons, bolts, or cliff-scarring devices are allowed. Check in with the park office for a climbing permit, and follow their safety rules and regulations. From Gastonia, US 321 leads to Crowder's Mountain State Park. Follow the signs. *522 Park Office La., Kings Mountain; 704/853–5375.*

REED GOLD MINE STATE HISTORIC SITE

map page 217, B-2/3

One Sunday in 1799, 12-year-old Conrad Reed played hooky from church, wetting a line in Meadow Creek instead. For penance, he pried a pretty yellow stone from a creek bed, and lugged it to his family's cabin. It served as a doorstop until 1802, when a visitor took a gander at the 17-pound toe-stumper. "Gold!" he shrieked.

"Nein," muttered Conrad's father, who took the stone to a Fayetteville jeweler, just in case. Gold! Reed sold the ingot for $3.50, and raced home with the news. Gold in Cabarrus County!

Farmers dropped their plow lines, teachers shelved their books, merchants folded their aprons. Armed with picks, pans, and provisions, they poured into the Carolina gold fields around Cabarrus County. America's first gold rush was on, and eventually 115 pounds of gold enriched the Reed family's coffers. Today, at the Reed Gold Mine State Historic Site, the pay dirt surfaces in buckets from April to November, ready to be panned in flowing water. A modest fee buys the use of a pan, two pans of dirt, and a few pointers.

The visitors center, open year-round, offers a film and exhibits on gold mining. The park includes a restored mine area, 19th-century stamping mill, 1850s Engine House, and numerous trails.

This restored stamping mill is one of the exhibits at Reed Gold Mine State Historic Site.

Modern prospectors pocket gold here, but as for striking it rich: "If gold was that plentiful," drawls the owner of a nearby commercial mine, "I'd be down there panning it myself." *9621 Reed Mine Rd., Midland; 704/721–4653.*

NASCAR: LIFE IN THE FAST LANE

As you head northeast from Charlotte on NC 49, if the traffic runs bumper-to-bumper and you're cruising among an inordinate number of drivers in black cowboy hats, you're headed for one of the biggest parties in the state: a NASCAR race at the **Lowes Motor Speedway,** in Concord.

Over a half-million race fans surge to the Speedway each year to cheer their favorite drivers around the 1.5-mile track. For super events like Memorial Day weekend's Coca-Cola 600—the third-largest sports event in the U.S.—they cruise in a day early and camp, living on hot dogs and beer until the races begin. *5555 Concord Pkwy S.; 800/455–3267.*

NASCAR wears the same blue-collared work shirt it's worn since North Carolina moonshiners gunned the engine on the sport in the 1930s. During Prohibition NC bootleggers made deliveries up and down the East Coast,

NEW TO NASCAR'S SMALL TRACKS?

First time at a small race? OK, there are a few things you need to know.

WHAT TO BRING.

Bring seat cushions, preferably some commemorating an NC racing legend, like the late Dale Earnhardt or Richard Petty. **Do** bring earplugs or buy them at the track, especially for any children among you. These races are loud.

WHERE TO SIT.

If you're visiting one of the small tracks scattered across North Carolina, avoid sitting just inside the last turn, where it looks like the cars are careening down your throat. These are exciting seats, but while you'll have a great view of the bumps and a fabulous view of the wrecks, you may also eat a lot of liberated tire tread. Try sitting about halfway up the stands instead, in seats with a view of both turns.

WHAT TO EAT.

Chances are, at a small race, the racetrack menu offers burgers, hot dogs, fried chicken, fries, chips, soft drinks, earplugs, headache medicines, and—perhaps—fried bologna sandwiches. If you are bold, try the fried bologna and bright yellow mustard on white bread. As one fan puts it, "What's a race without a fried bologna sandwich?"

FLAGS

Flags control the action on the track. It's important to know what the flags mean if you want to understand the race.

- A green flag starts or restarts the race. When you see it come out, grab your earplugs.

- A yellow caution flag usually means clutter on the track. (At some tracks, a yellow and red flag means oil on the track.) When the yellow flag's out, the drivers take slow laps, and once-large leads dwindle to only a few feet, making for a tighter race. It also gives drivers time to "pit," or go in for a pit stop.

- A red flag stops the race.

- A blue flag with a diagonal orange stripe signals a driver to let a faster driver pass. Drivers can ignore this one if they want.

- A black flag means the driver has broken a rule or is driving a dangerous car, and must "pit." If a driver ignores the black flag for five laps, he (or occasionally she) gets the black flag with a white X on it.

- The black flag with a white X means you're out of the race.

- The white flag means one lap to go.

- The checkered flag means victory. First-, second-, and third-place drivers see this one as they cross the finish line.

stocking bars from Connecticut to Florida. After unloading in Florida, they raced on Daytona's beach and circular track, creating a NASCAR tradition of going nowhere very, very fast.

Today National Association of Stock Car Auto Racing drivers enjoy the status of country music stars, and their races fuel conversation at country stores, workplaces, and kitchen tables across the state. Knowledgeable fans argue the strategy of two-tire changes vs. four-tire changes, compare pit crews, relive crashes, cheer the drivers who walk away from those crashes, and mourn those who do not.

Big race tickets go almost as fast as NASCAR's winning cars, selling out months in advance at more than $100 a seat. Speedway tour vans putter around the track on non-race days; half-day race car–driving classes including face-stretching laps in a stock car, start at around $300 a day.

For information on the big races like Winston Cup Series, Busch Series, and Craftsman Truck Series or for a complete schedule of races, write to NASCAR, at P.O. Box 2875, Daytona Beach, FL 32120-2875 or check www.nascar.com.

LIFE IN OTHER LANES

Unless you time your visit specifically to coincide with a huge race, it's hard to catch a big-ticket NASCAR event in town. The big races move from location to location, and when you look at an individual speedway, the big races are few and far between.

Do not despair. NASCAR drivers have to start out sometime, and somewhere. For many drivers, that "sometime" is Saturday night, and that "somewhere" is one of the scores of smaller racetracks that pepper the Carolina countryside. No matter where you are, you're probably not more than 50 miles from an auto racetrack of some kind.

You might catch one of the less glamorous NASCAR events there, you might catch a stock car race (or two or three), you might even luck in on a demolition derby. While major NASCAR events take several hours to run their course, a local track might offer a buffet of five short races in one evening. These races are often free for kids and always modestly priced for adults.

For information on local races, do a little online research or stop at a local gas station and ask the mechanic. If he doesn't have a car in the event, he probably knows someone who does.

SIGHTS OF INTEREST TO NASCAR FANS

There are scads of race-related venues in this region, including a self-guided tour of places dear to the heart of the late racing legend Dale Earnhardt, Sr. For info on all of them, contact the **Cabarrus County CVB.** *3003 Dale Earnhardt Blvd., Kannapolis; 800/848–3740.*

RICHARD PETTY MUSEUM
map page 217, C/D-1

South of Greensboro on peaceful US 220B is the Richard Petty Museum—the equivalent of Lourdes for NASCAR fans. The museum includes six race cars driven by the seven-time Winston Cup Champion. The cars are various makes and models, says the museum's director and curator. "Whatever went fast in that year is what he drove." *142 West Academy St., Randleman; 336/495–1143.*

MOORESVILLE'S RACE SHOPS *map page 217, A/B-1/2*

The small town of Mooresville on I-77 is home to race shops that keep Ricky Rudd, Kyle Petty, and Rusty Wallace in the driver's seat. Many of the region's 48 shops welcome visitors. The Cabarrus County visitors center (800/848–3740; www.visitcabarrus.com) has schedules and information.

THE NORTH CAROLINA AUTO RACING HALL OF FAME *map page 217, A/B-1/2*

This hall of fame welcomes around 150,000 race fans a year to its 30-car museum. Follow the state signs on I–77 to exit 36. *119 Knob Hill Rd., Mooresville; 704/663–5331.*

DALE EARNHARDT, INC., SHOWROOM *map page 217, B-2*

Fans of the late Dale Earnhardt may want to visit this free museum, which includes Earnhardt's famous "number 3 car." The museum also highlights the achievements of several other Dale Earnhardt, Inc., drivers, including Dale Earnhardt, Jr. *1675 Coddle Creek Hwy. (Hwy. 3), Mooresville; 877/334–9663, 704/662–8000.*

Cabarrus County's race shops give visitors the green flag year-round.

Salisbury grew up at the intersection of the Trading Path and the Great Wagon Road (now I–85 and Route 70). Walking Salisbury's peaceful tree-lined streets today, it's hard to imagine this was home to a notorious Civil War prison, but it was.

Salisbury Prison was built for 1,000 men, but by late 1864 ten times that many languished within its walls. One of them, Major Abner Small, wrote, "I saw, shuddering as I looked, the dead-cart on its morning rounds, and in it God's images tiered up like sticks of wood." Over 5,000 unknown Union soldiers who died here, of disease, hunger, and cold, rest at the Salisbury National Cemetery— the largest number of unknown dead from any Civil War prison.

The Confederates opened the prison gates in January 1865, but no one told the Union's General George Stoneman. His cavalry thundered into Salisbury, burning the prison, factories, businesses, and railroad facilities. But he spared the

courthouse and homes, including the **Josephus Hall House,** home to the prison's chief surgeon. It's now a museum filled with mid-Victorian furnishings and accessories. *Open weekends. 226 S. Jackson St.; 704/636–1502.*

Thanks to Stoneman's restraint, Salisbury's 30 square-block west historic area, downtown, includes numerous pre–Civil War Greek Revival and Federal-style homes, and an 1855 Greek Revival county courthouse (now a museum). To reach the historic district, take exit 76B off I–85 down

Hall House, in Salisbury, was once home to the chief surgeon of a Civil War prison, located outside town.

Salisbury National Cemetery contains the bodies of 5,000 unknown Union soldiers.

Innes Street until Fulton Street. The town offers walking tours year-round, and guided tours on the second weekend of October. Pick up information at the **Rowan County CVB** (204 E. Innes St., Suite 120; 704/638–3100).

IN THE SALISBURY AREA

The hills around Salisbury are as thin-skinned and hard-boned as a 10-year-old's knobby knees. Here and there slabs of gray slate and granite jut through thin, grassy pastureland. Among ranch-style brick homes and double-wides, old clapboard farmhouses stand back from the roads, surrounded by huge, hunkered-down old barns, silos, and milking sheds.

Not long ago, men pitched hay from the barn lofts, children ushered cows across pastures, and women urged cows into milking stalls. Today dairy farming isn't so much a family operation as a corporate one. Most folks make a living in the area's growing factories.

Germans settled this area. Cleveland's and Rockwell's stately stone churches, which date from the 1700s, are among the staunchest architectural reminders of that ancestry. (Both welcome visitors.)

Place names here have a literal bent. **Rockwell** grew up around a rock well; **China Grove** was named for a grove of chinaberry trees. The area's oldest house is the 1766 Old Stone House in **Granite Quarry.** Diamond Jim, legendary Manhattan financier, once lived in **Gold Hill,** a rowdy little mining town whose 19th-century prospectors lifted over $2 million in gold from the earth. The town, which nodded off for a century or so, is waking up. Parts are under restoration; the park contains three old gold mines and a small museum.

Faith, population 600, throws the state's biggest Fourth of July party.

In **Spencer,** weather permitting, you can hop a restored steam-driven train at the **North Carolina Transportation Museum** (411 S. Salisbury Ave.; 704/636–2889), a museum in what was once the Southern Railway Company's largest repair facility. At the giant roundhouse, where a mammoth Lazy Susan spun wheezing engines and crippled cabooses over mechanic's pits, several handsome old trains have been upfitted, painted, and polished one more time: pug-faced engines, bullet-fast silvery trains, elegant cars built for window-shade romance, highbrow cars that conveyed the royalty of a newly industrialized nation.

NC 801 winds southwest of Salisbury to White Road and **Thyatira Presbyterian Church,** the home of two eyewitnesses to a Revolutionary War scene.

A steam engine repair shop at Spencer's Transportation Museum.

In 1781 military lines seesawed so unpredictably here that Elizabeth Steele, who ran a popular Salisbury inn, never knew who might stop by for dinner. Her portraits of King George and Queen Charlotte smiled on Cornwallis's men when they were in town, and she turned the portraits' royal faces to the wall when Patriots bivouacked nearby.

One night General Nathaniel Greene stopped by for dinner. When he described his soldiers' poverty, Mrs. Steele plunked down a sack of money. The grateful general scrawled on the back of the king's portrait, "O, George! Hide thy face and mourn." Today the eyewitness portraits hang in Thyatira Church. Outside, a stone monument marks Mrs. Steele's grave.

From Salisbury, 150 heads west through farming communities and hardwood forests to **Mooresville,** known for its NASCAR garages, and **Lake Norman.** An early avenue of commerce, the Catawba River and its neighbor to the east, the Pee Dee River, today connect a stepped series of vast man-made lakes that once powered the largest concentration of textile factories in the world. Lake Norman is North Carolina's largest inland body of water, with 520 miles of shoreline. It's known for its boating, swimming, and skiing, and for its vacation and residential homes. The fishing here is outstanding.

Lake Norman, North Carolina's largest man-made body of water, generates two commodities for the people of Piedmont North Carolina: electricity and recreation. If you've got a boat to launch, a stroke to perfect, or a line to wet, Lake Norman is the best bet in the Southern Piedmont.

The 32,475-acre lake is one of 11 lakes Duke Power created on the Catawba River at various locations and at various times. Its waters serve two hydroelectric stations and McGuire Nuclear Station.

More to the point, anglers say, the freshwater fishing may be the best in the state. Sailing, waterskiing, and swimming round out the list of water activities.

You'll find plenty of public and commercial accesses along the 520-mile shoreline, including two bank fishing areas and eight public boat access areas provided by Duke Power. The region also includes 21 marinas, a dozen or so championship golf courses, lakefront restaurants, booming residential developments, and more shops than you can shake a credit card at.

Sailing regattas are fairly common; so are festivals, including the Loch Norman Highland Games (spring) and the Carolina Renaissance Festival (weekends, October through November).

Over in Huntersville, you'll find the **Historic Latta Plantation** (5225 Sample Rd.; 704/875–2312), which is the last Catawba River plantation open to the public, and the **Carolina Raptor Center** (6000 Sample Rd.; 704/875–6521), with its eagles, ospreys, falcons, and owls. Other gateways to Lake Norman are Cornelius, Davidson, Denver, and Triangle.

Lake Norman's several parks include **Lake Norman State Park,** 32 miles north of Charlotte. (Take exit 42 off I-77 and follow the signs.) Here you'll find a smaller lake whose summer offerings include access to a sandy beach and swimming area, and canoe rentals. The park also offers a couple of hiking trails, picnic areas, boat access to Lake Norman, and tent and trailer campsites.

About the fishing: On Lake Norman anglers cast for crappie, bluegill, yellow perch, catfish, and three varieties of bass: largemouth, white, and striped. You'll need a North Carolina fishing license. You can purchase one in just about any hardware or sporting goods store.

For more information, call or drop by the **Lake Norman Chamber of Commerce** in Cornelius. *19900 W. Catawba Ave. (exit 28 off I–77); 704/892–1922 or 800/305–2508.*

The North Carolina Zoological Park is one of the largest walk-through habitat zoos in the nation.

NORTH CAROLINA ZOOLOGICAL PARK *map page 217, C/D-1/2*

Off Highways 220B and 159, south of Asheboro, lies the **North Carolina Zoological Park,** one of the nation's largest walk-through habitat zoos. A million visitors a year come here to visit the creatures and habitats of Africa and North America. The zoo is home to over 1,100 animals representing 200 species.

The most recent habitat addition, the Watani Grasslands, re-creates an African grassland. Here, as in Africa, the grasslands are home to elephants, rhinos, ostriches, and gazelles. Visitors take a "walking safari" through the habitat, observing those animals and others in a re-created "natural" environment.

This zoo occupies 1,500 acres by the gentle Uwharrie Mountains. The 500 developed acres re-create habitats from African bushlands to the Sonora Desert. The Africa habitats include a chimp exhibit Dr. Jane Goodall called the best in North America.

Explore this natural habitat zoo on foot or by tram. Spring and fall are the best times to visit, since animals (and humans) are more active in moderate temperatures. If you come in August, visit the arctic section of North America's Rocky Coast at midday—it's air-conditioned for the polar bears. *4401 Zoo Pkwy; 336/879–7000 or 800/488–0444.*

At Owens Pottery in Seagrove, Boyd Owens mixes local clay by hand.

SEAGROVE *map page 217, C/D-2*

Seagrove, a little town at the intersection of NC 220 and 705, is nationally known for its traditional pottery. But when people mention Seagrove potters, they're generally referring to several small, very laid-back communities along 705. In fact, they're so laid-back, they're attitudinally horizontal.

The tiny town of Whynot, which went nameless for years, finally got its name from a community debate: "Why not this name?" "Why not that one?"

Whynot won by a landslide.

And at a pottery near Westmoore a sign in the shop reads, "If no one is here to wait on you, please come to the back porch and yell."

Clearly, you don't want to come to Seagrove in a hurry. Talk to people about their work and the weather, and expect a few easy delays as you explore NC 705 and its winding tributaries. They lead to potters' shops, tiny log-cabin museums, and groundhog kilns with walls of firewood neatly stacked nearby. You'll find scores of potters along these roads. In fact, you can easily spend a day carrying an inexpensive wealth of pottery to your car.

A visit to the **North Carolina Pottery Center** can help you organize your Seagrove visit and give you some insight into the history and ongoing tradition of pottery making in the state. In addition to exhibits on NC potters,

Earthenware made by Ben Owen—Boyd Owens's second cousin, and Ben Owen III's grandfather—at Jugtown Pottery, ca. 1950. (Cameron Art Museum, Wilmington)

Throwing a ring pot at Earth Spirit Pottery in Seagrove.

you'll also find maps pinpointing area and state potteries. A display of works from over 90 local potteries can help you zero in on the ones you like best. *233 East Ave.; 336/873-8430.*

Several families of English potters settled this area in the mid-1700s, drawn by rich clay deposits and plenty of pine trees, which stoke up red-hot fires in the kilns. Mildred Teague Moore, whose family has turned pots here since the 1700s, sells her wares from one of the several one-room shops lining Highway 705 at Westmoore.

"A hundred years ago, just men were potters," she says. "It was kind of a man's type thing."

Seagrove potters turned out oceans of utilitarian pots: storage jars for fruit, milk, pine tar, whiskey. They made butter churns, chamber pots, dinnerware. They even made grave markers.

Whiskey jugs were big business until Prohibition and Mason jars killed the market. "Years ago, it got down to where there weren't more than five or six potters here," Moore says.

The community has revised and revived, with a new generation of art-school-trained potters leading the way. Ben Owen III, for example, turned his first pot here at his grandfather's knee. Owen, who continues a family tradition of incorporating simple Asian forms and bold color into his art, earned his BFA at East Carolina University, in Greenville, North Carolina. Visit his studio, Ben Owen Pottery, on Highway 705 near Westmoore. (The cousins of Ben's grandfather changed their last name from Owen to Owens; hence the occasional confusion about Ben Owen Pottery and M. L. Owens Pottery.)

Westmoore Pottery, around the corner on Busbee Road, reproduces colonial designs.

At Jugtown Pottery, a couple of miles down Jugtown Road, the log-cabin shop is filled with pottery, tapestries, and handblown glass. Beyond the small garden of old-timey purple iris, yarrow, and phlox, in a small museum pottery exhibits and photos explain the long life of Jugtown Pottery, created in 1921 by Raleigh artists Jacques and Juliana Busbee to market North Carolina pots in their Greenwich Village Tea Room.

Their marketing skills marked the first revival of Seagrove pottery. The second revival was sparked by tourists driving up from Pinehurst and Southern Pines. There are a few home-style restaurants in the area, or you can pack a lunch.

UWHARRIE NATIONAL FOREST
map page 217, C-2

The Uwharrie National Forest, which curls west of US 220, attracts people with a taste for solitude. Hikers come for the 20-mile Uwharrie Trail, and nine shorter hiking and interpretive trails. Nature lovers also know the park for its deer, quail, ducks, wild turkeys,

Pine trees along Parson's Branch Trail in the Birkhead Mountain Wilderness of Uwharrie National Forest.

foxes, and rabbits. Fishermen, canoeists, and vacationers know Badin Lake for its large-mouth bass, white bass, bream, perch, and sunfish.

The Uwharrie Mountains, which once towered thousands of feet above the park floor, have worn away to around 900 feet. Even their name, Uwharrie, is beyond memory—a word borrowed from the Suala Indians who once lived here, perhaps.

Settlers plundered these hills' veins for gold, silver, lead, and copper, and exhausted the thin soil with their crops. The Civilian Conservation Corps reforested this land in the 1930s. Today mountain laurel, pines, hardwoods, dogwood, sourwood, wildflowers, and ferns form a gentle canopy along the slopes and stream banks.

Family and primitive campgrounds, accessible by hiking and bridle trails, are open year-round. The Uwharrie Mountains are especially beautiful in October, when the leaves change. *Enter the 46,888-acre forest through Troy.*

TOWN CREEK INDIAN MOUND   *map page 217, C-3*

NC 109 to Mt. Gilead and NC 73 wind east through fields and forests once tended by members of the Pee Dee culture, who moved to this area around AD 1000.

The reconstructed temple at Town Creek Indian Mound.

An interior of the temple on the mound.

The people lived in villages, pulled fish from stone fish traps at the river's edge, and hunted the forests here for around 400 years. Where tractors rumble through cotton and soybean fields today, they probably hoed corn, pumpkins, gourds, and squash and grew bright yellow sunflowers. On a sharp bluff overlooking the fork of Town Creek and Little River, they built a palisaded temple complex, placing a thatch-roofed temple on a stepped pyramid. They celebrated important feast days here, and played ceremonial ball games. Only priests lived here, to keep the temple.

The members of this culture vanished around AD 1400. Some researchers suspect that they simply exhausted the area's natural resources, then moved on to other town sites.

At their rebuilt temple complex, Town Creek Indian Mound, an interpretive center and film introduce visitors to the Pee Dee culture and guided tours offer a firsthand look at the temple, priest's dwelling, and ceremonial grounds. *509 Town Creek Mound Rd., Mt. Gilead (follow signs off Hwys. 73 or 731); 910/439–6802.*

GETTING AROUND

In the Southern Piedmont several of the main interstates go through Charlotte, the region's commercial heart. Looking north from Charlotte, I–85 connects Charlotte to Kannapolis, Salisbury, Thomasville, High Point, and Greensboro. Looking south, I–85 veers toward Gastonia and then into South Carolina.

NORTH CAROLINA QUILTS

The quilts below are part of the North Carolina Quilt Project, which documents quilts and quiltmakers in the state. Over 10,000 quilts have been documented: those below represent seven varieties.

(Photos and text courtesy Ruth Haislip Roberson.)

TREE OF LIFE
(above) A masterpiece medallion quilt in chintz appliqué. By Sarah Alexander Harris Gilmer, 1826.

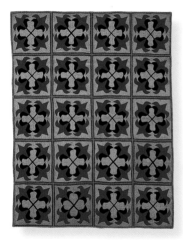

TULIP QUILT
(above) Made in a red and green pattern popular in the latter half of the 19th century. Made by machine and quilted one block at a time. By Joyce Shearin Coleman, 1880s.

DOUBLE IRISH CHAIN
(above) Made by a mother for her four-year-old daughter. By Amelia Rosetta Arey Rothrock, 1851.

FRIENDSHIP BASKET

(above) This quilt has the names and birthdates of each person making a block. Made in the Stone Mountain Community for Sarah Royal, 1939.

CRAZY QUILT

(above) Scraps from a grandfather's carriage shop made into motifs of starfish, birds, butterflies, and flowers. By Laetitia Brown Gibbs, 1890.

AMERICAN EAGLE

(above) By Hazel Reece, 1967.

MELON PATCH QUILT

(above) A home-dyed quilt—this one made from home-dyed sugar sacks. By Mary Midgett Bridgman, 1902.

A GREAT DRIVE IN SOUTHERN PIEDMONT

Seagrove is a great drive-to destination. This tiny community of traditional potters calls to folks once for its interesting history, twice for the pleasing landscape, and three times for the excellent pottery shopping. Add it to a trip to the North Carolina Zoological Park, and you've got a very pleasant day trip.

From Asheboro, I–73 and I–74 will take you south in a hurry, but 220A will take you south at a more leisurely, scenic clip. Beyond the community of Ulah, take a left on tiny 159 and then right on the 159 spur to the North Carolina Zoo-logical Park. Spend a couple of hours "on safari" in Africa, and then explore this zoo's North American habitats.

From here, backtrack to 220A, and head south toward Seagrove. Stop by the NC Pottery Center to get oriented, and if you're hungry, give one of the local cafés a try. Spend the afternoon exploring the scores of shops along the main drag, and tucked away on the side roads and in the hollows. If your Christmas shopping isn't done by the end of the day, feel free to come back tomorrow.

At Gastonia 321 branches north off I–85 and heads for Hickory and that region's furniture manufacturers.

I–77 gives you a straight shot from Charlotte to Mooresville and to Statesville, and beyond.

At the eastern edge of the Southern Piedmont, 220 gives you a drop from Greensboro, in the north, all the way down to Rockingham near the South Carolina border, and beyond.

Across the northern rim of the region almost all the major highways connect with I–40, North Carolina's primary east–west traffic artery.

The major thoroughfares in the Piedmont are some of the busiest in the state. When you have time, forsake them for the smaller, less traveled roads running parallel. They're not as fast, but they're gentler on the nerves and easier on the eyes.

A row of daffodils rise from red clay to brighten a barnyard near Lincolnton.

LOCAL FAVORITE PLACES TO EAT

Blue Restaurant and Bar. Hearst Tower, corner of 5th and College Sts., Charlotte; 704/927–2583. $$$

The Blue is known for Mediterranean-spiced cuisine and Southern-spiced jazz, all at the same upscale venue. The most popular entrée might be the beef tenderloin à la Blue, topped with Gorgonzola. The late-night live jazz (Wednesday through Saturday) is accompanied by a light late-night menu, which includes Provence-style lobster or crab cakes finished with basil oil and a citrus beurre blanc.

Price's Chicken Coop. 1614 Camden Rd., Charlotte; 704/333–9866. $

No frills and fried. For great fried chicken on the fly, line up with the folks at the counter and snag a take-out box. (Everything is takeout here, by the way.) A typical box here includes a quarter of a fried chicken, a pile of fried potatoes, coleslaw, a roll, and two hush puppies. If you're a giblet person, you're in luck. Price's boxes up liver and gizzard dinners, too. They also serve barbecue and sandwiches.

Mert's Heart and Soul. 214 N. College St., Charlotte; 704/342–4222. $-$$

This casual eatery in the heart of Charlotte dishes up down-home Southern cooking and Low Country-, and Gullah-inspired dishes. The wide selection ranges from fried chicken to blackened pork chops to veggie plates. Or consider Mert's Famous Salmon Cakes Dinner: fresh salmon blended with Cajun Trinity (green peppers, onions, and celery), with rémoulade. Don't overlook the very popular macaroni and cheese. Or consider the Creole: popcorn shrimp in a spicy sauce, served over a bowl of seasoned rice. Brunch starts at 9 on weekends, making this one of the few uptown restaurants open on Sundays.

Twin Tops Fish Camp. 4574 S. New Hope Rd., Gastonia; 704/825–2490. $-$$

Fish-camp ambience means yellow-pine chairs, bare tables, and a waitress who calls you "Sugar" and pirouettes from kitchen to table with plates of steaming seafood balanced on her outstretched arm. You might get food served on the same kind of plates they used in your elementary school cafeteria—the round, three-sectioned ones—but they never dished it out like this at school: a mountain of golden fried fish, fries, coleslaw, and a tumble of hush puppies.

LOCAL FAVORITE PLACES TO STAY

Ballantyne Resort. 10000 Ballantyne Commons Pkwy., Charlotte; 704/248–4000. $$$$

This resort has luxury guest rooms and a 20,000-square-foot spa and health facility, but it may be best known for its excellent golfing. The tree-lined, par-71 golf course frequently shows up on best-of lists: Golf Digest's readers rank it as a 4.5-star "best place to play." If your swing lacks zip, take heart. The on-site Dana Rader Golf School is one of the best golf schools in the country. The 214 luxurious rooms have marble entrances, 10-foot ceilings, and floor-to-ceiling windows; there's also a 35-room group retreat lodge. Some rooms have balconies overlooking the golf course's rolling hills. The highly rated Gallery Restaurant specializes in aged prime steaks.

Duke Mansion. 400 Hermitage Rd., Charlotte; 704/714–4400 or 888/202–1009. $$$-$$$$

James B. Duke bought this mansion in 1919 and expanded it to use as a home for his daughter, Doris. While he lived here, Duke envisioned many enterprises that helped shape the Carolinas, including Duke University, Duke Power, and the Duke Endowment. This Colonial Revival mansion is now home to a nonprofit, 20-room historic inn listed on the National Register of Historic Places. The guest rooms also feature reproduction period furnishings and antiques. All of the second-floor rooms have Southern sleeping porches, now for sitting. Proceeds are used to help preserve this elegant old property.

Rowan Oak House. 208 South Fulton St., Salisbury; 704/633–2086. $$

An afternoon on a wraparound porch, an evening in one of four charming, antiques-filled Victorian guest rooms, a candlelight breakfast. If that's not enough to flag your attention, Lowe's Motor Speedway is just 25 miles away. The Rowan Oak House, built in 1901, is in Salisbury's historic district near museums, antiques shops, and fine restaurants.

VanLandingham Estate Inn & Conference Center. 2010 The Plaza, Charlotte; 704/334–8909. $$$

This California-style bungalow, built in 1913 by Ralph and Susie VanLandingham, sits in five acres of gardens. Many of the furnishings were originally brought to the house from Atlanta's Majestic Hotel, which Susie VanLandingham's family owned. The inn includes nine guest rooms and one suite, library, solarium, and reading parlor. The most popular suite—and the inn's most romantic, with a fireplace and Jacuzzi—is the McGloohon suite. The inn and garden are listed on the National Register of Historic Places.

THE SANDHILLS

 The Sandhills lie east of Charlotte, between the Cape Fear and Pee Dee Rivers. They owe their unique character to a prehistoric ocean whose receding tides and snapping winds left white sand dunes baking in the sun.

Early Scots farmers, who watched the sandy soil trickle through their fingers, named the area the Pine Barrens and moved on. Nothing, it seems, grew easily in the Sandhills except long-leaf pines. Today the Pine Barrens are anything but barren, having given birth to three unique North Carolina cultures: Fayetteville's spit-and-polish military tradition; the golf-and-polo culture of

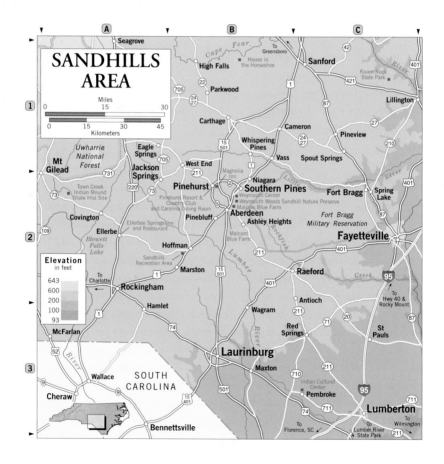

A hiking trail traverses the long-leaf pine forest in Weymouth Woods Sandhills Nature Preserve.

Pinehurst, Aberdeen, and Southern Pines; and the culture of the Lumbee people, the largest Native American tribe east of the Mississippi.

NC 211 takes you from the Seagrove area into Pinehurst and Southern Pines. You'll know you've crossed into the Sandhills when long-leaf pines begin crowding the roadside, growing in soil the color of ash and bone. This drive's dotted by unpainted board-and-batten houses, and hills behind them rise and fall like the pale, prehistoric ocean floor they are. The pristine white-stucco gas station with the cupola lets you know you've entered Pinehurst—"a whole 'nother world."

If you happen across an out-of-place mound of bare, sandy earth while you're exploring the Sandhills (or anywhere else, for that matter), avoid it like you'd avoid a trip to the emergency room.

It may be one of the millions of fire-ant hills now dotting the Carolina countryside. Fire ants, recent immigrants from parts south, came by their names honestly: their bite burns like fire. Many people are allergic to them and require medical aid if bitten. Steer clear!

PINEHURST   *map page 248, B-2/3*

Driving into Pinehurst, the transformation from sandhills to an oasis of golf greens is magical—especially in April, when azaleas and dogwoods turn the area's 40-odd golf courses into a scrollwork of manicured gardens.

Pinehurst Resort and Country Club is one of the world's largest golf resorts.

Annie Oakley was one of the many celebrities to frequent the Pinehurst area over the years. (Darke County Historical Society)

That transformation is the legacy of Boston businessman James Walker Tufts, who hopped off the train one day in 1895 and bought 5,000 acres of stripped pinelands that were so inhospitable even wild hogs didn't care to live on them. He called its remnant dunes "sand traps," and hired landscape architect Frederick Law Olmsted to turn his Sandhills into a New England–style village, Pinehurst. Northerners flocked to the fresh-air resort, eager to trade blizzards for shirtsleeve winters. Tufts added a golf course, and in no time flat Pinehurst was the bee's knees.

Amelia Earhart buzzed in for a landing. Annie Oakley headed up the Pinehurst Gun Club. The Rockefellers, Du Ponts, and Morgans swung by. So did Bing Crosby and Douglas Fairbanks.

Tufts' golf course was the first of the 40-plus courses that today make the Pinehurst region one of the world's top golf resort areas. His Course No. 2, the annual site of the North/South Amateur, still ranks among the nation's top 10 courses.

Today the area hosts top tournaments, and the Pinehurst Resort and Country Club is one of the world's largest golf resorts. Golfers love Pinehurst for its history, and because they actually tee up on its tournament courses.

Golfers aren't alone in their regard for the Sandhills. Pinehurst's major tennis championships often include the U.S. Clay Court Championships. At Historic Pinehurst Racetrack, trainers take standardbreds through their paces year-round. Polo, fox hunting, harness racing, and Olympic trials are also staged here.

In addition, the 100-mile Tour de Moore, held each April, draws bicyclists from around the world. Olympic teams from the U.S. and Canada train here, but wobblier bicyclists take to the trails, too, crisscrossing parks on miles of gentle bike trails.

AROUND SOUTHERN PINES   *map page 248, B-2/3*

The villages around Pinehurst and Southern Pines are full of crafts shops, antiques shops, cafés, and late-19th-century historic districts.

The bullet-riddled 1772 **House in the Horseshoe,** near Sanford, is the area's most famous historic site.

During the Revolutionary War this country home, which sits in a horseshoe-shaped river bend, belonged to Whig Colonel Philip Alston and was the heart of his 6,936-acre plantation. Alston's militia and the forces of Colonel David Fanning skirmished here in 1781, ventilating Alston's homeplace and leading to his surrender. History marched on, but the bullet holes remain to tell the story.

Alston was murdered in South Carolina in 1791, and the House in the Horseshoe became home to North Carolina Governor Benjamin Williams. Now a State Historic Site, the home has been restored and furnished with late colonial and early Federal pieces. The site also includes a well house, corncrib, and a reconstructed loom house.

The picnic tables make this a good spot for lunch. *288 Alston House Rd., Sanford; 910/947–2051.*

The **Malcom Blue Farm,** east of Aberdeen, offers a look at early 1800s farm life on the Pine Barrens before golf greens found their way into the region. The modest 1825 house has been filled with articles of everyday living. Outside, Darlington oaks shade the grounds, which include a windmill, gristmill, water well, and several barns. The 7.5-acre site is a mere fraction of the 8,000-or-so acres Blue, a turpentine and lumber entrepreneur, once owned.

A 1985 museum will clue you in on the area's Scots settlers, mourning etiquette of the 19th century, local pottery, and Native American crafts. This site is generally open only in the afternoon; you may want to call before you come. *1177 Bethesda Rd., Aberdeen; 910/944–7558.*

GOLFING IN THE SANDHILLS

With more than 40 courses in the Pinehurst area, the Sandhills is the region to golf in North Carolina. Below are some of the area's finest courses.

PUBLIC

Hyland Hills Golf Club. 115 Fairway Ave., Southern Pines; 910/692–3752.
Good course for average player.

Legacy Golf Links. US Hwy. 15-501 S, 2 miles south of Aberdeen; 910/944–8825.
Interesting layout by Jack Nicklaus, Jr.

Little River Golf and Resort. 500 Little River Farm Blvd., Carthage; 910/949–4600.
Good golf in a country setting.

Mid Pines Golf Club. 1010 Midland Rd., Southern Pines; 910/692–2114 or 800/323–2114.
Classic scenic course by Donald Ross.

Pine Needles Golf Club. 1005 Midland Rd., Southern Pines; 910/692–8611.
Superb. Second only to Pinehurst.

The Pit Golf Links. 410 Pit Link La., off Hwy. 5, about ¼ mile past Sand Pit Road, Aberdeen; 910/944–1600.
A popular, challenging course.

Talamore Golf Resort. 1595 Midland Rd., Southern Pines; 910/692–5884.
Beautiful Sandhills course. Llama caddies available.

SEMI-PRIVATE

Deercroft Golf and Country Club. 30000 Deercroft Dr., Wagram; 910/369–3107.
Interesting, scenic, and challenging.

Foxfire Golf. 9 Foxfire Village, Jackson Springs; 910/295–4563.
Two 18-hole courses.

Longleaf Golf and Country Club. 10 N. Knoll Rd., Southern Pines; 910/692–6100.
Some holes play through the old horse track.

Pinehurst Resort & Country Club. Carolina Vista Dr., Pinehurst; 910/295–6811 or 800/795–4653.
Eight courses. No. 2, the crown jewel, is ranked first in North Carolina by Golf Digest.

Whispering Woods Golf Club. 26 Sandpiper Dr., Whispering Pines; 910/949–4653.
Two excellent courses.

Woodlake Country Club. 150 Woodlake Blvd., Vass; 910/245–4031.
Two fascinating lakeside courses.

The House in the Horseshoe is the region's most famous historic site. Bullet holes from the Revolutionary War are visible on the wall above the door and portrait.

NC 2, a peaceful passage lined with long-leaf pines, connects Pinehurst and **Southern Pines,** a picturesque village with a viable downtown, restaurants, bookstores, and offices. Flowers bloom along the track leading into its clean, well-tended railroad station, right in the middle of town. Southern Pines has long been home to artists and writers, including novelist James Boyd, author of *Drums.*

A year-round program in the arts and humanities is available at the **Weymouth Center,** a Georgian-style house situated on 24 acres in Southern Pines. Many notable writers have been guests here, including Thomas Wolfe, Sherwood Anderson, and William Faulkner. *555 E. Connecticut Ave.; 910/692–6261.*

At **Weymouth Woods Sandhills Nature Preserve,** on Ft. Bragg Road on the outskirts of Southern Pines, grows one of the Southeast's few remaining virgin, long-leaf pine forests. When the wind blows, this is a place of music. In fact, there's a special word just to describe a wind blowing through long-leaf pines: "susurrus." (The trees pronounce it, "soo-*sur*-rahs.")

Explore this 168-acre forest by a mile-long loop trail that begins at the visitors center and museum, at the top of the hill. The forest slopes down along the gentle hillside. Large hardwoods—mostly black oaks and hickories—have taken root in the forest's upper meadow. "At the lower end of the meadow you'll start running into the big, old-growth trees," says park superintendent Scott Hartley. "They're anywhere from 200 to 400 years old. Height-wise, they're upwards of 70 to 100 feet." A former state champion long-leaf pine towers beside the trail. "It's really fantastic," he says. "You get two people, and you still can't hug it."

Farther down the hillside meadow pines dominate. Sit beneath a pine, close your eyes, and listen. "It's almost like an instrument, the way the long-leaf needles sound when they move in the wind," Hartley says. "When the wind's real hard it sounds like a roar, almost like heavy surf." *1024 N. Ft. Bragg, Southern Pines; 910/692–2167.*

ROBESON COUNTY AND THE LUMBEE

Southeast of Pinehurst lies the traditional home of the Lumbee, the largest Native American tribe east of the Mississippi.

The Lumbee (Lum-*bee*) have been a puzzle since 1755, when settlers found an English-speaking society of Native Americans living here in English-style houses. Most Lumbee believe the settlers stumbled on a melting-pot nation made up of displaced tribes. Catawba, Tuscarora, Creek, Waccamaw, and Cheraw people escaped into this dense swamp, they say, adopting English as a common trade language. Others believe the tribe included the English-speaking descendants of Sir Walter Raleigh's Lost Colony, and runaway slaves.

The Lumbee lived peacefully with their neighbors until the racially charged 1830s. To survive, they hid their culture underground. Today the 40,000-member tribe has legal recognition from North Carolina, but not from the Bureau of Indian Affairs.

For Lumbee children growing up in a region known for poverty, drugs, and crime, the challenge is restoring a sense of culture and of self. "First you've got to make people proud," says Tony Clark, who teaches traditional dance to young Lumbee. "I always tell them: you've got to believe in yourself."

Each October the Lumbee Regional Development Association, in Pembroke, hosts a powwow across from UNC-Pembroke. The public is invited. Men, women, and children from various Native American tribes mill about in traditional regalia—feathers, bone breastplates, face paint, turtle-shell rattles, and bells. As the drums begin, the dancers begin their low, stately whirls . . . .

Many of the dancers dance for the sheer joy and pride of dancing. Others dance with an additional reward in mind: several thousand dollars in prize money, in adult and children's categories.

For information on the powwow, call The **Lumbee Regional Development Association,** which also maintains a calendar of events. *910/521–8602.*

The University of North Carolina campus at Pembroke was the first four-year college in the nation established for Native Americans (1887). It began the first American Indian Studies BA degree program in the US. The **Museum of the Native American Resource Center** includes artifacts from native peoples across North America, but emphasizes the Lumbee culture. The museum is in the Old Main building, on the UNC–Pembroke Campus. *10 miles west of the intersection of I–95 and US 74; 910/521–6282.*

Lumber River State Park winds along the Lumber River, roughly from Wagram to Fair Bluff. The cypress-stained river is a state-designated Scenic River.

Park officials offer night hikes, birding tours, and guided canoe trips, but you can drop a canoe or small boat and explore the cypress-lined shores on your own. Move quietly, and you may see deer peeping over the riverbanks.

This outbuilding, with its generous chimney, originally served as a kitchen for Wright Tavern, built in 1816 in Rockingham County. It stood apart from the tavern in case of a kitchen fire.

Fishermen with North Carolina licenses pull in black crappie, red breasts, bass, and catfish. (Those without licenses land hefty fines.) Two rare minnow-size fish, the sandhills chub and pinewood darter, haunt the waters in the northern park.

This park includes nature trails, drive-in camping, and canoe-in campgrounds. Bring your own canoe. *South from Lumberton on NC 41 to Fairmont, then 12 miles east on NC 130; turn onto Creek Rd. and follow signs; 910/628–4564.*

GETTING AROUND

The Sandhills claim only one major highway, I–95, which moves north-south along its eastern edge.

US 1 takes you from Sanford to Southern Pines and Pinehurst, or from Pinehurst south to South Carolina. Most travel here is on IBRs—Itsy Bitsy Roads. Slow down and enjoy the view.

LOCAL FAVORITE PLACES TO EAT

Carolina Dining Room. Pinehurst Resort, Pinehurst; 910/235–8433. $$$$

This elegant old jewel, which opened in 1901 to welcome Pinehurst Resort's early guests, overlooks the resort's gardens and West Lawn. The dinner menu changes seasonally, but favorites include the potato-crusted sea bass, pan-seared mountain trout, and slow-roasted Carolina pork chop. This is one of the country's last "scratch kitchens," where all soups, stocks, etc., are made in-house. The black-and-white photos on the walls give you the flavor of early Pinehurst life. The dining room is in the Carolina Inn (see Local Favorite Places to Stay).

Ellerbe Springs Inn and Restaurant. 2537 US 220, Ellerbe; 910/652–5600. $$

If you like generous portions and country cooking–meat loaf, fried chicken, fresh vegetables, homemade breads and homemade cobblers—Ellerbe Springs Restaurant is a good bet. This 1857 Greek Revival–style resort inn has three fireplaces in its dining room. The inn's 50-acre grounds and five-acre pond make for a nice after-dinner walk.

Lob Steer Inn. 625 Southeast Service Rd., Southern Pines; 910/692–3503. $$$$

The lobster tail and rib-eye plate is the most popular choice at this casual joint with a fireplace for chasing the chill on cold autumn and winter nights. All the breads are made on the premises; the baked cheese biscuit bread may be the best. The menu focuses on seafood and beef, but you'll find a smattering of chicken and pork entrées, too. Autographed photos of some fellow diners, who have included famous NASCAR drivers and well-known golfers, hang in the lobby.

The Magnolia Inn and Restaurant. Corner of Magnolia and Chinquapin Rds., Pinehurst Village; 910/295–6900. $$

Built in 1895 and opened as an inn in 1896, The Magnolia takes you back to the days when Pinehurst was a port-of-call of the wealthy industrialists of the early 20th century. Magnolias and long-leaf pines grace the grounds of the glistening white Victorian inn. A fireplace warms the dining room in winter; in fair weather guests often dine on the wraparound porch. Try the free-range chicken breast with Creole-mustard demi-glace or the most popular entrée, Chilean sea bass with fingerling potatoes and lump-crab hash.

LOCAL FAVORITE PLACES TO STAY

Many of the most interesting places to stay in the Sandhills reflect the area's resort-rich history. As you might expect, most area resorts and B&Bs offer golf packages.

The Carolina. Pinehurst Resort and Country Club, 1 Carolina Vista Dr., Pinehurst; 910/295–6811. $$$$

Pinehurst Resort's historic centerpiece inn has 220 elegant guest rooms with marble-tiled bathrooms and flat-screen televisions. If you're feeling regal, consider the 1,700-square-foot Presidential Suite, with a living room, dining room, study, wet bar, and a private entrance onto the West Lawn. Golf packages at the 2,000-acre resort, home to the state's top-ranked course, are popular, but Pinehurst also has excellent spa, tennis, and croquet facilities, as well as a gated pool area. You can create your own mini-putting course at the putting green.

Holly Inn. Pinehurst Resort and Country Club, 155 Cherokee Rd., Pinehurst; 910/295–6811. $$$$

Pinehurst founder James W. Tufts opened the village's first hotel on New Year's Eve, 1895. Twenty guests checked in. Their $3 a day gave them access to electric lights, steam heat, telephones, a solarium, a billiards room, and an orchestra. These days the National Historic Landmark with 89 rooms and suites is one of the golfing region's finest historic inns, following a $31 million restoration completed in 1999. Details echo the inn's early days, from the botanical prints and images on the floors and walls, to the Tiffany lamps, to the rocking chairs in the guest rooms. The inn offers access to all Pinehurst Resort amenities: swimming, fitness center, and sporting venues. The on-site 1895 Grille serves dinner and a breakfast buffet.

Inn at the Bryant House. 214 N. Poplar St., Aberdeen; 910/944–3300 or 800/453-4019. $$

This Southern Colonial Revival inn was built in 1913, and has operated as a tourist home ever since. Listed on the National Historic Register, it has 10 rooms: eight in the main house and two in the carriage house. The District, a large corner room, is one of the inn's most popular guest rooms. Like other rooms in this inn, it's filled with antiques and reproductions. Some rooms (including the District) have fireplaces. The inn occupies an acre of gardens and lawns in the heart of Aberdeen's historic district. Although the many golf courses nearby may be its biggest draw, the porch offers its own relaxing charm.

THE APPALACHIANS

 The westernmost eighth of North Carolina lies within the Appalachian Mountains, one of the oldest mountain ranges in the world. North Carolina's geologic braid of time-gentled mountain ranges is noted for broad vistas, pristine forests, thundering waterfalls, and vast tracts of protected lands.

The Blue Ridge Mountains, the easternmost range of North Carolina's Appalachians, run parallel to the coast, northeast to southwest. Immediately behind the Blue Ridge, which rises sharply from the Piedmont floor, lies a mountainous tableland of forests, pastures, valley farmland, and clear, rushing streams.

Along North Carolina's border with Tennessee, the Great Smoky Mountains rise in ranges parallel to the Blue Ridge, like rails on the same geologic railroad. Both the Blue Ridge Mountains and the Great Smoky Mountains draw their names from the blue-gray haze that veils them.

To the south, near Asheville, the cross-ranges begin. These short, choppy ranges— the Black Mountains, Craggy Mountains, Cowees, Nantahalas, Pisgah Ledge, Balsams, Plott Balsams—run perpendicular to the Blue Ridge, providing North Carolina's most rugged mountain scenery and the tallest peaks east of the Mississippi.

The idyllic Mill Creek Valley is nestled in the Norton area of the Appalachian Mountains.

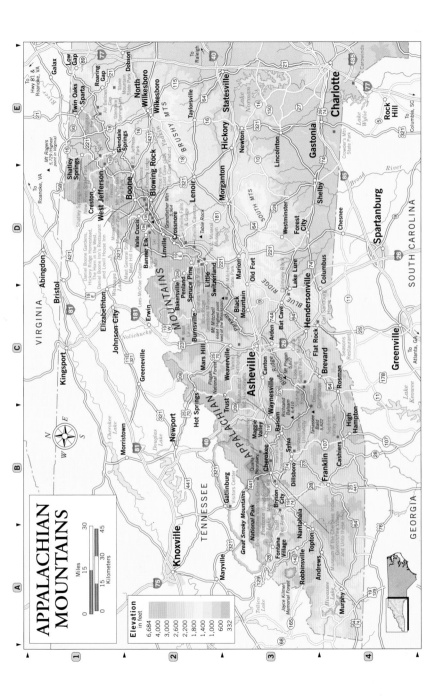

APPALACHIAN MOUNTAINS

Elevation
in feet

6,684
4,000
3,000
2,600
2,200
1,800
1,400
1,000
600
332

Miles
0   15   30   45

Kilometers
0   15   30

Asheville, population 74,000, stands as the mountains' lone city. It's known for its artists' communities, rich resort history, and art-deco architecture. In general, though, the Appalachians are made up of scenic drives, small towns, quiet hamlets, expansive parklands, hardscrabble homesteads, and used-to-be villages.

GEOLOGY, HISTORY, AND A WAY OF LIFE

How did the Appalachians come to be here? The Cherokee, who have lived here for thousands of years, say that one day long ago the Great Buzzard swooped low over the new earth. His wings brushed the impressionable earth, creating the mountain ranges that rise and fall, and then fade into the sky.

Geologists envision a wilder scenario.

About 450 million years ago a migrating continental fragment collided with an underwater landmass, sending layers of earth thousands-of-feet thick skidding over the lip of the raw North American continent. The earth folded and creased, bellowed and roared, pushing the Appalachians to their feet. Below the surface, superheated rock changed the continent's very blood.

The land rose, dipped to become an ocean bed, and rose again. Twice more over the next 250 million years landmasses collided, pushing up mountains taller than today's Alps. Over the next 200 million years, time softened the mountains' edges. Freezing water sheered boulders and mountainsides, tree roots split stones, and spring rains swirled away tons of pebbles and sand.

Today's Appalachians are the hearts of those towering peaks. Most are made of granite and greenstone. Some are remnants of the old continent: gneiss, schistose, and quartzite. Quartzite, the hardest of them all, forms the heart of the tallest mountains.

Earth forces have also given North Carolina more gems and minerals than any other state.

The Cherokee once mined mica in Mitchell County. Today commercial mines harvest mica, feldspar, and ultra-pure quartz in the same region, while rock hounds search for emeralds, rubies, garnets, amethyst, and sapphires that tumble from the earth's pockets.

A MATTER OF ALTITUDE

Sky-side, these mountains support a wealth of life.

The mountains' unusual diversity of plant life has sent botanists into quiet frenzies since 1775, when William Bartram "discovered" the flame azalea. (Part of Bartram's pathway is now a trail in Nantahala National Forest.) Botanists have

Over the millennia the
myriad streams and rivers
have gradually worn the
once-towering Appalachians
down to gentle peaks.

FLOWERS OF THE APPALACHIANS
as may be seen from the Parkway

Phlox bloom May through June near mileposts 4, 79–82, 163–4, 200–2, 219–21, 339, and 370–80.

Mountain laurels bloom late May through June near mileposts 130, 163, 348, 380–81.

Catawba rhododendrons bloom in June near mileposts 45, 77–83, 130, 239, 247, 267, 348–50, 364.

Black-eyed Susans bloom in July and are common in fields and along roadsides.

Azaleas bloom May through June near mileposts 139, 144–5, 150, 164–6, 217–21, 308–10, 368–80, 412–23.

Trilliums bloom April through May near mileposts 175, 200–16, 339–40, 365.

Carolina lilies bloom April through May near milepost 439.

Tulip poplars bloom April through May in low woods and coves.

recorded, named, and sketched oceans of flowering shrubs, wildflowers (1,500 species in Smoky Mountain National Park alone), lichens, and fungi species. Plus, they chortle, more tree species live in the North Carolina Appalachians than in all of Europe.

In the mountains, altitude determines two big environmental factors: temperature and rainfall. The temperature drops about three degrees for every 1,000-foot climb up a mountainside, and temperature helps define ecological communities.

Then there's rain. In North America only the forests of the Pacific Northwest receive more rainfall than the southern Appalachians, though the amount of rain is uneven. Asheville, which lies in a valley, receives 40 inches of rain a year; a few miles to the south, Transylvania County's mountains receive 100 inches each year. (This helps explain why Transylvania County is home to the state's most spectacular waterfalls.)

Thanks to differences in temperature and moisture, a 6,000-foot mountain may harbor 16 different forest types—complete with trees, shrubs, ferns, wildflowers, fungi, and lichens—one stacked atop another as the altitude rises.

This lush plant kingdom supports an equally lush wildlife community, from black bears, to hawks, to rattlesnakes, to mud puppies, to trout, to fireflies and migrating Monarch butterflies. Volumes have been written on the plants and wildlife of the Appalachians.

THE CHEROKEE

The first known stewards of these mountains were the Cherokee, who once occupied the Appalachians from the Ohio River south to Alabama. When Europeans first visited North Carolina's mountains in 1540, they found around 25,000 Cherokee living in a land the Cherokee called *Shaconage,* "Land of the Blue Mist."

The Cherokee lived in villages of perhaps 50 small log homes centered on a town square and large council house. The seven-sided council house acknowledged the seven clans within a society where clan membership and property were passed down matrilineally. (A boy looked to his mother's brother for his sense of place in society.) Neighboring Shawnee occasionally skirmished with the Cherokee—over hunting lands rich with buffalo, deer, bear, and wild turkeys. For the most part, though, the Cherokee lived quietly, much of their sustenance coming from gardens planted in corn, melons, beans, and tobacco; and from wild plants gathered for food as well as for medicine and trade. Cherokee women wove baskets of oak strips and reeds, and they cooked in pots of clay. They fashioned robes of animal skins and ceremonial headdresses of sacred eagle feathers.

The Cherokee wove a mythology as intricate as their basketry, explaining their relationship to plants, animals, other tribes, a race of little people, and giants. When they fell ill, they consulted healers, who gathered herbs and talked with their god, who listened. And why not? The Cherokee believed themselves to be the *Yun Wiya,* the "real people" of the world.

Spanish explorer Hernando de Soto visited the Cherokee in 1540, lured by fables of gold and silver mines. His murders made an impression: as late as 1890, a Cherokee who killed an eagle immediately identified himself to other powerful eagle spirits as a Spaniard, in case they took revenge on him and his people.

Scots rather than Spaniards finally settled the North Carolina highlands, looking not for gold, but rich soil. From the mid-1700s on, Scots and Germans surged down the Great Wagon Road claiming valley lands farmed by the Cherokee, and pushing the Cherokee into the hills. A local boy named Daniel Boone soon blazed a Wilderness Road to Tennessee, leading settlers deeper into the mountains. The Cherokee struggled to change with the times. They adopted a legal code and a Supreme Court. Sequoyah, a Cherokee silversmith, designed an alphabet for his language; within two years, most Cherokee could read and write. They published a newspaper and wrote a constitution.

But by 1828 some 30 treaties with the Cherokee had been signed and broken, and North Carolina's Cherokee found themselves elbowed into the rugged, southwest corner of the state. Gold, which had lured de Soto to their land in 1540, now sealed their fate.

When prospectors struck gold in Georgia's mountains in 1828, settlers clamored for Indian land. President Andrew Jackson signed the Removal Act, demanding that all Native Americans east of the Mississippi move to the new Oklahoma Territory.

The Cherokee insisted on their legal right to stay. In Congress Davy Crockett, Daniel Webster, and Henry Clay argued in

Sequoyah—Cherokee warrior, silversmith, and painter— invented the Cherokee alphabet in 1821. He created a system of 86 symbols, adapting letters from English, Hebrew, and Greek. (The Thomas Gilcrease Institute of American History and Art, Tulsa, Oklahoma)

PRIVATE BURNETT REMEMBERS

This is my birthday, December the 11th, 1890, I am eighty years old today . . . I grew into manhood fishing in Beaver Creek and roaming through the forest hunting the Deer the wild Boar and the timber Wolf . . . On these long hunting trips I met and became acquainted with many of the Cherokee Indians, hunting with them by day and sleeping around their camp fires by night. I learned to speak their language . . .

The removal of the Cherokee Indians from their life long homes in the year of 1838 found me a young man in the prime of life and a Private soldier in the American Army. Being acquainted with many of the Indians and able to fluently speak their language, I was sent as interpreter into the Smoky Mountain Country . . . in the chill of a drizzling rain on an October morning I saw them loaded like cattle or sheep into six hundred and forty-five wagons and started toward the west.

One can never forget the sadness and solemnity of that morning. Chief John Ross led in prayer and when the bugle sounded and the wagons started rolling many of the children rose to their feet and waved their little hands good-by . . .

* * *

Being a young man I mingled freely with the young women and girls. I have spent many pleasant hours with them when I was supposed to be under my blanket, and they have many times sung their mountain song for me, this being all that they could do to repay my kindness . . . They are kind and tender hearted and many of them are beautiful.

—**John G. Burnett,** 2nd Regiment, 2nd Brigade, Mounted Infantry, *The Cherokee Removal Through the Eyes of A Private Soldier,* 1838–39

their behalf. The U.S. Supreme Court ruled in their favor. Chief Junaluska, who had saved Jackson's life at the Battle of Horseshoe Bend in 1812, now asked President Jackson for help.

For the first and only time, a U.S. president turned his back on a Supreme Court decision. He forced the Cherokee on a 1,200-mile death march known today as the Trail of Tears. A few hundred Cherokee hid in the mountains, eking out a living until 1899 when Congress chartered the 56,000-acre Qualla

Boundary, commonly known as the Eastern Cherokee Reservation. Today around 11,000 descendants of its original 1,000 residents live there.

HARDSCRABBLERS AND HOLIDAYMAKERS

With the Cherokee driven away or in hiding, white settlers claimed the Appalachian countryside. The rich bottomlands had been settled by traders, merchants, and farmers. Still settlers came—Scots, Germans, the Irish. These "hardscrabble farmers" clung to the high mountainsides, scrabbling to stay alive.

Another, wildly contrasting lifestyle emerged, too.

As early as the late 1700s, wealthy lowlanders summered in the North Carolina mountains, trading summer's deadly malarial fevers for the cool mountain air. As tuberculosis rates climbed in the lowlands, health resorts flourished, with Asheville leading the way. People came to the mineral springs, boardinghouses, and spas, hoping to cure everything from hiccups to brain tumors.

The members of this Appalachian family, photographed in the 1930s by a Farm Security Administration photographer, are testimony to the "hardscrabble" life many of the state's mountain residents endured before and during the Depression. (Library of Congress)

The Civil War came and went, with the relatively slave-free mountains dressing sons in both blue and gray. Now the railroad puffed through the highlands. George Vanderbilt (1862–1914) hopped off the train in Asheville, brushed the cinders from his coat, and took a good look at the scenery. He liked what he saw. He built an opulent, 255-room chateau outside town, importing European artists, craftsmen, and foresters to create his 120,000-acre Biltmore Estate.

Suddenly everybody who was anybody wanted a place in the mountains. Mansions went up on mountaintops, gardens sketched themselves along mountainsides, geometric ponds lolled in the valleys. Cream-colored roadsters packed with well-heeled outlanders purred along the switchbacks leading to the old resort towns: Flat Rock, Cashiers, Asheville, Blowing Rock. But roads winding from those towns and high into the mountains crossed economic chasms as stunning as Nantahala Gorge.

The stock market crash of 1929 sent the resort economy into a downhill skid. Millionaires lost millions, but across the economic chasm, where farm income averaged $86 a year, there wasn't much to lose. As banks drew their shades and resorts closed their doors, hardscrabble farmers planted their corn and carded their wool, and wondered what all the fuss was about.

THEN CAME THE PARKWAY

Over 25 million people drive the Blue Ridge Parkway each year, making it America's most popular scenic drive. In North Carolina the Parkway meanders from the Virginia border, down along the rim of the Blue Ridge Mountains, to Asheville. There it swerves west, past Cherokee and the Qualla Boundary, to the Great Smoky Mountains National Park.

Before the Great Depression a description of that route would have been a real knee-slapper. The Parkway crosses regions then known for mud roads, oxen-pulled sleds, and mule-drawn wagons. Folks built their own cabins, ground their own corn, and shot their own squirrels.

So why a Parkway? The National Park Service wanted to connect Shenandoah National Park, in Virginia, with the Great Smoky Mountains National Park, draped across the North Carolina–Tennessee border. More important, President Franklin D. Roosevelt wanted to put America to work, and a 477-mile project was bound to help in that regard.

In September 1935 a blast of Red Diamond dynamite and a shower of mountain stones christened Parkway construction. The *Asheville Citizen* reported: "More than 100 men started work on the Parkway at the Carolina–Virginia line

Rhododendrons bloom beside the entrance to the Parkway's Craggy Pinnacle Tunnel.

The Brinegar Cabin, whose owner refused to budge when the Parkway was being built.

above Low Gap Monday morning, this being the first 12-mile section of the Parkway. . . . The men were secured from the relief and unemployment rolls of Alleghany County . . . ."

Of course, not everyone was glad to see FDR's steam shovels, trucks, and dynamite coming 'round the mountain. Most people who found themselves on the government's broad right-of-way had to move—lock, stock, and hen house. Caroline Brinegar, however, closed her cabin door and refused to budge.

How did the Federal government fare in a standoff with the aged mountain woman? You can still visit Mrs. Brinegar's mountain home, where for years she raised squash, potatoes, pole beans, corn, tomatoes, and mountain flax as tourists' Studebakers puttered along the Parkway, outside her back door. The Park Service now makes good use of the homestead. Today the park's ubiquitous costumed interpreters demonstrate the chores and crafts Caroline Brinegar refused to do someplace else.

It took 52 years to complete the Parkway. Workers chiseled roads around, along, and through mountainsides; Italian stonemasons fashioned graceful arched underpasses, tunnels, and sweeping walls; engineers built spectacular roadside balconies from mountain rubble; and landscape architects artfully hid every inch of scar on the mountains' altered faces with rhododendrons, laurels, and wildflowers.

Hints of forgotten homesteads do remain. The apple trees that perfume April mornings are gifts from settlers who woke up here morning after morning, stretched, and snuggled back beneath their quilts, never dreaming a Parkway would bring millions of outland visitors to their cabin door.

DRIVING THE PARKWAY

Today the Parkway includes a host of campgrounds, hiking trails of various difficulty (from stroll-alongs to puff-alongs), historic sites, orchards, fishing streams, nature walks, museums, waterfalls, and overlooks.

This place is rich in wildlife. Groundhogs, or "whistle pigs," stand paunch-bellied and limp-wristed by the side of the road, like tiny, inquisitive old men. Bear and wild turkeys live in the forests; deer graze by the road as foxes, possums, skunks, squirrels, and other small fry scurry through the woodlands. In spring over a hundred species of birds migrate through or nest here.

The seasons stroll majestically up and down the North Carolina mountains, and the Parkway is a great place (but certainly not the only place) to watch their stately procession.

Spring awakens in the valley in early April, and wanders up the mountainside trailing native greens, the pristine white of the flowering dogwood, and the pinks of service berries, redbuds, and mountain laurel. Summer climbs in lusher, deeper greens and the royal purple of the Catawba rhododendron.

In September, autumn brushes the mountaintops with a faint, reddish gold that descends to the valley like a long, voluptuous blush: sumac, dogwood, gums, and sourwoods; buckeyes, birch, tulip poplars, beech, hickory, and sassafras; mountain ash, maples, and red oaks.

Before autumn brushes her fingertips across the valley one last time, winter begins its slow, pale drift down the mountains, returning to the valley until spring is born again.

DIRECTIONS, SIDE ROADS, AND TIPS

Parkway directions are easy, since all sites have a milepost number. Milepost 0 marks the northernmost point of the Parkway, in Virginia. Off the Parkway, directions can be trickier. But despite their lust for deadpan (*see* Buncombe

Deadpan sidebar, in Asheville), most mountaineers give good directions. To understand the directions, you must know two things.

Number One: "Up" means uphill, not north. "Down" means downhill, not south. If someone tells you to "Go up Highway X," they mean drive up the mountain on Highway X even if you head south to do it.

Number Two: Roads are scarce. "Take the next paved right" may mean turn right a half-hour down (or up) the road. If this kind of uncertainty makes you nervous, ask for travel times.

You could say that mountain drives come in three varieties: Parkway, Off-Parkway, and Off-Off-Parkway. Off-Parkway highways and roads twist and turn their way to tiny Carpenter Gothic churches with unexpected frescoes, general stores with potbellied stoves, barn dances with potbellied fiddlers, crafts fairs, gemstone mines, gourmet restaurants, gourmet trout streams, wildlife walks, and whitewater gorges.

Off-Off-Parkway drives are the dotted blue roads on the road map. They're usually graveled, two-lane roads—but, as one local explains, "sometimes the lanes lie on top of each other."

There are no gas stations or restaurants along the Parkway, but you'll find abundant turn-offs that take you into towns with both. Restrooms are plentiful in the picnic areas and museums.

Depression-era workers chiseled the Blue Ridge Parkway into scores of mountainsides, including this one: Craggy Mountain.

The view from Waynesville Overlook at Milepost 441 is typical of the many extraordinary vistas along the Blue Ridge Parkway.

The **Blue Ridge Parkway Destination Center,** near Asheville, provides exhibits on the Parkway's recreational opportunities and the region's nature and culture. *Blue Ridge Parkway, milepost 384; 828/271–4779.*

Wherever you're going on the Parkway, slow down! The Parkway is a lush, twisty, scenic drive but not a fast one. The speed limit is generally 45; don't go faster. (If you're in a hurry, take a parallel route.) Take advantage of the scenic overlooks, and watch out for drivers who've stopped to admire the bears, the trilliums, the leaves, etc. Use your horn before you enter a blind curve, and give the right of way to drivers coming downhill. Courtesy counts. Nod to cows, wave to everybody else.

Parts of the Parkway close when it snows, and parts are extremely foggy at times because you're driving through clouds. Go to a museum or go into a valley; the fog will clear. Many travel-related businesses in the North Carolina mountains close around the first of November and don't reopen until Spring. Take this into consideration when planning your visit.

There are no billboards along the Parkway, but there are plenty of historic and informational plaques and markers. Take time to read them. Enjoy the scenery.

OUTDOOR RECREATION

About two-thirds of North Carolina's mountains lie within a tremendous patchwork of protected areas, including the Great Smoky Mountains National Park, the Parkway, two national forests, and several state parks. In addition, the private economy is based almost entirely on tourism, and small businesses are eager to help you do just about anything you'd want to do in the mountains: from whitewater rafting, mountain biking, and downhill skiing to enjoying the rocking chairs on the front porch of a cozy mountain inn.

For anglers, the North Carolina mountains are a promised land of fast-flowing, well-stocked, and wild trout streams. In fact, there are around 2,100 miles of public mountain trout waters in North Carolina, and they're loaded with brown, brook, and rainbow trout. You can get a complete list of those waters, with rules and regulations, from the **North Carolina Wildlife Resources Commission** (888/248–6834; www.ncwildlife.org).

Fishermen need a license, available at area stores and via phone or online from the North Carolina Wildlife Resources Commission. Anglers under 16 can fish without a license, but any accompanying adult must have a license. To fish on the Cherokee Reservation you need a tribal license, available at shops in and near

Cherokee. Check the state and tribal regulations before casting your hand-tied fly upon the waters, or you may land more than a trout.

By the way, fisherfolks don't need a license to fish in a private pond. The mountains abound with ponds stocked with fat, easily duped trout sold by the pound.

THE UNSPOILED PROVINCES: ASHE AND ALLEGHANY, THE NORTHERN COUNTIES *map page 261*

Not long ago, the easiest way to get to North Carolina's northernmost mountains was to be born there. Today most visitors take NC 89 from Mt. Airy instead.

Heading west from Andy Griffith's hometown, the hillsides grow steeper, the soil grows thinner, afternoon's blue shadows lie flatter against the earth.

Near **Dobson,** a farmer has draped the mountainside with neat garlands of bright green Christmas trees. His neighbor devotes her felt-green pastures to horses and black-and-white Holsteins. By a white frame house in the bend, a seamstress advertises handmade quilts.

At **Low Gap,** NC 89 slips beneath the Blue Ridge Parkway's arched stone overpass, and heads into Alleghany County.

Alleghany County remains relatively innocent of ski slopes, artsy shops, and upscale restaurants. (In fact, Sunday drivers might want to pack a picnic.) The architecture tends to be frugal and hardworking, like the people, and constructed from materials close at hand: timber and stone.

Old settlements here include sixth-generation extended families. Newer houses sit with their backs nestled against hillsides, for warmth. Here and there older, plain-faced clapboard houses sit a ways up the mountain, their gray tin roofs pulled up into tight buns. In the valleys, tiny, white, steepled churches—most of them Baptist of one bent or another—dot the countryside.

Scots, Germans, and Brits settled this land in the late 1700s, drifting south along river valleys into hunting grounds claimed by the Shawnee and Cherokee. Most built one-room log cabins with fieldstone chimneys and rear-shed kitchens.

They positioned their homes carefully, building halfway up a hill or in a valley to ward off winter winds, and near a stream or spring for water and power. They planted apple orchards, and named places so you'd know when you got there: Air Bellows, Roaring Gap, Low Gap, Laurel Springs.

In Alleghany and Ashe counties the main industries rely on the land: livestock, burley tobacco, Christmas trees, timber. The barns are sprawling affairs—broad, elegant structures with diamond-shaped vents near their peaks.

A view over the New River Valley from Luther Rocks in Ashe County's Mt. Jefferson State Park.

The Unspoiled Provinces' backcountry roads wind along dancing rivers and up undeveloped mountains. Road posts with four-digit numbers are public roads; roads without number posts are private drives.

ROARING GAP AND SPARTA   *map page 261, E-1*

Roaring Gap, east of the Parkway on US 21, was settled in 1780 by a runaway servant, Absalom Smith, and his ex-boss's daughter Agnes. They named their new home Roaring Gap, because the rock formations amplify the howl of the winds. (The private golf resort, built in 1926, also carries the name Roaring Gap.)

West of the Parkway, Sparta's townscape benefits from the work of an Italian stonemason who came to build the Parkway and settled in Alleghany's county seat. Much of the cut stonework throughout the mountains reflects the skill of Parkway stonemasons, or locals who learned the art from them.

In Sparta you can sit in on some mountain music at the **Alleghany Jubilee** (25 N. Main St., Sparta; 336/372–4591) on Tuesday and Saturday nights. You might also want to drop by **Alleghany Arts and Crafts** (36 N. Main St.; 336/372–1776), an art co-op featuring woodworking, quilts, and paintings by local artists. Stop by the **Alleghany County Chamber of Commerce** (58 S. Main St.; 336/372–5473) for information on both.

NC 93 TO NEW RIVER STATE PARK map page 261, E-1

US 221 heads west from Sparta. Veering north on scenic NC 93, you'll see Stratford Road on your left; **Mangum Pottery's** small sign is down Stratford a ways, on your right. The steep gravel path winds up through the rhododendrons, poplar, oaks, and dogwood to the shop of Bet Garrison and Robin Mangum. Mangum Pottery is best known for its red glazes and autumnal raku, but the work here is extremely varied. Visitors watch these artists throw pots and build sculptures from the feet up. *Open Apr.–Dec., Turkey Hollow La.; 336/372–5291.*

Backtracking to NC 93, this country road wanders past a tractor graveyard, where ancient metal skeletons rust away, putters along the twisting section of road tended by the Piney Creek Dirty Fingers Garden Club, and then cuts over to **New River State Park.** *358 US 221 N. Access Rd.; 336/982–2587.*

This 26.5-mile Scenic River, the heart of North Carolina's newest state park, offers some of the best easy canoeing in the mountains. The New is actually one of North America's oldest rivers. Thomas Jefferson's father, who surveyed the western North Carolina–Virginia line, apparently named it after a Mr. New, who drowned here.

The New River, on the western side of the Eastern Continental Divide, flows north. Its clear, greenish water rolls through a valley of rhododendron, pines, and dogwood. Paddlers have taken a shine to the New, which offers a relaxed paddle—Class I rapids with a couple of Class II runs near the Virginia line. Private outfitters along the river offer canoes, shuttle service, etc.

THE SPRINGS map page 261, D/E-1

South on NC 16 lie Ashe County's mineral springs—popular health resorts from the late 1800s until the Depression.

A left on Healing Springs Road leads along a mountain stream and a row of easygoing, 1930s-era cabins. Folks stop by the springhouse to trade gardening tips and load up on the free, mineral-rich waters. (Three ladies from Tennessee cruise in regularly with exactly 52 gallon jugs—the record for jugs packed, precisely, into one car. Don't distract them.)

A little farther down NC 16 you'll find **Shatley Springs.** Martin Shatley discovered Shatley Springs in 1890, when a dip in its waters cured a life-threatening skin disease. Thousands have flocked to the springs since, to cure skin diseases, digestive problems, rheumatism, and nervous twitches.

People still come to take the waters, but more drop by to hike the buffet line at the Shatley Springs Inn (*see* Local Favorite Places to Eat at the end of this chapter).

NC 16 and US 221 lead to the **New River General Store and Outfitters,** a 1928 mercantile with sassafras candy, a hand-cranked coffee grinder, rental canoes, and a defunct two-seater outhouse in the back room, overhanging the river. *10725 US 221 N; 336/982–9190.*

AIR BELLOWS GAP *map page 261, E-1*

Back on the Parkway, **Caroline Brinegar's cabin**—which she refused to vacate for the Parkway—bustles. Brinegar, a well-known weaver, used "tromp as writ" patterns for her four-poster loom. This "sheet music" told her which foot treadles to tromp to create a specific pattern. (Docents will demonstrate it for you.) *Blue Ridge Parkway, milepost 238.5; no phone.*

Doughton Park bears the name of the U.S. congressman who helped finagle the Parkway out of Tennessee's mountains and into North Carolina's, bringing Depression-era jobs and a long-term tourism industry with it. Nature lovers know Doughton Park for its campfire programs and nature walks. *Blue Ridge Parkway, milepost 258.5; no phone.*

GLENDALE SPRINGS *map page 261, E-1*

It's no accident the Parkway runs so near the front door of the **Glendale Springs Inn** (*see* Local Favorite Places to Stay at the end of this chapter). Congressman Doughton, who helped route the Parkway, was part owner of the inn.

Colonel D. W. Adams built this National Registry inn in 1895. Some visitors' Model Ts did wheeze up the cutbacks on Old 16 (now a very scenic, one-lane gravel drive with more back-and-forth than a belly dancer). But the resort never quite caught on.

Instead, it's been a bit of everything for tiny Glendale Springs: inn, post office, circuit courthouse, general store, wedding chapel (the preacher lived upstairs), and moonshine-stocked dance hall.

From 1935 to 1938 the mildly scandal-ridden inn headquartered Parkway engineers and stonemasons. The inn reopened after a restoration in the early 1990s, gourmet dining and ghost included. But the most popular area destinations for guests are the frescoes in two tiny churches—one within walking distance of the inn, the other in West Jefferson, 9 miles down the road.

ALONG THE NORTHERN PARKWAY

This section of the Parkway winds its way south from Boone to Grandfather Mountain. The popular drive is known for its scenic overlooks and nature trails, among other things. Venture off the Parkway a little to explore a cavern or to visit some of the best-known ski resorts in the state.

BOONE   *map page 261, D-1/2*

Boone, the home of Appalachian State University, is a right-this-minute college town from its ski goggles to its hiking boots. Set tight in a mountain valley and surrounded by forest, it is a compact town of brick buildings, wide sidewalks, and lush vegetation. (Its less appealing condo and mall area is southeast of town on Highway 321 going toward Blowing Rock.)

As you'll notice as you head into town, Boone is surrounded by evergreen and deciduous forests filled with mountain laurel and rhododendron. You may also notice fields of dark-green evergreens planted in neat rows on the mountainside—Christmas trees.

North Carolina is the nation's number-one producer of Christmas trees. You'll find more than 20 Christmas-tree farms in the countryside around Boone. Many offer a cut-and-choose program. For a map and information, contact **NC High Country Host** (1700 Blowing Rock Rd.; 828/264–1299).

Boone, population 15,000, welcomes around 16,600 ASU students each year.

(You might like to know that Appalachian State graduate Mark Stroud has designed most of the maps in the Compass American Guides, including those in this book.)

The restored 1875 home of one of the school's founding trustees, Edward Francis Lovill, has been reincarnated as one of the area's nicest inns, the Lovill House Inn (*see* Local Favorite Places to Stay at the end of this chapter).

At the center of downtown are King Street's student-oriented shops. As a gateway to North Carolina's ski resorts, Boone is more visitor conscious than small towns to the north. Something's always going on, from arts festivals to crafts demonstrations, to the Appalachian Summer Festival.

The Appalachian Summer Festival, held in late June and July, includes chamber music, jazz, popular singers, and arts workshops.

The *Southern Farmer's Almanac* once christened Boone the Firefly Capital of America. Glowworm-watching (there are thirty varieties) is one form of Boone nightlife June through August. You'll find another form of nightlife in King Street

ASHE COUNTY'S FRESCOES

In 1973 Faulton Hodge came to Ashe County to pastor two tiny Episcopal churches. He found Holy Trinity, in Glendale Springs, standing empty, one wall caved in. Nine miles away, in West Jefferson, St. Mary's 13 members worshiped in a church badly in need of repair. To make matters worse, Hodge had a budget the size of a mustard seed.

Then at a party he met artist Ben Long, who suddenly announced he wanted to paint a fresco in Hodge's church—for free. To create a fresco, Long explained, the artist places a thin mixture of lime and sand on a wall and brushes pigments into the wet wall. While studying the technique in Italy, Long said, his spirit had been told to paint a church fresco in North Carolina. And since he and Hodge had crossed paths . . .

Long began his work. For St. Mary's he wanted to paint an expectant Mary. He scanned every face he met, searching for a model. One day he spied a barefoot girl walking along a road. "That's her!" he thought, and asked to sketch her. When he had finished, he finally asked her name. "Mary," she said, walking away.

As people came to watch Long paint, the church took on new life. He began a second work, *John the Baptist*. Then, as people filed into the church to pray, he created a tremendous crucifixion/resurrection scene, *The Mystery of Faith*.

While Long finished his work at St. Mary's, Hodge stood in Trinity's churchyard, wondering if he should destroy the Glendale Springs church he couldn't afford to repair, and sell the property. A car pulled up and a stranger got out, saying he'd come to see his mother's childhood church. He looked at the tumbled-down wall. "What do you reckon it would take to fix her?" he asked. Hodge guessed: $1,500. The man wrote a check, hopped in his car, and drove away. The repairs cost $1,400, leaving $100 for supplies for Long's finest fresco, *The Last Supper*.

Long worked on this piece for three months, using locals as models for all the figures except Christ and Judas. Even a dog who dozed in the church found a home in the fresco.

Some people see Ben Long's frescoes as miracles of faith, some as a revival of a Renaissance art. One thing is certain: his art resurrected these beautiful old Carpenter Gothic churches.

From the Parkway, take Rte. 163 to Ashe County. Holy Trinity Church in Glendale Springs is off Rte. 16, about 2½ miles north of Rte. 163; 9 miles farther on Rte. 163 is West Jefferson. St. Mary's Church is only about a half mile off the highway at 400 Beaver Creek School Rd.

A fresco titled *The Last Supper* adorns a wall in Holy Trinity Episcopal Church in Glendale Springs.

Twenty to 40 inches of snow may be expected to fall each winter in the mountains around Boone.

pubs. King Street is also known for its art galleries and shops. If it's local music you crave, King Street is again a good option. Look for the **Concert on the Lawn Series** at the Jones House Community Center (604 W. King St.; 828/262–4576). The series hosts local musicians, primarily playing traditional music.

Near the community center is an old **Mast General Store** (630 W. King St.; 828/262–0000)—not the original, but one of the oldest, as you can tell from its creaky floors and old-fashioned counters. The *Mountain Times,* a free tabloid available in local businesses, explains what's going on in town.

Daniel Boone Native Gardens is a great place to stretch your legs. Paths meander beneath an arbor trailing clematis and through a sunken garden, rockery, sweet-smelling fern garden, and several other small gardens. The log hunting cabin with the mossy roof may have once belonged to Daniel Boone's father, Squire Boone. Near his cabin you can picnic on a broad lawn or admire the trilliums, jack-in-the-pulpit, beeches, wild roses, wild larkspur, and bloodroot. *651 Horn in the West Dr.; 828/264–6390.*

This park area includes Hickory Ridge Homestead and *The Horn in the West,* a summertime drama performed outdoors, depicting the role Daniel Boone and

SKIING IN THE APPALACHIANS

HIGH COUNTRY RESORTS

High Country Host (800/438–7500), a visitor information center in Boone, offers general information on High Country resorts and operates a 24-hour ski line (800/962–2322) from mid-November to mid-March.

Appalachian Ski Mountain.
Near Blowing Rock; 800/322–2373.

Popular with families and beginners. The outdoor ice-skating rink has spectacular views.

Sapphire Valley Ski.
Sapphire; 800/743–7663.

A 425-foot vertical drop.

Sugar Mountain Resort.
Banner Elk; 800/784–2768.

The largest North Carolina ski area; 18 slopes and a 1,200-foot vertical drop.

Ski Beech.
Beech Mountain; 800/438–2093.

Highest ski area in the eastern U.S. and a lively resort with restaurants, shops, and an ice-skating rink.

FARTHER WEST

Cataloochie Ski Area.
Maggie Valley; 800/768–0285.

A good place for beginners, families, and groups. A top elevation of 5,400 feet and 10 slopes, some of which are quite challenging.

Wolf Ridge Ski Resort.
Mars Hill; 800/817–4111.

Snowboarding and a ski school.

The Unaka Mountains in Pisgah National Forest.

A toy maker demonstrates
a handmade top.

RUNNING THE NOLICHUCKY

Adventurous travelers can sign up for a white-water rafting trip with one of several outfitters in the Appalachians. Boone's **High Mountain Expeditions** caravans rafters west through Erwin, Tennessee (a little town where folks either once hanged a circus elephant for murder or tell tall tales), to a put-in on the rambunctious Nolichucky River. *828/295–4200.*

The "Chucky" slices through protected lands in North Carolina and Tennessee, periodically roaring and then drifting through a beautiful, forested gorge. Nature regulates the flow on this undammed river, so rafters get the fastest ride in early spring, when melting snows send the river's Class IV–V rapids cartwheeling along.

After a safety lecture and a few practice paddles—forward, back, and rest—rafts of four or five paddlers each launch themselves upon the Nolichucky.

White-water rafting brings with it definite risks and a stack of release forms. It also offers views you'll never see through a windshield, and a feel for the rivers that sculpted this land.

In white water, you travel at the speed of change.

At your elbow, the water molds itself into a perfect emerald sculpture, poised to dive across a boulder. At your side, a stone's smooth, freckled face peeps through parted waters. Behind you, rapids hang in the air like hawks with windswept wings.

By the end of a five-hour paddle, folks who hunched and lurched their way over the first rapids ride like swivel-hipped cowboys on wild horses, leaning slightly back, relaxed, sensing the river's dance.

---

other North Carolina mountaineers played in the Revolutionary War. **Hickory Ridge Homestead** includes 18th-century buildings typical of a Watagua County farm. Demonstrators cook over the cabin's fire, hang hams in the smokehouse, pitch hay in the barn, and create traditional homespun in the weaving house. The museum sells local crafts. *591 Horn in the West Dr.; 828/264–2120.*

Tweetsie, a gussied-up old steam engine that once huffed through these mountains, has retired to a modest track just outside Boone on 421. The East Tennessee & Western North Carolina Railroad, or ET&WNC laid tracks through this region in the mid-1880s, bringing in visitors and supplies as it tugged iron ore out to market. Local wits soon renamed the ET&WNC the "Eat Taters & Wear No Clothes." The nickname Tweetsie, honoring the engine's two-toned whistle, stuck instead. Today Tweetsie puffs serenely along three miles of track through an "Old West" amusement park that's open mid-May through October. *300 Tweetsie Railroad La., between Boone and Blowing Rock; 800/526–5740.*

VALLE CRUCIS *map page 261, D-1/2*

The biggest thing south of Boone is the **Mast General Store** in Valle Crucis. This is the first Mast General Store, founded in 1883, the sire of the Mast Generals scattered through the mountains. You'll know it by its oak floors, glass-fronted showcases, wooden nail bins, coffee barrels, splay-toed rakes, beehives, and wire fly swatters.

Near the potbellied stove in the middle of the store a checkerboard stands between two chairs, ready for a game: red Coca-Cola bottle caps squared off against the gold caps snapped from bottles of Blenheim Ginger Ale.

Of course, times change. This venerable old mercantile stocks tourist items—like antique toys, old-fashioned kitchen gadgets, and herbal remedies—and the old-timey cash register disguises a computer screen. But that sweet, dusty odor in the back room isn't the smell of the $200 hiking boots sold here, it's chicken feed. And the trapdoor by the cash register? Owner W. W. Mast once took chickens in trade for the hardware, coffee, and salt on his shelves. He dropped his squawking, wing-flapping profits through the trapdoor before his customer could back out of a done deal. *3565 Hwy. 194 S; 828/963–6511.*

Speaking of wing-flapping and squawking, for a few weeks each summer Valle Crucis is also home to a bagpipers' school. You might find its students, along with crews of stout-legged hikers and other relaxed visitors, at the 19th-century Mast Farm Inn Restaurant (*see* Local Favorite Places to Eat at the end of this chapter), whose excellent dishes rely on organic vegetables from its garden. The inn and general store are both listed on the National Register of Historic Places.

BANNER ELK *map page 261, D-2*

To reach Banner Elk, head south from Valle Crucis on NC 194—a Scenic Highway so relentlessly twisted you can read road signs meant for cars going in the opposite direction. After 12 miles of emerald-green pastures, broad-shouldered barns, and old stone churches you will have wound your way into Banner Elk.

(above) The Natural Blend Honor Market in the Bryson City area sells honey, sweets, and condiments, using the honor system; payment is made through a slot in the door.
(below) The Appalachians are host to a number of rural general stores and specialty shops. Inside the Mast General Store, you can still buy marbles by the pound.

WOOLLY WORMS AND WEATHER

Edgar Tuft would have little trouble recognizing Banner Elk today—unless he visited in mid-October. The Woolly Worm Festival, which attracts about 15,000 humans and scores of prancing caterpillars each October, is Banner Elk's answer to the National Weather Service.

Mountain legend says the 13 stripes on the back of an Isabella moth caterpillar foretell freezes, snowfalls—even high-low temperature patterns. In fact, farmers once moved their cattle from upland pastures after reading the crawlers' fluffy hides.

Since thousands of caterpillars patiently putter about the countryside in October, each wearing distinctive stripes, the big question is, which worm wears the truth? In Banner Elk they figure fastest is truest.

They race the contenders in heats, allowing early winners to soak up the festival's entertainments and crafts until one glossy beauty inches its way to victory in the final heat. Weather Channel fans take note: the winning worm's stripes, as deciphered by a qualified "worm reader," are on the money 80 percent of the time.

This peaceful hamlet on the Elk River is noted for the massive ski resorts on nearby mountaintops and for picturesque **Lees-McRae College,** which was willed into existence by Edgar Tuft, a Presbyterian minister who arrived in the valley in 1895 and made its people's welfare his life's work.

Tuft rolled up his starched shirtsleeves, beginning a church during his first summer there, and finishing it during his second stay. Over the next years the indefatigable minister founded and funded an orphanage and Lees-McRae College, whose dressed-stone buildings adorn a lovely, small campus area.

BLOWING ROCK   *map page 261, D-2*

Blowing Rock shocked missionary Edgar Tuft, who visited in 1895:

> I never was more surprised than when I saw [Blowing Rock]. I thought my work would be almost altogether among country

people. But Blowing Rock has four or five big hotels and they say sometimes there are as many as a thousand people there, from all parts of the country . . . .

Blowing Rock, a resort village across the Parkway, is still known for those old resorts, fine restaurants, golf courses, and for **Blowing Rock.** Winds sweep up the 3,000-foot cliff overhanging Johns River Gorge, creating an updraft that returns handkerchiefs and other light objects tossed over the cliff. An observation tower and a visitor center (432 Rock Rd.; 828/295–7111) help get you oriented.

MOSES B. CONE MEMORIAL PARK   map page 261, D-2

There are two great places to buy crafts on the Parkway, and **Parkway Craft Center** at Cone Park is one of them. (The other is near Asheville.)

This brilliant white mountaintop mansion and its graceful grounds were once home to textile magnate Moses Cone and his wife Bertha. You've probably never heard of Moses Cone, but you know his work. In fact, you may be sitting on it. Cone put the "blue" in blue jeans. The denim that rolled from his North Carolina textile mills earned him millions and the title "Denim King."

At Blowing Rock, an upsweep of wind brings handkerchiefs back to their owners' hands.

The Cone Manor House near Blowing Rock.

In 1897, drawn by the mountain air, the Cones raised the roof on a 20-room mansion, crowning their 3,516-acre estate. Moses also built 25 miles of carriage trails for Bertha, threading them through extensive rhododendron and mountain laurel plantings. He added white pines and hemlocks to their forests, transported enough New England sugar maples to make the mountains crimson in October, and added an orchard of 40,000 apple trees.

The Cones' guests rocked on the porch, admiring the view. Today tourists rock on the same porch, admiring the same view, and chatting with a guild craftsman who weaves a delicate basket, using white oak strips cut days before. Out on the carriage trail, two denim-clad young men clip-clop by on Tennessee Walkers, the horses' gait as smooth as the rocking chairs'.

Most of this house, with its Tiffany windows, hardwood floors, and magical angles, is closed to visitors. No matter. The art of the Southern Highland Handicraft Guild, on the first floor, more than makes up for it.

Don't expect hillbilly jokes and Taiwan-made "mountain crafts" here. As you wander through these high-ceilinged rooms you'll find pottery of subtle design, handblown glass, and textiles in ancient mountain patterns and in colors that would make Joseph drop his coat of many colors and kick it behind the door.

The pottery of Michael Sherill represents the vibrant style of contemporary Appalachian art.

Fine jewelry, wooden toys, hand-stitched quilts, and Cherokee baskets line the shelves. In one room a weaver talks with inquisitive travelers as she overspins three handspun fibers on her spinning wheel, creating a vibrant multi-textured yarn.

You can buy a thousand dollars' worth of art in this shop or simply browse through, enriching your life with the clear, earthbound arts inspired by highland life. *Blue Ridge Parkway, milepost 294; 828/295–7938.*

PISGAH NATIONAL FOREST   *map page 261, B/C-2/3*

Now the Parkway heads south into Pisgah National Forest, the oldest of North Carolina's four national forests.

On a map, the main section of Pisgah's nearly half-million acres look like a child's footed pajama pants tossed to the floor. One rumpled leg dips and folds along the North Carolina–Tennessee border; the other leg, bent at the knee, follows the Parkway. You'll pass through yet another section of the Pisgah National Forest if you leave Asheville, heading toward Tennessee.

Travelers who simply drive the Parkway may notice little difference heading into Pisgah National Forest, since the Parkway remains undeveloped. But travelers who venture Off-Parkway will find themselves in a land of rich mountain forests and tiny, picturesque towns.

⇨ National forests offer travelers fewer amenities than national parks, and more backcountry access. Pisgah National Forest maintains 40 recreation areas. Hiking, fishing, camping, and nature study are perennially popular. (Thirty-nine of North Carolina's 55 species of wild orchids live within this park.) Bicycle access, limited to paved auto routes in parks, includes designated trails, abandoned railroad beds, and old logging roads. *For information, contact the Pisgah National Forest office at 828/257–4200 or 828/877–3265.*

PRICE PARK   *map page 261 D-1*

Today this park, one of the Parkway's most popular, offers easy and strenuous mountain hiking trails, trout fishing in a stocked pond, nature walks, and boat rentals. During the Civil War it provided a hideout for bushwhackers, draft dodgers, and escaped Union POWs making their way to Union-held Tennessee—often with the help of the fairly infamous Keith Blalock and his wife "Sam." Together, the Blalocks wrote an odd chapter in North Carolina history.

White-water rafting is one of the more popular recreational activities in the region.

Keith, a Union sympathizer, was drafted into the Confederate Army. His dedicated wife stuffed her hair under a soldier's cap and reported with her husband, joining Col. Zebulon Vance's 26th Regiment. The tent-mates made good soldiers. The trouble was, given their political sensibilities, they were fighting on the wrong side.

So after a respectable time, Keith rolled in poison oak, convinced army doctors he had an incurable skin disease, and went home to die. A few days later, the nimble-fingered "Sam" needed only 15 seconds and three buttons to convince startled physicians her enlistment had been a mistake.

The Blalocks moved into a cabin on Grandfather Mountain and lived happily ever after, cheerfully skirmishing with pro-South neighbors and helping Union soldiers to safety until war's end. *Blue Ridge Parkway, milepost 296; no phone.*

LINN COVE VIADUCT   *map page 261, D-2*

In 1983 Linn Cove Viaduct, at milepost 304, became the last section of Parkway to go into place. It is one of the most sophisticated bits of environmental engineering on the planet.

The viaduct snakes along the side of Grandfather Mountain without disturbing the protected habitat below. To achieve that end, engineers designed 153 different precast highway segments, each 8.6 feet long and weighing 50 tons, and extended the highway piece-by-piece over the 90-foot drop. From the trail below you can look up at this state-of-the-art construction.

Down a ways, US 221 leads from the Parkway to Grandfather Mountain, a quartzite giant whose trails, nature preserve, and swinging bridge make it a popular stop.

GRANDFATHER MOUNTAIN   *map page 261, D-2*

The Cherokee called Grandfather Mountain (US 221 N, just south of Blue Ridge Parkway milepost 305; 800/468-7325 or 828/733-4337) "Tanawha," for the golden eagles that rode its wind currents. Europeans, who settled the valleys, named the quartzite giant for the bearded man they saw profiled in its ridges.

Andre Michaux scrambled up Grandfather in 1794, scouting the boundaries of France's New World. "Reached the summit of the highest mountain in all of North America," he wrote in his journal, and burst into song.

His song, as it turns out, was about 40 miles off-key. Mt. Mitchell, to the south, is actually the highest peak east of the Mississippi. Nonetheless Grandfather—the highest on the Blue Ridge—has been a favorite hiking spot since Michaux's day.

A mountain cougar on Grandfather Mountain.

Grandfather Mountain provides habitat for more globally rare species than any other mountain east of the Rockies. Its abrupt rise from the valley floor creates climates supporting 16 distinct ecological communities. In them live 42 rare and endangered species, 17 of them globally imperiled—including the peregrine falcon, funnelweb tarantula, Heller's blazing star, Blue Ridge goldenrod, bent avens, and Gray's lily.

Black Rock Nature Trail is a favorite with birdwatchers, who have spotted 147 bird species on the mountain. The cliffs host one of the South's largest flocks of ravens. The Cherokee believed ravens were burned glossy black as they tried to steal fire from the gods. These ebony acrobats, which nest two-thirds of the way up sheer cliff faces, swoop, spin, dip, and back-flip from the mountainsides.

A nature museum, cafeteria, and gift shop, which together form a visitor center, are located halfway up the mountain. At the outdoor wildlife habitats, a mountain cougar with smoke-gray face and soot-lined eyes leaps gracefully to a rock ledge, and his mate. Deer, otters, eagles, woodchucks, and bears busy themselves in other habitats. Check for a schedule of nature lectures while you're here.

Continue up the mountain to reach the **Mile High Swinging Bridge,** the country's highest suspension footbridge. You'll find another visitor center here. Winds gusting through this 80-foot ravine keep the bridge rocking. In the ravine below is a perfect wind-created bonsai garden of gray stone, pale lichens, sand myrtle, and dwarfed red spruce, which bow and shield their faces from the wind. From the other side of the bridge, high on a black rock riverbed wrenched sideways a billion years ago, is a fine view of the countryside thousands of feet below.

The trails that lead from Grandfather's upper parking area make for challenging hiking and backpacking. Some take a few hours, some take days. All require good boots. Follow the park's safety rules and regulations, and watch the weather.

Each July the sweet, wild drone of the bagpipe swirls across the face of Grandfather Mountain as Campbells, MacLeods, MacRaes, Stewarts, MacDonalds, and scores of other Scottish clans file into the meadow, tartans unfurled, for the country's largest **Highland Games** (828/733–1333). Everyone's invited "be ye Scot or be ye not."

Thousands of spectators and competitors pour in for the torchlight parade, traditional Highland athletic events, Highland dancing, piping, drumming, Scottish fiddling, sheep herding, and Scottish harp playing.

SOUTH OF GRANDFATHER MOUNTAIN

From the parking lot at **Lost Cove Cliffs** (Blue Ridge Parkway, milepost 310), at nightfall, you can look for the Brown Mountain Lights. These mysterious star-like lights appear low on the horizon, twinkle brighter as they move near, and then fade away only to reappear and repeat their hesitant dance. Scientists have attributed the lights to Tweetsie (a theory that bit the dust when the train stopped

In July everyone's invited to Grandfather Mountain for the country's largest Highland Games, "Be ye Scot or be ye not."

Grandfather Mountain, at 5,964 feet, is the tallest peak in the northern half of the state's Appalachians.

running) and to refracted automobile lights. Others suggest there are ghosts or hardworking moonshiners afoot.

Just beyond Lost Cove Cliffs is **Linville Falls** (Blue Ridge Parkway, milepost 316.4). Poet A. M. "Chucky Joe" Huger probably blazed the first trails to the most dramatic set of falls on this stretch of the Parkway.

An easy trail from the River Bend parking area (milepost 316.4) leads to the base of the falls, where sycamore, butternut, and ironwood shade the riverbanks. Slightly more difficult trails lead up through an old-growth forest of hemlock and pines to a series of overlooks that show off the falls and the 14-mile forested gorge that descends to the Catawba Valley.

Taking the easy trail, **Erwin's View**—where pale pink rhododendron lean over the outcroppings to face the white waters below—offers the best view of the river, which curves and tumbles down the broad upper falls, pools, and somersaults down a narrow chasm. Catching its breath, it scrolls 30 feet down the gray cliffside into a deep, emerald pool.

Maps from the visitor center at Linville Falls detail other trails, from easy to strenuous, that offer views of these famous falls and gorge.

Just south of the falls, the Parkway again crosses US 221. If you love textiles, follow the signs west to the **Weavers Room at Crossnore,** where you can watch weavers re-create and preserve historical Appalachian patterns; their wares are for sale in the gift shop. This organization works with children from families in crisis; proceeds from the gift shop help support the private nonprofit children's home and school. You can see one of Ben Long's frescoes in the chapel. *100 DAR Dr., Crossnore; 828/733–4305.*

LINVILLE CAVERNS *map page 261, D-2*

"Here is one of the few chances of a lifetime to observe openly one of the usually hidden, but almost irresistible, forces of nature: the work of underground water. This water, often in mere traces, is the silent sculptor producing patterns of great beauty in stone," writes geologist Henry S. Brown.

Fishermen, not geologists, discovered these caverns in 1822. When their prey swam upstream into a mountainside, they followed, finding a vast maze of water-carved corridors and chambers. Their torchlight danced across geologic formations that resembled draperies, grape clusters, the capitol dome, giant bats with spread wings. They squeezed through narrow walkways and edged along the rim of a bottomless pool as tiny Eastern Pipistrelle bats fluttered overhead.

Trout still occupy NC's only public-access caverns, but their waters are now lit by guides' flashlights as visitors explore this work-in-progress.

The caverns' dolomite stone—the compressed exoskeletons of tiny sea creatures—was deposited here when this was the sea floor, millions of years ago. After the earth shifted, fresh groundwater ran through the earth, carving the cavern.

Dripping groundwater shapes more than caverns; it also creates a frizzled hairstyle known as "cave hair." Wear a hat. *19929 US 221 N; 828/756–4171.*

SPRUCE PINE AREA *map page 261, C/D-2*

The **Museum of North Carolina Minerals,** at the intersection of the Parkway and NC 226, offers solid, uninspired information about North Carolina's vast mineral wealth. Good background, true, but the most exciting introduction waits in gemstone "mines" near Spruce Pine and Little Switzerland. *Blue Ridge Parkway milepost 331; 828/765–2761.*

In North Carolina's rocky soul rest more minerals than in any other state, and you'll find most of them (57) in the Spruce Pine Mineral District, one of the richest districts in the country. Some mines contain as many as 45 separate minerals and gems, gifts from a young earth's uneven temperament. At **Spruce Pine's Mineral and Gem Festival** (828/765–2117) some 50 dealers offer everything from geodes to cut gems to fossils. The August festival also includes gem-cutting demonstrations and mine tours.

Today commercial mica, feldspar, and ultra-pure quartz mines dot this rugged countryside. Mitchell County yields around 35 percent of the feldspar produced in the United States—and used in everything from toilet bowls to false teeth.

Native Americans mined mica here—using the glittery, reflective mineral for personal ornaments and grave decorations—but mica's not the only pretty mineral in these hills. Tiffany's ran Crabtree Emerald Mine for years, beginning in 1883. Since 1884 Wiseman Mine has brought to light some of the best-colored aquamarine in the United States. The area produces buckets of gem-quality emeralds, aquamarine, clear quartz, amethyst, citrine, rose quartz, smoky quartz, tourmaline, garnets, and sapphires—mostly by-products of commercial mines.

Rockhounds can't visit the commercial mines directly, but gemstone-mining operations buy their ore by the truckload, doling it out bucket-by-bucket to customers who search through it at the outfits' flumes. Most evaluate your find for free, and cut your stones for a fee.

Emerald Village, a popular mine near Little Switzerland, offers by-the-bucket gemstone mining at a sheltered flume, a mining museum, and a stonecutting and gem-setting shop. *331 McKinney Mine Rd.; 828/765-6463.*

Blue Ridge Gemstone Mine, near Little Switzerland, also has a reputation for rich, local pay dirt and no-pressure advice. Part of its flume flows through a greenhouse-type building, offering shelter from the elements; part is under the sky. *Leave the Parkway at Little Switzerland; Chestnut Grove Church Rd. loops under the Parkway; take the first paved left; 828/765-5264.*

The earliest known illustration of mining in the state dates to 1833 and shows men digging for gold. At that time North Carolina was sometimes called the Golden State. (North Carolina Collection)

GEMSTONE MINING

Haven Peaden scoops a trowel of dirt and stones from a 10-gallon bucket onto her screen, and lowers it into the flume's fast-flowing water. As she joggles the screen, a cloud of clay drifts away, leaving a jumble of stones.

Propping the screen against the flume, she discards a few chunks of granite. When a golf-ball-size amethyst rolls to the bottom of the screen, she plunks it in the bag at her side and lifts the screen to the sunlight. There's an emerald! A small ruby . . . a three-inch quartz crystal. . . . And what's that? Uncertain, she drops it into her bag.

An hour later, Haven leans against gemologist Dick Johnson's counter. "We have three kinds of stones in the mountains," says the owner of Blue Ridge Gemstone Mine. "Gems worth cutting, gems that aren't worth cutting, and real pretty rocks."

"It would be well worth your while to have these cut," he says, scooping two rubies, a small sapphire, an emerald, and a piece of citrine into a small plastic bag.

The gemstones too small or uneven to cut include the amethyst, a rose quartz, a chunk of tourmaline, and a handful of tiny rubies, emeralds, and garnets. They get their own bag.

"And these are your pretty rocks," he smiles, pushing a small avalanche toward her. These are bound for a terrarium, but occasionally pretty rocks have more glamorous fates. Down the counter, a woman who plucked a pretty rock from the flume sits down hard after learning the black-blue stone she nearly tossed is a 477.5-carat sapphire.

Few will strike it rich at a gemstone mine, but most will strike it pretty. And if you count the calming of the mind, the joy of discovery, and a realization of the earth's generosity so crystal-clear you can put it in your pocket, more people strike it rich at these flumes than you might imagine.

ALONG HIGHWAY 226 *map page 261, C/D-2*

As Highway 226 and its smaller tributaries wind through Mitchell County they pass a host of tiny towns with odd names. "It was easy to name a town in those days," Muriel Earley Sheppard wrote in *Cabins in the Laurel,* in 1935. "When the government in Washington was ready to establish a post office, whoever filled out the application blank wrote in whatever name occurred to him." Loafer's Glory needs no explanation. Relief was named for a tonic sold at Squire Peterson's store.

Sheppard noted others: "Ledger, Daybook, Wing, Bandana, Lunday, Hawk, Plumtree, Staggerweed, Poplar, and a host of like names are scattered through Toe River Country." (Toe River's name, which she didn't seem to find odd, echoes the Cherokee capital, Estatoh.)

Last but not least, the name **Penland** is synonymous with fine art–quality crafts worldwide. Miss Lucy Morgan founded Penland School in 1929 in a little building of donated logs. In it she helped local women rekindle the art of hand weaving, and marketed their work to the "outside world."

Today Penland, on NC 226 between Ledger and Spruce Pine, offers classes in textiles, printmaking, ceramics, glass, metal, wood, and photography. Studios stand open; the student at the potter's wheel or loom may be a great-grandmother or an artist who just pocketed his first driver's license.

Miss Lucy's is now an international school; its graduates' work resides in museums all over the world. Check out the gallery first. *Conley Ridge Rd.; follow the signs; 828/765–6211.*

A display of glass and ceramic works in the Penland Gallery.

Unpaved backcountry roads
in the Appalachians are ideal
for hiking and bicycling.

South of Penland, the Parkway heads into the Black Mountains, a mighty quartz-ite cross-range of North Carolina's highest peaks—including Mt. Mitchell, the highest peak east of South Dakota's Black Hills. The range's name springs from the shadow-green hemlock, spruce, and pine tinting the mountainsides.

Mt. Mitchell State Park, an island within the Pisgah National Forest, is, like Grandfather Mountain, a U.N.-designated biosphere. (To gain this status, an area must already be protected, have unique ecological significance, a history of scientific study, and provide for scientific education.) To visit, take NC 128 at milepost 355 off the Parkway. The drive climbs 5 miles almost to the mountain's summit.

An easy trail from the parking area leads to the summit. The observation tower on top overlooks the cloud-draped Black Mountains and surrounding countryside.

Treks of varying difficulty make up an 18-mile trail system. You may notice evergreens dying at higher elevations; scientists don't yet know exactly why, but some suspect pollution, others, natural causes. North Carolina's oldest state park includes a seasonal campground, restaurant, concession stand, and interpretive center. *828/675–4611.*

BLACK MOUNTAIN
map page 261, C-3

The town of Black Mountain, just off the Parkway on NC 9, experienced a "New Age" boom in the 1980s. This small

This 1857 lithograph shows Elisha Mitchell, who fell to his death near the falls. The mountain, the highest in the eastern United States, was named as a memorial to Mitchell (North Carolina Collection)

Rime ice coats a tree along the Appalachian Trail in Yancey County. Mt. Mitchell rises in the distance to a height of 6,684 feet.

town's restored historic district has become a busy neighborhood of antiques shops, crafts shops, boutiques, and cafés.

Historically, the town is known for Black Mountain College, a progressive but short-lived liberal arts school that flourished here from 1933 until 1957. Buckminster Fuller developed the geodesic dome while teaching here. Other faculty included artists Josef and Anni Albers, choreographer Merce Cunningham, and composer John Cage. Writer Francine du Pleissix Gray studied here; Albert Einstein was a guest lecturer. The **Black Mountain College Museum & Art Center** (56 Broadway, Asheville; 828/350–8484) focuses on the school's contributions to modern arts.

ASHEVILLE AREA   *maps pages 306 & 310*

Asheville, home of UNC-Asheville, has been a resort town since almost forever. It was hip in the 1700s, and remains hip today. Its arts community sizzles, its architecture inspires, its restaurants grab rave reviews . . . and it's got the mountains, with all that they imply. Even its history is a little cooler than that of the rest of the state.

Low-country plantation owners began summering here in the late 1700s, trading malaria's fevers for the Cherokee's cool, untainted air. By the mid 1800s Asheville was known for its middle-class boardinghouses and fresh-air tuberculosis "cures." (Author Thomas Wolfe grew up in one of those boardinghouses.)

With the opening of the railway in 1880, Asheville welcomed a more sophisticated set of visitors—among them George Vanderbilt, who fell in love with the countryside and stayed, importing architects and craftsmen to build a 255-room chateau and gardens at his Biltmore estate.

As the Vanderbilts' friends visited, Asheville's fortune shot skyward. By the 1920s Asheville was, irrefutably, the cat's meow. It looked the role.

With Biltmore complete, architects, stonemasons, and other craftsmen turned to other projects: St. Lawrence Catholic Church, a domed basilica with Spanish baroque towers; an Italian-influenced art-deco Baptist church; the stately Cathedral of All Souls. Influential guests promenaded in front of the mammoth Battery Hotel. Inspired by an infusion of culture and cash, city fathers sank a fortune into art-deco skyscrapers and public buildings.

Then came the fall. The crash of 1929 stifled the city's luxury-based economy, saddling Asheville with the highest per capita debt in the nation. After the furor of the Roaring 20s the silence was deafening. For nearly half a century civic leaders

A crowded stagecoach stands in front of the Eagle Hotel in Asheville, circa 1880. (Courtesy Pack Memorial Library, Asheville)

could barely afford to swing a wrecking ball. As a result, much of Asheville's fine old architecture still stands.

VISITING ASHEVILLE TODAY

Pack Square, downtown, has been a good place for travelers to stretch their legs since the early 1800s, when the stagecoach deposited travelers here. Its architecture is a patchwork of old and new. Inside, the emphasis is on new.

Like many buildings on the square, **Pack Place** is a relic of the early 1900s, Asheville's boom years. It illustrates Asheville's adaptive use policy of recycling older buildings. Pack Place is home to the **Asheville Art Museum** (2 S. Pack Sq.; 828/253–3227), which showcases 20th- and 21st-century American art. Other residents include the Colburn Gem and Mineral Museum and The Health Adventure, an interactive science and health museum.

From Pack Square you can stroll east on Patton Avenue to **City/County Plaza,** an area noted for its beautiful and sharply contrasting art-deco and classical architecture.

If you walk west a few blocks to Haywood Street and turn right you'll find yourself in a lively downtown area of restaurants, bars, alternative movie houses, and specialty shops. **Biltmore Avenue** is at the heart of the gallery district. **The Asheville Area Arts Council** (11 Biltmore Ave.; 828/258–0710) can hook you up with an art walk or get you started on a self-guided tour of the 30 or so galleries in the neighborhood.

Asheville's restored 1929 **Grove Arcade** (1 Page Ave.) has reclaimed its place as Asheville's downtown public market. Its

The Buncombe County Courthouse, an art-deco classic at City Hall Plaza.

BUNCOMBE DEADPAN

Everybody knows buncombe means malarky. Few people realize the term was coined to define the verbiage of a politician from Asheville—the county seat of Buncombe County, North Carolina. But it doesn't take visitors long to realize mountain people take their buncombe seriously.

They will look you dead in the eye and swear their cows have two short legs and two long, to allow them to graze the mountainside; that their cousin (uncle, grandfather) fell out of a particularly steep cornfield and broke his neck; or that if you look hard enough, you'll see the North Carolina–Tennessee line painted across the bottom of the Nolichucky River.

Don't try to make them stop. History proves it won't work.

shops include Appalachian crafts and furniture, clothing, and cafés. In the River Arts District, beyond the Broad River, you'll find the homes and studios of a number of emerging artists and musicians.

Asheville's music scene is always humming. If you want to hum along, you might want to check out the **Orange Peel Social Aid and Pleasure Club.** It's known for its eclectic calendar—ballet to burlesque, and rock operas to dance nights. *101 Biltmore Ave.; 828/225–5851.*

The 426-acre **North Carolina Arboretum**, outside town, takes advantage of the mountains' diverse environments, creating gardens at different altitudes to showcase the flora of the entire state. The arboretum, which opened in 1997, includes theme gardens, wildflowers, a greenhouse, overlooks, and an Appalachian quilt garden laid out in patterns that duplicate traditional quilts. *100 Frederick Law Olmsted Way; 828/665–2492.*

THOMAS WOLFE MEMORIAL

Today visitors walk up the steep front steps of old 48 Spruce Street, knock on the door, and step straight into the pages of Thomas Wolfe's autobiographical first novel, *Look Homeward, Angel.* It almost wasn't so. In the late 1990s an arsonist torched the

29-room boardinghouse once run by Wolfe's entrepreneurial mother, Julia Westall Wolfe, nearly robbing Asheville of one of its most important historic sites.

Thanks to a $2.4 million restoration effort, Wolfe's boyhood home again welcomes guests. The restoration reflects the house as it looked in 1916. This is the house Wolfe used as a model for Dixieland in his novel. You'll find a modern visitors center next door; guided tours leave from there. If you'd like to pay your respects more directly, Wolfe's grave is in historic Riverside Cemetery. *52 N. Market St.; 828/253–8304.*

BILTMORE ESTATE *map page 306, A/B-2*

Biltmore is remarkable for its architecture, its extravagance, and the 50,000 pieces of art, furnishings, and antiques inside. Much of the original collection is intact.

Vanderbilt commissioned landscape architect Frederick Law Olmsted to design his grounds and formal gardens, and architect Richard Morris Hunt to help plan

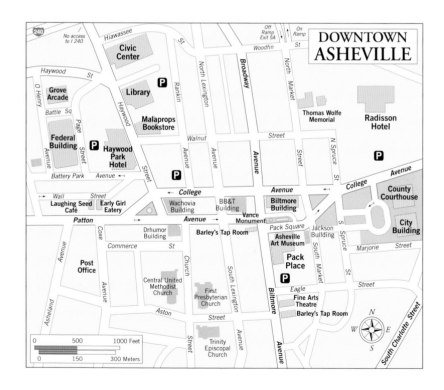

NOTABLE ASHEVILLE WRITERS

Today, of course, **Thomas Wolfe** is one of Asheville's most honored sons. But when *Look Homeward, Angel* first hit the bookstores in 1929, Asheville went pale with fury. Wolfe, who assumed Ashevillians would be delighted to find themselves described down to their imperfect belly buttons, was startled by his neighbors' death threats. He steered clear of his hometown until 1937.

Wolfe isn't the only writer who had a difficult relationship with Asheville. Short-story writer **O. Henry** (William Sidney Porter), who married an Asheville native, hated the place. "I could look at these mountains a hundred years and not get an inspiration—they depress me," lamented the master of the twist ending. He returned to his beloved New York, where he died in 1910, but he rests in Asheville's Riverside Cemetery—suggesting that his wife, too, had a flair for surprise endings.

As for **F. Scott Fitzgerald,** who spent a lot of time womanizing in this mountain town, Ashevillians still sneer.

Happily, Asheville has a better relationship with modern writers, including novelists **Gail Godwin, Wilma Dykeman, Charles Frazier,** and **John Ehle**—Asheville natives all. Thanks in part to the presence of **The University of North Carolina** at Asheville and nearby **Warren Wilson College,** the mountains around Asheville are thick with writers. Their latest work is carried at **Malaprops** (55 Haywood St.; 828/254–6734), a bookstore and coffee shop.

⊕ ⊕ ⊕

his house, a 255-room chateau, the largest home in America. Hundreds of workers toiled from 1890 to 1895 to complete the house and grounds.

Standard tours take you through the public sections of the house and some of the family's living quarters as well as some of the servants' quarters. Don't overlook the winery while you're here. It's the most-visited winery in America, welcoming a half-million visitors each year.

George Vanderbilt. (Courtesy Biltmore Estate, Asheville, North Carolina)

You can easily spend a day at Biltmore, especially when the gardens bloom; at a brisk trot you need three hours to tour house, gardens, and winery; five if you lunch at Biltmore restaurants.

You won't rub elbows with the Vanderbilts here, but you will rub elbows—especially during peak seasons (summer, October, and Christmas) and at peak hours.

The most tranquil time to visit: early in the morning. See the house first and then the grounds. Ticket prices here change seasonally, but are generally $45–$55 on weekdays and $55–$65 on Saturday. Look for discounts and deals on the Web site. *1 Approach Rd.; 800/543–2961; www. biltmore.com.*

Biltmore Village, a cluster of upscale shops and high-end galleries, occupies the stately old employees' quarters outside the Biltmore gates. *Take NC 25 off I–40 south of downtown.*

Biltmore House in 1902. (Library of Congress)

The Library at the Biltmore House.

Relaxing on the veranda at the Grove Park Inn not long after the resort opened in 1913.
(Courtesy Grove Park Inn)

GROVE PARK INN *map page 306, B-1*

While Vanderbilt boosted land prices on the south side of town, Edwin Wiley Grove looked north toward Sunset Mountain. Later he recalled, "The dream of an old-time inn came to me—an inn whose exterior, and interior as well, should present a homelike and wholesome simplicity. . . ." The Midwesterner had the bucks to back the dream. With the catchy slogan "Makes Children & Adults Fat as Pigs," his Grove's Tasteless Chill Tonic had made millions.

Four hundred builders signed on at $1 a day to build the inn. The stonemasons—many of them Biltmore veterans—began construction, making sure only uncut stone faces showed, inside and out.

The 156-room inn went up in a little over a year. Workers hoisted 120 tons of boulders into the 36-foot-wide chimneys at each end of the 120-foot Great Room. As exterior walls rose, roofers capped the building with a swooping red-tile roof. Roycroft craftsmen hammered out copper lamps and light fixtures and no-nonsense Arts and Crafts furniture. A bowling alley, indoor pool, and billiards room took shape.

The Grove Park Inn, one of Asheville's most historic and storied inns, houses the world's largest collection of Arts and Crafts furnishings.

Since 1913 its doors have swung open for heads of state, inventors, and everyday travelers. Harry Houdini, Béla Bartók, and Enrico Caruso stayed here. So have Presidents. Thomas Wolfe, who hated the place, never slept here. But in a page that could have been ripped from one of his own Jazz Age novels, F. Scott Fitzgerald began haunting the inn in 1935. Between visits to a local asylum to visit his wife Zelda, he romanced any young woman who crossed his path.

Some suspect the pink-clad ghost in the inn's Palm Atrium, near Fitzgerald's old room, is Zelda. Whoever she is, she's often spotted, and known for pranks.

Today the **Grove Park Inn Resort and Spa** (*see* Local Favorite Places to Stay at the end of this chapter), listed on the National Register of Historic Places, is home to the world's largest collections of Arts and Crafts furnishings, and to the Horizons restaurant.

FOLK ART CENTER *map page 306, B-1/2*

Remember Cone Memorial Park, near Blowing Rock, the first great place on the Parkway to buy crafts? Well, this is the second great place. It, too, features the work of the Southern Highland Handicraft Guild.

Inside this modern building you'll find crafts made in the highlands of nine southern states, along with a museum of modern, creative adaptations in craft mediums. Appalachian craft designs, which immigrated to America with Scots, English, German, and Irish settlers, remained virtually unchanged in isolated, hardscrabble communities until the late 1800s. In 1895, when missionary Frances Louisa Goodrich accepted a handwoven coverlet as a gift from a mountain woman in Madison County, the gift inspired an industry.

The vegetable-dyed Double Bowknot coverlet convinced Goodrich to begin Allanstand Cottage Industries, and to revive and market the mountaineers' crafts. In 1908 Goodrich opened an Asheville showroom. Allanstand Shop, which the Southern Highland Handicraft Guild has operated since 1931, is a vital part of today's Folk Art Center. Today the Southern Highlands' multimillion-dollar crafts industry preserves and expands on traditional Appalachian crafts. This shop offers great browsing, and wonderful art.

The Southern Highland Handicraft Guild sponsors two crafts fairs at the Asheville Civic Center each year, one in July and one in October. The guild also sponsors a shop called Guild Crafts, on Tunnel Road in Asheville. *Blue Ridge Parkway, ½ mile east of Asheville; 828/298–7928.*

OUTDOORS

On the French Broad River, which strolls through Asheville, you can enjoy gentle rafting, kayaking, and tubing. (Area outfitters also arrange trips to wilder waters.) **Chimney Rock Park** rates high with those who appreciate gorgeous views, wheeze-free hiking, and easy access. (An elevator inside the granite mountain zips visitors to its crest.) An easy trail leads to the bottom of its 400-foot waterfall. You can see nearby Lake Lure from the observation platform. *Hwy. 74, 25 miles southeast of Asheville; 800/277–9611.*

HENDERSONVILLE   map page 261, C-3

Hendersonville, southeast of Asheville on US 25, is a 19th-century resort town whose small downtown historic district is loaded with antiques shops, many of them on Main Street. Hendersonville is also home to a large antiques mall, **Needful Things** (10 Francis Rd.; 828/696–8745).

The best place to browse and catch up on hearsay: the **Curb Market,** known for great-grandma entrepreneurs who make and sell hand-labeled jars of watermelon preserves, bread-and-butter pickles, apple butter, pickled beans, chutney, and heaven knows what else. They also sell aprons, fresh vegetables, wheat bread,

The view from Chimney Rock reveals Lake Lure.

Indian corn, dried gourds, grapevine wreaths, birdhouses, rugs woven from stocking toes—even buckeyes. *221 N Church St.; 828/692–8012.*

FLAT ROCK *map page 261, C-3/4*

Flat Rock has been an upscale resort from birth, conceived by Charlestonians as an elite summer retreat from the heat of the Southern lowlands. The town's history shows in Flat Rock's inns, B&Bs, old homes, and golf courses; and at St. John in the Wilderness Church, where headstones bearing prominent Low Country surnames pepper the cemetery. (The church is less than a mile north of Carl Sandburg's home, Connemara, on US 25.)

Flat Rock Playhouse, aka the State Theater of North Carolina, stages Broadway and London hits and consistently rates as one of the 10 best summer-stock theaters in the United States. Performances run through the summer and well into the fall. *Intersection of Hwy. 25 South and Little River Rd.; 828/693–0731.*

Carl Sandburg, one of America's greatest poets and biographers, spent the final 22 years of his life on the outskirts of Flat Rock. He and his wife Lillie lived in a rambling, white-clapboard house, **Connemara,** which they bought from the family of Charles Memminger, the first Secretary of State for the Confederacy. The center of a 240-acre farm, it overlooks rolling pastures, ponds, a barn for Lillie's prizewinning goats, and the Blue Ridge. This National Historic Site offers guided tours of the house every day except Christmas. The grounds, trails, and farm are open at no charge; the goat barn lies within bleating distance of the house. *1928 Little River Rd.; 828/693–4178.*

FROM ASHEVILLE TO THE GREAT SMOKY MOUNTAINS

From Asheville, the Parkway winds through some of North Carolina's most rugged mountains and spectacular scenery as it heads west, through Cherokee, to the Great Smoky Mountains National Park.

THE LAND OF WATERFALLS

Route 64, as it heads west from Hendersonville into Nantahala National Forest, unites a strand of picturesque resort towns: Etowah, Brevard (known for its white squirrels), Lake Toxaway, Sapphire, Cashiers, and Highland. This is the Land of the Waterfalls, which you can also access via 276 from the Blue Ridge Parkway south of Asheville.

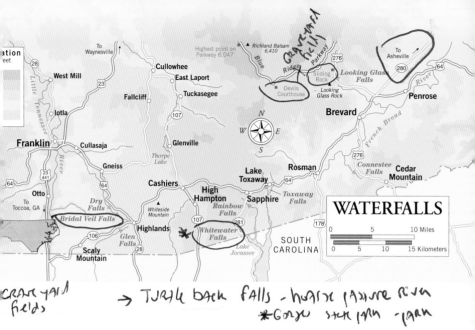

→ TURN BACK FALLS - HORSE PASTURE RIVER
*GORGE STATE PARK - PARK

CRAVE YARD fields

More than 250 spectacular waterfalls make Transylvania County's Parkway and Off-Parkway drives among the most popular in the Appalachians.

Why so many waterfalls? Two reasons.

These mountains are the first to greet heavy rain clouds rolling north from the Gulf of Mexico. They trap the clouds, which drop around 100 inches of rain here each year before they lighten up and pass on.

This flood splashes down on mountains that rise nearly 5,000 feet in elevation from one side of the county to the other. The result? "From upland coves water rushes headlong in leaps and splashes to the valley floor below, over countless cascades, cataracts, chutes, falls, jumps, runs, shoals, slides, slips, and spills," writes Transylvania County photographer Jim Bob Tinsley in his book *The Land of the Waterfalls.*

Among the most famous of the area's many falls are the 411-foot Whitewater Falls, the highest falls in the eastern United States; Bridal Veil Falls, famous for its lacy cascades; and Sliding Rock, where visitors slide like playful otters along a 60-foot natural waterslide plunging into a breathtakingly cold pool below. You can drive right up to Bridal Veil Falls on US 64 near Highland. Whitewater Falls, on NC 281, requires a short walk from an overlook. It's an easy walk from the parking area to Sliding Rock, located on 276 near Brevard. Caution: Always stay on the marked trails or in areas designated as safe.

Whitewater Falls measures
411 feet—the highest in the
eastern United States.

NANTAHALA NATIONAL FOREST

South of Asheville, beyond the Cradle of Forestry, the Parkway passes through a small section of Pisgah National Forest and enters **Nantahala National Forest.** North Carolina's largest national forest, Nantahala includes over 517,000 rugged acres in the southwest corner of the state. Nantahala means "Land of the Noonday Sun"; if you drive or raft down the Nantahala Gorge, you'll understand why. Sunlight slips in only at noon. This national forest offers a wealth of backcountry adventure—hiking, rafting, horseback riding, camping, and mountain biking. *For information, contact the Nantahala Ranger District, 90 Sloan Rd., Franklin; 828/524–6441.*

Commercial outfitters in Asheville and Nantahala make good use of the Nantahala National Forest, which is known for hiking, camping, and bridle trails. **Tsali Recreational Area,** within the national forest, is one of the nation's most popular mountain-biking spots, with around 40 miles of biking trails. *For information, contact the Cheoah Ranger District, 1070 Massey Branch Rd., Robinsville; 828/479–6431.*

DEVIL'S COURTHOUSE   map page 261, B/C-3/4

This marked overlook on the Parkway inspires legends. Settlers swore the devil judged souls in a cavern beneath this rocky summit. The Cherokee believed this cavern to be the dance hall of a sensitive, slant-eyed giant named Judacalla, who lived in this secluded hideaway with a Cherokee woman.

If the Cherokee were right, Judacalla had some view. His roof offers a 360-degree look at the French Broad, Tuskaseigee, and upper Pigeon River valleys. (The Cherokee called Pilot Mountain, visible from here, *Tsuwahtuldee.* In a village inside the mountain, they said, people lived a life of song, dance, and feasting.)

A strenuous half-mile climb takes you to the top of Devil's Courthouse. Most visitors are content to admire the view from the overlook. *Blue Ridge Parkway, milepost 422.4.*

THE DRIVE TO CHEROKEE   map page 261, B/C-3

From Devil's Courthouse, the Parkway turns west toward Cherokee, through a land increasingly rich in Cherokee history and tradition. On **Tanasee Bald,** travelers can still see where the giant Judacalla cleared the mountain for farmland. (Tanasee Bald borrowed its name from the Cherokee village Tanasi. So did the State of Tennessee.)

Bears were once plentiful in the North Carolina mountains. The Cherokee believed the first bears were lazy men, transformed into animals for punishment. The names of a string of Parkway stops—Bear Pen Gap, Bear Trap Gap, and Bear Trail Ridge—are reminders of the once-plentiful bruin loafers. At Rabb Knob Overlook (milepost 441.9) you can see the sites of what used to be a Cherokee village. The village was decimated by U.S. troops in the 1700s.

At Balsam Gap, US 23 leads north to **Waynesville,** named for Revolutionary War General "Mad Anthony" Wayne. The town is home to the **Museum of North Carolina Handicrafts** (49 Shelton St.; 828/452–1551), whose exhibits focus on heritage crafts, including jewelry making, woodworking, and China painting.

From here you can take a detour on NC 209, a welcome respite from heavy Parkway traffic. It cruises through Luck (population 4), and Trust (population 3, if you count the dog). Then it slips up the undeveloped mountainside, past a tiny meditation chapel. From Waynesville it's also a short hop to US 19 and **Maggie Valley,** with its shops and winter ski slopes.

CHEROKEE

The drive down US 19 into **Cherokee** offers a jarring assortment of billboards, out-of-kilter shops, bingo joints, motels, theme parks, and bizarre Old West photo opportunities—clear reminders that 75 percent of the Cherokee tribe's revenues come from tourism, including **Harrah's Cherokee** (777 Casino Dr.; 828/497–7777). North Carolina's only casino features 2,400 video gaming machines.

Be patient. Straight ahead in town lie two culture-oriented Cherokee stops.

The **Museum of the Cherokee Indian** traces this important tribe's history and art via computer-generated imagery, stone artifacts, textiles, mythology, basketry, and jewelry. The Qualla Arts & Crafts Mutual, Inc., adjacent to the museum, showcases and sells the work of 300 Cherokee craftspeople. The 20-foot hand-carved redwood statue outside the museum depicts Sequoyah, who created the Cherokee alphabet in 1821. *589 Tsali Blvd.; 828/497–3481.*

Oconaluftee Village, a re-creation of a 1750 Cherokee village, reflects the research of anthropologists from the University of Tennessee, UNC Chapel Hill, and the University of Georgia, as well as traditions recorded by the Cherokee themselves.

In the cabins, shelters, and open-air workplaces, Native American artisans demonstrate traditional Cherokee crafts. An older woman deftly interweaves strips of white oak and river cane to create an angular, lidded basket whose decorative design is older than memory. Beneath another shelter, where coals smolder on a poplar log, a gray-haired gentleman patiently chops away the charred wood with a sharp stone ax, hollowing a canoe.

As visitors watch and ask questions, Cherokee women shape pots in the same way their great-grandmothers did, carefully pressing a sharp pattern of lines into the pots' blank faces. A red-shirted young man tips a reed dart with thistle down. Another craftsman carves a ceremonial mask from soft, pale wood.

A group of schoolchildren follows a nature trail to a Cherokee garden of squash, corn, gourds, beans, and herbs. Meanwhile, in the seven-sided Cherokee Council House, a guide explains the Cherokee's democratic political system and spiritual beliefs.

The Cherokee saw themselves as living in a complex spiritual universe, in a world suspended between two others: a world of perfect order, above, and a world of total chaos, below. In their Middle Earth, they tried to balance the extremes.

Several million visitors have learned about the Cherokee people's traditional art, lifestyle, and beliefs here since this village opened in 1952. The outdoor drama *Unto These Hills,* staged in the amphitheater next door (mid-June–mid-August), has a broader scope. It follows the Cherokee from Hernando de Soto's visit to the Trail of Tears, and the beginnings of the Eastern Cherokee tribe. *Village open May 15–Oct. 25. Hwy. 441 N; 828/497–2315.*

QUALLA BOUNDARY

During the Trail of Tears era a few hundred Cherokee escaped the government's corrals and guarded trails and hid in the mountains. They became the forebears of the Eastern Band of Cherokee who now occupy the Qualla Boundary, better known locally as the Cherokee Indian Reservation.

Will Thomas, an adopted Cherokee, bought the reservation lands in the 1800s for the tribe. Today the 11,000-member Eastern Band occupies the sovereign, 56,000-acre land. Of them, about 10,000 live on the reservation. Its community names echo the names of the ancient clans: Yellowhill, Birdtown, Painttown, Snowbird, Big Cove, and Wolftown.

Reservation roads are public roads. Trout fishing (with a tribal license), hiking, and water sports are allowed in designated areas. Inquire at the **Cherokee Visitor Center** (498 Tsali Blvd.; 828/497–1056 or 800/438–1601), across from the Museum of the Cherokee Indian.

Tom Branch Falls thunder through a dappled afternoon in Great Smoky Mountains National Park.

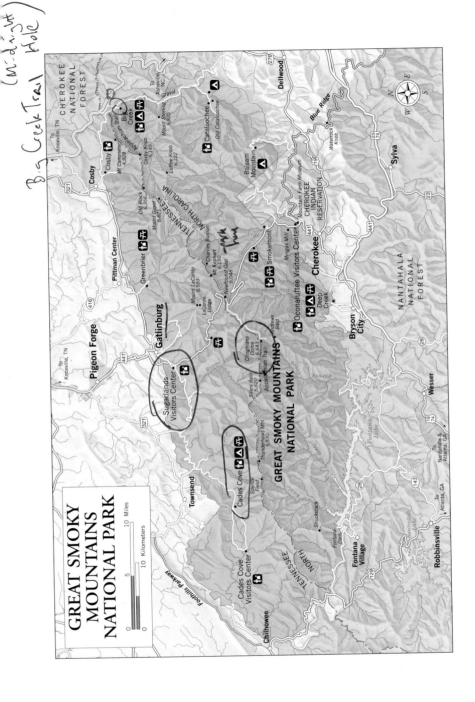

Big Creek Trail (midnight hole)

GREAT SMOKY MOUNTAINS NATIONAL PARK

0 — 5 — 10 Miles
0 — 5 — 10 Kilometers

GREAT SMOKY MOUNTAINS NATIONAL PARK

GREAT SMOKY MOUNTAINS NATIONAL PARK

More than nine million people a year visit the Great Smoky Mountains National Park, the best-used national park in the country. It's also the end point (or starting point) of the Blue Ridge Parkway. The 520,408-acre park lies draped across the state border, with 60 percent of its land falling within North Carolina and 40 percent in Tennessee.

Cherokee provides the gateway for visitors entering the park from North Carolina. The **Oconoluftee Visitor Center,** 2 miles north of Cherokee, has maps, general information, and a few exhibits. This is also the place to pick up permits for campgrounds or backcountry camping. *1194 Newfound Gap Rd.; 828/497–1904.*

Visitors generally drive through the park for the view, or to trailheads for hiking, mountain biking, canoeing, etc. Overnight accommodations in the park generally involve tents and blankets of stars.

More than 1,500 species of flowering plants, 200 species of birds, 50 fish species, and 60 species of mammals occupy the park's forests, balds, historic sites, streams, and rivers. A whopping 27 species of salamanders scurry through the park, among 2,000 varieties of mushrooms. But bears still get all the glory.

Some 1,500 black bears live here—fishing by a stream, plundering through a rhododendron slick, ambling along a berry-rich trail. Black bears, which weigh 200–400 pounds, may be black, brown, reddish, or even a cinnamon color. Of course you know not to feed them, but you might not know it's not wise to tempt them, either.

Park bears have come to like packaged foods. If they spot a snack, they want it; if they want it, they get it. Unless you want a convertible, don't leave canned food, cookies, or coolers stored in sight in your car. (Bears, who are not wily consumers, will also go for anything that looks like packaged foods. Put cans of tennis balls, cooler-shaped cases, etc. in the trunk.) Follow park suggestions for storing food when you camp or park. And if a bear does swipe a snack, don't try to get it back.

The Great Smoky Mountains National Park's popular scenic drive moseys along bumper-to-bumper during peak seasons—especially in summer and in autumn, when the leaves change. Those who seek serenity should visit at other times.

HISTORIC SITES

One of the park's best historic sites lies just across the NC–Tennessee border. In the 19th-century village of **Cades Cove,** complete with its churches, homes, and businesses, you can almost see settlers strolling along the one-lane road that loops through the valley and hear them joking as they trudge up the mountainside or bustle about the fireplace getting dinner on the table. At dusk, when herds of whitetail deer saunter down to graze in the cove's rich bottomland, this is the most peaceful spot in the park.

On the less-developed North Carolina side of the park, interpreters reenact farm life at **Mountain Farm Museum,** near the Oconaluftee Visitor Center.

The Mountain Farm Museum is a working farm made up of buildings moved here from throughout the park: a log house, apple house, barn, springhouse, and working blacksmith's shop. Demonstrators are on hand. A June program highlights "women's work," from quilting to soap making to weaving. In September a mountain-life exhibit demonstrates everything from making apple butter to making bluegrass music. A couple of easy walking trails leave from here in case you'd like to stretch your legs and treat yourself to some mountain scenery. *1194 Newfound Gap Rd.; 828/497–1904.*

HIKING AND CAMPING

More than 800 miles of trails lead to the park's waterfalls, meadows, and overlooks. They range from strenuous climbs to easy, quarter-mile quiet walkways.

The **Appalachian Trail,** which dips along the North Carolina–Tennessee border, passes along 68 miles of the park's highest ridges on its 2,100-mile stretch from Georgia to Maine. Each year around 100 hikers trek the entire trail, but most opt for a smaller slice of the outdoors.

Hikers can step onto the Appalachian Trail at Clingman's Dome, Newfound Gap, Fontana Dam, or Big Creek Campground. The most popular stretch is the eight-mile walk from Clingman's Dome to Charlie's Bunion and back. This trail, which explores a spruce and fir forest with outstanding vistas, has an elevation gain of only 980 feet.

Ten developed campgrounds are tucked away in the park. (Three take reservations: 800/365–2267.) You'll find 100 primitive campsites on the ridges.

BRYSON CITY AREA   map page 261, B-3

US 19 wanders along the Great Smoky Mountains' southern boundary to easygoing Bryson City, the home of Horace Kephart, who wrote *Our Southern Highlanders* and helped preserve Great Smoky Mountains National Park from lumber companies gnawing their way across the mountainsides.

Autumn colors cascade down the mountainside to the
door of the Methodist Church in Cades Cove.

A section of the Appalachian Trail as it rises over a summit in Madison County.

Bryson City is also the departure point for the "Road to Nowhere," a highway that simply and famously stops en route to the resort community of Fontana Lake. (Government funding dried up before it was finished.) The **Great Smoky Mountains Railroad,** on the other hand, chugs all the way from Bryson City to Dillsboro and Andrews, tugging passenger cars through remote, spectacular scenery. *226 Everett St.; 800/872–4681.*

US 19 continues south through the tiny community of Nantahala, a good place to catch a backcountry excursion or rafting trip. US 129 cuts northwest to Robbinsville.

ROBBINSVILLE   *map page 261, A-3*

Cherokee Chief Junaluska rests, at last, near the small town of Robbinsville. When President Andrew Jackson forced the Cherokee from their homeland, Chief Junaluska—like other Cherokee—walked 1,200 wintry miles to Oklahoma, along the Trail of Tears. Thousands of his people died of exposure and exhaustion along the way. Many years later Junaluska walked back to North Carolina, to live his last years in his homeland.

A highway marker on Main Street reads:

At 6,643 feet, Clingman's Dome is the tallest peak in the national park, and only 41 feet shy of Mt. Mitchell.

JUNALUSKA
CHEROKEE INDIAN CHIEF, BRAVE WARRIOR UNDER
ANDREW JACKSON AT HORSE SHOE BEND, IN CREEK WAR, 1814.
GRAVE ONE MILE SOUTHWEST.

From Robbinsville, you can head southwest on US 129 and then NC 141 to the crafts-rich area known as Brasstown, and John C. Campbell Folks School. Or, you can follow the unsurpassed twists and turns of the Cherohala Highway (NC 143/TN 165) between Robbinsville, North Carolina, and Tellico Plains, Tennessee. If highways can be double-jointed, this one is. Ninety-nine of its twists exceed 90 degrees. Most of its elevations exceed 4,000 feet; many rise above 5,000, making it one of the region's loftiest drives.

Drive this highway with a sunset softening the sky ahead of you and a full moon rising at your shoulder, and you feel like Tanawah—a golden eagle soaring between two worlds.

A conductor and engineer of the Great Smoky Mountains Railway take a break at the train depot in Dillsboro. The train runs from Dillsboro to Bryson City and back, and from Bryson City to Natahala Outdoor Center and back.

Slickrock Creek brings the enduing harmony of stream and stone to Nantahala National Forest.

JOYCE KILMER MEMORIAL FOREST *map page 261, A-3*

The Cherohala Highway (NC 143/TN 165) writhes within 3 miles of Joyce Kilmer Memorial Forest, whose virgin forest is the largest in North Carolina.

This wilderness area is known for its giant tulip poplars, hemlock, sycamore, oak, basswood, maple, birch, and beech. Spruce, pine, and cedars dwell in this forest, whose understory is a mosaic of wildflowers, ferns, mosses, lichens, rhododendron, laurel, and flame azalea.

This forest, unlike most North Carolina forests, has never been "harvested." This is the same, uninterrupted forest the Cherokee walked through hundreds of years ago. It holds an ancient spirit.

When plants were first made by a force now forgotten, the Cherokee believed, the Great One told them to stay awake for seven nights, as young men did when praying for their medicine. Nearly all stayed awake the first night, but on the second night they began falling asleep, one by one. After seven nights, only the cedar, pine, spruce, holly, and laurel remained. To reward their endurance, the Great One made them evergreen, and made them plants of healing.

The sun sets over the Smoky Mountains, as viewed from Heintooga Overlook.

Measuring the largest hemlock in the state of North Carolina, located in Joyce Kilmer Memorial Forest.

Today people come to Joyce Kilmer Memorial Forest to follow gentle paths along tumbling streams. They come to lean against the cool, strong trunks of giant poplars, and to rest beneath the gnarled, muscled arms of ancient oaks.

Most of all, they come to feel the enduring rhythm of uninterrupted life. Nowhere is that rhythm clearer than in the cathedral of this ancient forest. *Cheoah Ranger District; 828/479–6431.*

GETTING AROUND

Only one interstate highway braves the NC mountains: I–40 winds its way from the Piedmont into Asheville and then northwest toward Knoxville, TN. The Blue Ridge Parkway is hugely popular with tourists; if you want to move at a brisker north-south pace, consider US 221.

LOCAL FAVORITE PLACES TO EAT

ASHEVILLE

Barley's Tap Room. 42 Biltmore Ave.; 828/255–0504. $

Housed in a cavernous downtown storefront with its original pressed-tin ceilings, Barley's offers delicious microbrews and great food, especially pizza. Families, businesspeople, and artists come here. This book's photographer, Jim Hargan, recommends a lunch of calzone and a Highland Gaelic Ale. There's live bluegrass and jazz on Tuesdays and Sundays.

Bistro 1896. 7 Pack Square SW; 828/251–1300. $$$

This popular bistro has plenty of patio seating overlooking Pack Square, as well as dining rooms inside. Try the Cajun-inspired fried green tomato Napoleon, or the Chicken Bel-Air with sun-dried cherries and walnut-encrusted goat cheese. Brunch is served Sunday.

Early Girl Eatery. 8 Wall St.; 828/259–9292. $-$$

Come to this casual restaurant for Southern cooking made from scratch. The most popular dinner might be pan-fried chicken with herb gravy, squash casserole, and grilled asparagus. For dessert, try the Italian cream cake. They have daily specials, and breakfast is served all day.

Gabrielle's. 87 Richmond Hill Dr.; 828/252–7313. $$$$

This upscale restaurant at Richmond Hill Inn serves continental cuisine. A typical entrée is North Carolina flounder with braised red cabbage, celery-root puree, and French lentils with apples and Dijon mustard. Ask for a table in the sunporch dining room—the view of Asheville is great. No lunch.

Moose Café. 520 Brevard Rd., Asheville; 828/255–0920. $

Moose Café takes full advantage of the western North Carolina farmers' market, which happens to be next door. Fresh local veggies, hot scratch-made biscuits with apple butter, buttermilk fried chicken. Home-cooked, don't-have-to-dress-up-for-them meals are dished up in this bustling eatery, which has excellent service.

Laughing Seed Café. 40 Wall St.; 828/252–3445. $$

A creative international, vegetarian menu features "mostly organic" local produce and locally brewed beers. The most popular entrée at this casual, hip eatery just may be the curried tempeh Napoleon—or perhaps the wild-mushroom enchiladas. Chances are this place will be packed; if you've got a wait, head downstairs to Jack in the Wood, a smoke-free pub.

ELSEWHERE IN THE APPALACHIANS

Daniel Boone Inn's Restaurant. 130 Hardin St., Boone; 828/264–8657. $$

If your grandmother didn't cook this way, you're probably not from around here. Meals start with soup or salad, and mosey on to a family-style meal: three meats and five vegetables, biscuits, preserves, desserts, and tea. The fried chicken is notoriously tasty. Breakfast includes eggs, bacon, sausage, ham, grits, stewed apples, redeye gravy, cream gravy, cinnamon bread with preserves, juice, and coffee, and costs under $10.

Eseeola Lodge Dining Room. Near the intersection of US 221 and NC 105, Linville; 828/733–4311. $$$$

The Eseeola Lodge opened in 1892; their dining room has been famous ever since. If you drop in for breakfast, consider the trout and eggs. The dinner menus rotate but might include boneless rack of lamb with scalloped potatoes and seasonal vegetables or coq au vin. You'll fit right in with a coat and tie. Closed November–mid-May.

Mast Farm Inn Restaurant. 2543 Broadstone Rd., Valle Crucis; 828/963–5857. $$$$

This easygoing restaurant in a restored 1885 farmhouse is noted for its Southern contemporary cuisine. Ninety percent of the vegetables come from the garden down by the river. The menus varies, but a popular entrée is the Watauga County pork and Ashe County cheese in a pastry from Deep Gap, white and wild basmati rice, and sesame green beans from near the New River. Homemade breads and desserts round out the menu.

Seasons Restaurant at Highland Lake Inn. Highland Lake Rd., Flat Rock; 828/696–9094. $$$

This restaurant's slogan is "from the garden to your plate," and, with a 2-acre organic garden out back, that's no joke. A perennial favorite is the North Carolina rainbow trout topped with celery and a tomato, artichoke, black olive, eggplant, caper, and chickpea étouffée. Vegetarian entrées include vegetable-saffron risotto and organic oyster mushrooms. The list of 150-plus wines is well chosen.

The Shatley Springs Inn. 407 Shatley Springs Rd., Shatley Springs; 336/982–2236. $–$$

Shatley Springs' huge, rustic 1930s-style restaurant dishes up its Southern cooking to about 10,000 visitors a month. A breakfast of a ham biscuit and cup of coffee will set you back three or four dollars. Lunch or supper plates—say, chicken pie, fresh baked apples, sweet cabbage, biscuits, and tea—are moderately priced. Rumor is that FDR used to eat here ... maybe because of the homemade desserts.

In a valley near Sylva, a red barn admires a pond and split-rail fence.

LOCAL FAVORITE PLACES TO STAY

Glendale Springs Inn. 7414 NC 16 (Blue Ridge Parkway, milepost 259), Glendale Springs; 336/982–2103. $$

Since 1895, this inn has been a bit of everything for Glendale Springs: post office, courthouse, general store, wedding chapel, and moonshine-stocked dance hall. Today it offers nine beautifully restored guest rooms, parlors, a fine dining room, and a well-behaved ghost.

Grove Park Inn Resort and Spa. 290 Macon Ave., Asheville; 800/438–0050. $$$$

For nearly a century, this inn—on the National Register of Historic Places—has been the place to stay in Asheville. It's home to the world's largest collection of Arts and Crafts furnishings, and to the highly rated Horizons restaurant. The 512-room resort includes a world-class 43,000-square-foot spa and a century-old, restored Donald Ross golf course.

Inn on Biltmore Estate. Biltmore Estate, Asheville; 800/441–3812. $$$$

George Vanderbilt might feel at home in this 213-room luxury hotel, whose design was inspired by English and French manor houses. The inn provides shuttles to various sights, and arranges outdoor activities and spa services. The dining room serves regional cuisine. The views of Biltmore Estate are excellent.

Lovill House Inn. 404 Old Bristol Rd., Boone; 828/264–4204. $$$$

This restored 1875 farmhouse sits on 11 quiet, wooded acres in Boone. The six-room inn serves a full breakfast. Ask for the Bristol Room if you like a wood-burning fireplace. Every guest receives lifetime porch-sitting privileges on the wide front porch.

Mast Farm Inn. SR 1112, Valle Crucis; 828/963–5857. $$$$

This relaxed country inn, noted for its antiques and hospitality, is listed on the National Register of Historic Places as "one of the most complete and best preserved groups of nineteenth century farm buildings in western North Carolina." Choose from restored rooms in an 1885 farmhouse, historic cabins, or cottages.

Richmond Hill. 87 Richmond Hill Dr., Asheville; 828/252–7313. $$$$

This Queen Anne–style mansion, built in 1889 for Ambassador Richmond Pearson and his wife Gabrielle, is one of Asheville's most elegant inns. In the historic mansion are 11 rooms and one suite. The most popular accommodation is a corner room that was originally Gabrielle's. The property also includes nine newer Shaker-style cottages, two modern family cottages, and rooms in a garden pavilion.

PRACTICAL INFORMATION

AREA CODES

Triangle Area: 919. Northern coastal plain and Outer Banks:252. Southern coastal plain and southern Piedmont: 910. Northern Piedmont: 336. Appalachians: 828.Charlotte and environs: 704.

BEST TIMES TO GO

The best time to visit North Carolina? It depends on where you're headed. Sun worshippers head for the Outer Banks in summer, so come at other times if you don't like crowds. Summers along the coast are hot—but the islands will generally be a few degrees cooler than the inland, thanks to ocean breezes. Winter temperatures are also tempered by the sea, but winter can be windy and raw.

If you don't like hot, muggy weather, visit the Coastal Plain in spring or fall. If you visit during a rare winter snowstorm, be forewarned: we flatlanders don't know how to drive in snow, and we rarely let that stop us.

The Piedmont is more moderate in humidity than the Coastal Plain, but still hot in summer. With its rolling hills and hardwood forests, the Piedmont tends to be most beautiful in the autumn. Snow is more frequent here than in the east.

The Appalachians are the only region that experience a prolonged winter. Snow falls every year. Summers are cool and pleasant, with temperatures rarely reaching

Near Rodanthe, a beached fishing boat waits patiently by a calm sea.

90°F. If you're touring, visit here May through late October, and expect plenty of traffic in the summer and in autumn's leaf season. Skiers visit in winter, of course.

HURRICANES

Ocean breezes create a pleasant summer climate on the islands, but occasionally breezes escalate and a hurricane slams ashore. If this happens, you want to be elsewhere. Island authorities call for a voluntary evacuation first. Leave immediately and let others make their way off when the evacuation becomes mandatory, probably the next day. You can always come back if the storm turns.

CLIMATE

TEMPS (F°)	AVG. JAN.		AVG. APRIL		AVG. JULY		AVG. OCT.		RECORD	
	HIGH	LOW	HIGH	LOW	HIGH	LOW	HIGH	LOW	HIGH	LOW
Hatteras	52	37	67	51	84	72	72	59	97	6
Wilmington	56	31	76	47	90	68	76	50	104	0
Raleigh	51	30	73	47	89	68	73	49	105	-9
Charlotte	49	30	71	48	89	69	72	50	104	-5
Asheville	47	25	68	42	83	62	68	44	101	-16
Mt. Mitchell	32	17	52	33	66	52	55	36	87	-34

PRECIPITATION (INCHES)	AVG. JAN.	AVG. APRIL	AVG. JULY	AVG. OCT.	ANNUAL	
					RAIN	SNOW
Hatteras	5.5	3.4	5.0	5.2	56.6	2
Wilmington	5.1	2.7	7.7	3.7	58	1.9
Raleigh	3.7	3.0	5.3	3.1	45.3	7
Charlotte	3.7	3.0	3.8	3.2	43	5.5
Asheville	3.4	3.2	4.3	3.6	47.1	15.6
Mt. Mitchell	5.8	5.8	7.0	5.1	74	58

GETTING THERE AND AROUND

BY AIR

NC has four international airports. Three are in the Piedmont.

Raleigh-Durham International (RDU) is between Raleigh and Durham (about 12 miles northwest of Raleigh and 14 mi southeast of Durham), off I–40. Piedmont Triad International (GSO) serves Winston-Salem, Greensboro, and High Point. It's 12 mi west of Greensboro, off I–40. Charlotte-Douglas International (CLT) is 8 miles west of downtown, off I–485.

In the east, Wilmington International (ILM) is 5 miles north of Wilmington, off Highway 117. The western part of the state is served by the Asheville Regional Airport (AVL). It's 18 miles south of the city on I–26.

Other regional airports include: Pitt/Greenville in Greenville (PGV), Craven Regional in New Bern (EWN), Albert J. Ellis in Jacksonville (JAX), Fayetteville Regional in Fayetteville (FAY), and Kinston Regional Jetport (ISO).

BY CAR

Driving is generally the most convenient way to explore the state. North Carolina's highway system is one of the largest state-maintained highway systems in the nation. The interstate highways are concentrated in the Piedmont.

I–40 runs roughly east–west across the middle of the state, connecting Wilmington, Raleigh, Greensboro, and Asheville. Other major highways include I–95, which runs north–south along the western edge of the coastal plain; I–85, which connects Charlotte with Greensboro and Piedmont cities to the north; I–77, which runs north–south in the western Piedmont, connecting Charlotte and Salisbury, among other cities; and I–26, which runs north–south, connecting Asheville to Columbia, SC. Get off of these highways when time allows, and enjoy the pace and scenery of the smaller highways.

The Blue Ridge Parkway, the state's most famous scenic drive, runs north–south through the Appalachians, where secondary roads are predictably both twisting and scenic.

TRAFFIC LAWS

In North Carolina everyone in the car, front and back seats, must use a seat belt. If you're traveling with children, check www.buckleupnc.org for complete child safety regulations. You'll need to make sure children up to 8 years of age and under 80 pounds use the appropriate child safety seats.

You can turn right on red after stopping, unless signs say otherwise. If it's rainy enough or misty enough to turn your windshield wipers on, the law is that you must also turn on your headlights.

Motorcyclists must wear helmets and operate their headlights at all times.

For complete information on North Carolina's driving regulations, check www.ncdot.org.

BY TRAIN

Two Amtrak (800/872–7245; www.amtrak.com) routes pass through North Carolina, providing service to 16 cities: Charlotte, Gastonia, Kannapolis, Salisbury, Fayetteville, Selma, Raleigh, Durham, Cary, Rocky Mount, Wilson, Southern Pines, Hamlet, Greensboro, Burlington, and High Point.

FESTIVALS AND SEASONAL EVENTS

Small-town festivals celebrate everything from herring (Jamesville) to fiddle playing (Union Grove), to the almost lost art of hollerin' (Spivey's Corner). The best offer a glimpse into the region's culture. The following are a few of the most entertaining and interesting festivals in the state.

APRIL

Grifton: Shad Festival
Grifton throws its Shad Festival the first week in April. North Carolina's oldest continually operating small-town festival celebrates a small, bony fish that spawns in Contentnea Creek, at the edge of town. *252/524–5168.*

Moses Cone Park, which once welcomed the kings and queens of North Carolina's textile industry, now welcomes horseback riders and art lovers.

Wilkesboro: MerleFest

This four-day acoustic and bluegrass music festival in late April honors the late Merle Watson, son of festival host "Doc" Watson. *336/838–6267; www.merlefest.org.*

Wilmington: North Carolina Azalea Festival

The weeklong event—NC's oldest city festival—in early to mid-April includes parades, garden tours, horse shows, etc. Wilmington is most beautiful when its millions of azaleas burst into bloom. *800/222–4757; www.ncazaleafestival.org.*

JUNE

Durham: American Dance Festival

This influential dance festival has premieres, performances, and backstage tours. June and July. *919/684–6402; www.americandancefestival.org.*

JULY

Grandfather Mountain: Highland Game and Gathering of the Clans

The largest Scottish Highland games in the United States are held at Grandfather Mountain, near Linville, each July, with dancing, sheepdog herding demonstrations, piping, and athletics. *828/733–1333; www.gmhg.org.*

AUGUST

Jefferson: Bluegrass and Old Time Fiddlers' Convention at Ashe County Park

This one-day competition, where visitors are welcomed to gather and listen to the music, has been a mountain music attraction for over a quarter of a century. Held the first Saturday of the month. *336/846–9550.*

SEPTEMBER

Benson: Mule Days

Hundreds of mules compete here, leaping tall fences, thundering around a dusty racetrack (or halfway around, depending on their moods). There's also a parade, carnival, rodeo, barbecue cook-off, and arts and crafts. The festival runs Thursday–Sunday the fourth full weekend in September. *919/894–3825; www.bensonmuledays.com.*

Durham: Bull Durham Blues Festival

One of the South's premier blues events. *919/683–1709; www.bulldurhamblues.org.*

OCTOBER

October's autumn color brings thousands of visitors to the mountains each year, so October is a big festival month. Among the best mountain festivals:

Asheville: Southern Highlands Crafts Guild Fair

Over 100 members of the prestigious Southern Highland Handicrafts Guild demonstrate and/or sell their work at North Carolina's best highlands crafts show. The fair also includes mountain music and dancing. Held twice a year, the third weekend in October and the third weekend in July. (The guild also has two shops on the Blue Ridge Parkway.) *828/298–7928; www.exploreasheville.com.*

Cherokee: Cherokee Indian Fair

A Native American arts and crafts show, Native American foods, an agricultural fair, stickball games, archery contests, blowgun contests, and dancing fill the calendar at this five-day fair. *800/438–1601; www.cherokeesmokies.com.*

DECEMBER

Harker's Island: Core Sound Decoy Festival

Decoy carving was once part of everyday life in coastal North Carolina. Today it's almost a lost art, and a high-dollar art at that. Artists and visitors come to sell and buy antique and new decoys, eat seafood, and check out competitions in decoy carving, retriever showing, and loon calling. First full weekend in December. *252/728–1500; www.decoyguild.com.*

PRICE CATEGORIES

RESTAURANTS (average cost of a main course at dinner or the equivalent)			
$$$$=over $25	$$$=$15-$25	$$=$10-$15	$=under $10

LODGING AND CAMPING (a single night's peak-season rate for a standard double room)			
$$$$=over $175	$$$=$100-$175	$$=$50-$100	$=under $50

VISITOR INFORMATION

VISITOR CENTERS

Asheville CVB and Visitor Center, *800/257–1300; exploreasheville.com.*
Boone CVB, *800/852–9506; www.visitboonenc.com.*
Cape Hatteras National Seashore, *252/473–2111; www.nps.gov/caha.*
Cape Lookout National Seashore, *252/728–2250; www.nps.gov/calo.*
Charlotte Visitor Info Center, *800/231–4636; www.charlottesgotalot.com.*
Cherokee Visitors Center, *800/438–1601; www.cherokee-nc.com.*
Croatan National Forest, *252/638–5628; www.nps.gov/nfsnc.*
Great Smoky Mountains National Park, *865/436–1200; www.nps.gov/grsm.*
Greater Raleigh CVB, *800/849–8499; www.visitraleigh.com.*
Greensboro Area CVB, *800/344–2282; www.visitgreensboronc.com.*
High Country Host, *800/438–7500; www.skithehighcountry.com.*
Outer Banks Visitor Bureau, *877/629–4386; www.outerbanks.org.*
Pisgah National Forest, *828/877–3265; www.nps.gov/nfsnc.*
Smoky Mountain Host of NC, *800/432–4678; www.visitsmokies.org.*
Uwharrie National Forest, *910/576–6391; www.nps.gov/nfsnc.*
Wilmington Cape Fear Coast CVB, *877/945–6386; www.capefearcoast.com.*

OTHER USEFUL WEB SITES

For scenic drives, check out **American Trails** (*www.americantrails.org*) and the **National Scenic Byways Program** (*www.byways.org*), part of the U.S. Department of Transportation.

The **Blue Ridge Parkway Association** (*www.blueridgeparkway.org*) provides information on driving this famed route and about campsites, hotels, restaurants, sights, and activities along the Parkway.

The **North Carolina Association of Festivals & Events** (*www.ncfestivals.com*) maintains a full list of statewide goings-on.

Explore the past in more depth with **North Carolina Historic Sites** (*www.nchistoricsites.com*) and the **North Carolina Office of Archives & History** (*www.history.ncdcr.gov*).

The **Appalachian Trail Conservancy** (*www.appalachiantrail.org*) is a resource for those looking to tackle the hiker's holy grail. **High Country Outdoors** (*www. highcountryoutdoors.com*) provides outdoors enthusiasts with information about western NC.

Santa's helper Mack Davis waves from the engine of the Great Smoky Mountains Railway.

North Carolina is unequivocally where barbecue originated, according to the **North Carolina Barbecue Society** (*www.ncbbqsociety.com*), an organization dedicated to preserving its history and culture.

North Carolina's main metro newspapers have a solid Web presence; check out their print or online versions. *Our State* magazine, meanwhile, highlights special events, local recipes, and Tarheel culture.

Asheville Citizen-Times: *www.citizen-times.com.*
Charlotte Observer: *www.charlotteobserver.com.*
Greensboro News & Record: *www.news-record.com.*
Our State magazine: *www.ourstate.com.*
Raleigh News & Observer: *www.newsobserver.com.*
Wilmington Star: *www.starnewsonline.com.*
Winston-Salem Journal: *www.journalnow.com.*

Balsam Mountains, Sylva. Old Jackson County Courthouse. Fountain at the bottom of the Courthouse Hill, steps leading up to the courthouse, dogwoods in spring bloom.

INDEX

ACKNOWLEDGMENTS

FROM THE AUTHOR

Many people have shared their time and expertise with me as I've written this book.

First, I thank R. L. Beasley, my fellow traveler and first reader, for his good-hearted support.

Although I visited several libraries as I researched this book, I'd especially like to thank Julie Hicks, formerly with Sheppard Memorial Library in Greenville, NC, who could always find the answers.

Southern hospitality is alive and well in North Carolina. Among the many people in Piedmont and western NC who assisted this flatlander in her research, I especially thank: Lynn Minges, of NC's Department of Commerce, Travel, and Tourism Division, in Raleigh; Michael Rouse of Smoky Mountain Host in Franklin; Millie Barbee of High Country Host in Blowing Rock; Ranger Frank Finley of the US Forest Service; Beth Sander of the Boone CVB; Alice Alexander Aumen of the Maggie Valley Chamber of Commerce; Marla Tambellini of the Asheville Area Chamber of Commerce; David Redman of Cherokee Tribal Travel and Promotion; Gail Murphy and Claudette Landwehrmann of the Greensboro Area CVB; Margaret Pike of the Winston-Salem CVB; Jim Sanders at Old Salem; Vickie Riddle, spokesperson for Gaston County; and Gina King of the Charlotte CVB.

Last but certainly not least, I thank: Kit Duane, former managing editor of Compass American Guides, for her patience, guidance, and encouragement; Chris Burt for his clear perspective; editors Barry Parr and Beth Burleson, whose thoughtful suggestions contributed to the clarity of this text; designer Debi Dunn for the balance she's given these pages; and expert reader Tom Ross, who caught my gaffes and righted my wrongs. Thanks also to editors Jennifer Paull and Shannon Kelly for their guidance and suggestions for the fifth edition of this book.

FROM THE PUBLISHER

All photographs in this book are by Jim Hargan unless noted below.

CHAPTER 1: CULTURE & HISTORY:

16, Katrina Leigh/Shutterstock. 19, Library of Congress Prints & Photographs Division. 21, North Carolina Museum of Art, Raleigh. 24, Library of Congress Geography and Map Division. 25, Friends Historical Collection, Guilford College, Greensboro, North Carolina. 26, State Capitol, Commonwealth of Virginia, The Library of Virginia. 28, National Museum of American History, Smithsonian Institute. 29, North Carolina Collection, University of North Carolina Library at Chapel Hill. 30, William S Powell, North Carolina Collection, University of North Carolina Library at Chapel Hill. 31, Southern Historical Collection, Julius A. Leinbach Papers. 33, North Carolina Collection, University of North Carolina Library at Chapel Hill. 34, Southern Historical Collection, University of NC (call #P-4132). 36 and 43 (top), Jack Moebs, Greensboro News and Record Photo Archives. 42 (top and bottom), North Carolina Collection, University of North Carolina Library at Chapel Hill. 43 (bottom), 19, Library of Congress Prints & Photographs Division.

CHAPTER 2: OUTER BANKS:

46, Bill Russ/NC Tourism. 48, North Carolina Collection, University of North Carolina Library at Chapel Hill. 50, Library of Congress, Prints and Photographs Division. 51, Southern Historical Collection, University of NC Library. 58, Southern Historical Collection, University of NC. 61 and 64, Library of Congress Prints & Photographs Division. 73, Cameron Art Museum. 76, William E. Elmore Collection (#PC-39/154), Special Collections Department, J.Y. Joyner Library, East Carolina University, Greenville, NC. 80, Patrick Johnson/Shutterstock.

CHAPTER 3: COASTAL PLAIN:

86 and 88, North Carolina Collection, University of North Carolina Library at Chapel Hill. 91, Cameron Art Museum. 100 and 101 (left and right), North Carolina Collection, University of North Carolina Library at Chapel Hill. 108, North Carolina Museum of Art, Raleigh. 113, Mary Terriberry/Shutterstock. 123, Zack Frank/Shutterstock. 128, North Carolina Office of Archives and History, Raleigh. 135, The North Carolina Maritime Museum. 140, Rare Book, Manuscript, and Special Collections Library, Duke University. 148, iofoto/Shutterstock. 156, North Carolina Collection, University of North Carolina Library at Chapel Hill.

CHAPTER 4: NORTHERN PIEDMONT:

170, The New York Historical Society. 174-75, Tabitha Marie DeVisconti Papers, 1705-1983, #480, East Carolina Manuscript Collection, Joyner Library, East Carolina University, Greenville, NC. 177, 179, and 180, Bill Russ/NC Tourism. 184, North Carolina Office of Archives and History, Raleigh. 190-91, Bill Russ/NC Tourism. 197, North Carolina Collection, University of North Carolina Library at Chapel Hill. 202, Anne S. K. Brown Military Collection, Brown University Library. 209, Moravian Archives, Bethlehem. 213, Library of Congress Prints & Photographs Division.

CHAPTER 5: SOUTHERN PIEDMONT:

218, University of Maryland Baltimore County, Edward L. Bafford Photographic Collection. 219, North Carolina Office of Archives and History, Raleigh. 237, Cameron Art Museum. 242-43, North Carolina Museum of History.

CHAPTER 6: THE SANDHILLS:

250, Bill Russ/NC Tourism. 251, Library of Congress Prints and Photographs Division.

CHAPTER 7: THE APPALACHIANS:

266 and 268, Library of Congress Prints and Photographs Division. 291, Regina Chayer/Shutterstock. 297, JustASC/Shutterstock. 300, North Carolina Collection, University of North Carolina Library at Chapel Hill. 304, N[athaniel] Jocelyn (artist) and D.C. Hinman (engraver), North Carolina Collection, University of North Carolina Library at Chapel Hill. 307, North Carolina Collection, Pack Memorial Public Library, Asheville, North Carolina. 312 (top), Biltmore Estate, Asheville, North Carolina. 312 (bottom), Library of Congress Prints & Photographs Division. 313, The Biltmore Company. 314, The Grove Park Inn Resort & Spa, Asheville, NC. 315, Eileen Morris/iStockphoto.

ABOUT THE AUTHOR

photo © R. L. Beasley

SHEILA TURNAGE, a native North Carolinian, is the author of scores of articles on North Carolina people and places. Those articles have been published by *Southern Living,* the *Atlanta Journal and Constitution,* the *Raleigh News and Observer, American Legacy Magazine,* and *Our State* magazine, among many others. She is the author of a children's book, *Trout the Magnificent* (Harcourt Brace Jovanovich), and of *Haunted Inns of the Southeast* (John F. Blair, Publisher). Her work has also been published by the *International Poetry Review* and *The Lincoln Center for the Performing Arts,* among others. Sheila Turnage lives on a farm on eastern North Carolina's coastal plain with her husband, Rodney L. Beasley, and a throng of friendly beasts.

ABOUT THE PHOTOGRAPHER

JIM HARGAN started his career as a photographer with both bachelor's and master's degrees in geography. After a 17-year stint in Florida as a specialist in urban planning, his interest turned toward photography, which seemed a natural way to blend observation of his surroundings with his academic background in geography. Jim practices freelance photography full-time from his home in the mountains of North Carolina, where he lives with his wife in the community of Possum Trot. His work has appeared in numerous magazines and books and on calendars and postcards. His signed and numbered art prints are purchased by businesses and private collectors and are represented by agencies worldwide.